ETHICS IN THE REAL WORLD

ETHICS IN
THE REAL WORLD

82 Brief Essays
on Things That Matter

• • •

PETER SINGER

PRINCETON UNIVERSITY PRESS
PRINCETON AND OXFORD

Copyright © 2016 by Peter Singer
Requests for permission to reproduce material from this work
should be sent to Permissions, Princeton University Press
Published by Princeton University Press, 41 William Street,
Princeton, New Jersey 08540
In the United Kingdom: Princeton University Press,
6 Oxford Street, Woodstock, Oxfordshire OX20 1TR

press.princeton.edu

All Rights Reserved

ISBN 978-0-691-17247-7

Library of Congress Control Number: 2016935598

British Library Cataloging-in-Publication Data is available

This book has been composed in Minion Pro

Jacket design by Faceout Studio

Jacket imagery courtesy of Shutterstock and Thinkstock

Printed on acid-free paper. ∞

Printed in the United Kingdom

1 3 5 7 9 10 8 6 4 2

... CONTENTS ...

··· INTRODUCTION ···

We all make ethical choices, often without being conscious of doing so. Too often we assume that ethics is about obeying the rules that begin with "You must not. . . ." If that were all there is to living ethically, then as long as we were not violating one of those rules, whatever we were doing would be ethical. That view of ethics, however, is incomplete. It fails to consider the good we can do to others less fortunate than ourselves, not only in our own community, but anywhere within the reach of our help. We ought also to extend our concern to future generations, and beyond our own species to nonhuman animals.

Another important ethical responsibility applies to citizens of democratic society: to be an educated citizen and a participant in the decisions our society makes. Many of these decisions involve ethical choices. In public discussions of these ethical issues, people with training in ethics, or moral philosophy, can play a valuable role. Today that is not an especially controversial claim, but when I was a student, philosophers themselves proclaimed that it was a mistake to think that they have any special expertise that would qualify them to addresses substantive ethical issues. The accepted understanding of the discipline, at least in the English-speaking world, was that philosophy is concerned with the analysis of words and concepts, and so is neutral on substantive ethical questions.

Fortunately for me—because I doubt that I would have continued in philosophy if that view had prevailed—pressure from the student movement of the late 1960s and early 1970s transformed the way moral philosophy is practiced and taught. In the era of the Vietnam War and struggles against racism, sexism, and environmental degradation, students demanded that university courses should be relevant to the important issues of the day. Philosophers responded to that demand by returning to their discipline's origins. They recalled the example of Socrates questioning his fellow Athenians about the nature of justice, and what it takes to live justly, and summoned up the courage to ask similar questions of their students, their fellow philosophers, and the wider public.

My first book, written against the background of ongoing resistance to racism, sexism, and the war in Vietnam, asks when civil disobedience is justified in a democracy.[1] Since then, I've very largely sought to address issues that matter to people outside departments of philosophy. There is a view in some philosophical circles that anything that can be understood by people who have not studied philosophy is not profound enough to be worth saying. To the contrary, I suspect that whatever cannot be said clearly is probably not being thought clearly either.

If many academics think that writing a book aimed at the general public is beneath them, then writing an opinion piece for a newspaper is sinking lower still. In the pages that follow you will find a selection of my shorter writings. Newspaper columns are often ephemeral, but the ones I have selected here discuss enduring issues, or address problems that, regrettably, are still with us. The pressure of not

[1] *Democracy and Disobedience* (Oxford: Clarendon Press, 1973).

exceeding 1,000 words forces one to write in a style that is not only clear but also concise. Granted, in such essays it is impossible to present one's research in a manner that can be assessed by other scholars, and inevitably some of the nuances and qualifications that could be explored in a longer essay have to be omitted. It's nice when your colleagues in philosophy departments appreciate what you are doing, but I also judge the success of my work by the impact my books, articles, and talks have on the much broader audience of people who are interested in thinking about how to live ethically. Articles in peer-reviewed journals are, according to one study, read in full by an average of just ten people.[2] An opinion piece for a major newspaper or a syndicated column may be read by tens of thousands or even millions, and as a result, some of them may change their minds on an important issue, or even change the way they live. I know that happens, because people have told me that my writing has changed what they donate to charity, or led them to stop eating animal products or, in at least one case, to donate a kidney to a stranger.

The essays in the opening section will shed some light on my approach to ethics, but it may be useful to say a little more here. Moral judgments are not purely subjective; in that, they are different from judgments of taste. If they were merely subjective, we would not think it was worth arguing about ethical issues, any more than we think that it is worth arguing about which ice cream flavor to choose. We recognize that tastes differ, and there is no "right" amount of garlic to put in a salad dressing; but we do think it is worth

[2] Asit Biswas and Julian Kirchherr, "Prof, No One Is Reading You," *Straits Times,* April 11, 2015, http://www.straitstimes.com/opinion/prof-no-one-is-reading-you.

arguing about the legalization of voluntary euthanasia, or whether it is wrong to eat meat.

Nor is ethics just a matter of expressing our intuitive responses of repugnance or approval, even if these intuitions are widely shared. We may have innate "yuck" reactions that helped our ancestors to survive, at a time when they were social mammals but not yet human and not capable of abstract reasoning. Those reactions will not always be a reliable guide to right and wrong in the much larger and more complex global community in which we live today. For that, we need to use our ability to reason.

There was a time when I thought this kind of reasoning could only be unraveling the implications of a more basic ethical stance that is, ultimately, subjective. I no longer think this. There are, as Derek Parfit has argued in his major work *On What Matters* (which I describe in the pages below in an essay entitled "Does Anything Matter?") objective ethical truths that we can discover through careful reasoning and reflection.[3] But for those who reject the idea of objective ethical truths, the essays that follow can be read as attempts to work out the implications of accepting the ethical commitment espoused by many philosophers in different terms, but perhaps best put by the great nineteenth-century utilitarian philosopher Henry Sidgwick:

> . . . the good of any one individual is of no more importance, from the point of view (if I may say so) of the Universe, than the good of any other; unless, that is, there are special grounds for believing

[3] Derek Parfit, *On What Matters*, 2 vols. (Oxford: Oxford University Press, 2013). For my own developing views on this issue see Peter Singer, *The Expanding Circle* (Princeton, NJ: Princeton University Press, 2011), and Katarzyna de Lazari-Radek and Peter Singer, *The Point of View of the Universe* (Oxford: Oxford University Press, 2014).

that more good is likely to be realised in the one case than in the other.[4]

Sidgwick was a utilitarian, and so am I. Once we start to question our evolved and culturally transmitted intuitive responses to moral issues, utilitarianism is, I believe, the most defensible ethical view, as I have argued at much greater length in *The Point of View of the Universe*, written jointly with Katarzyna de Lazari-Radek.[5] Nevertheless, in the essays that follow, I do not presuppose utilitarianism. That is because on many of the issues I discuss, my conclusions follow from many non-utilitarian positions as well as from utilitarianism. Given the practical importance of these issues, as a good utilitarian I ought to aim to write for the broadest possible audience, and not merely for a narrow band of committed utilitarians.

Some of the following essays address topics for which I am well known: the ethics of our relations with animals, questions of life and death, and the obligations of the affluent to those in extreme poverty. Others explore topics on which my views are likely to be less familiar: the ethics of selling kidneys, or of growing genetically modified crops, the moral status of conscious robots, and whether incest between adult siblings is wrong. Happiness, and how to promote it, plays a key role in my ethical view, so that is the topic of one group of articles. Among the more personal essays is the book's closing reflection on surfing, which has added to my own happiness.

Readers who know my work on some topics may be surprised by my views on other topics. I try to keep an open

[4] Henry Sidgwick, *The Methods of Ethics*, 7th edition (London: Macmillan, 1907), p. 382.
[5] See fn3.

mind, to be responsive to the evidence, and not simply to follow a predictable political line. And if you are not already persuaded that philosophers do have something to contribute to issues of broad general interest, I hope that this volume will convince you of that.

... ACKNOWLEDGMENTS ...

MANY, THOUGH BY NO MEANS ALL, of these pieces were written for Project Syndicate, a news service that provides a broad range of commentaries to over 450 media outlets in 153 countries. At the instigation of Andrzej Rapaczynski, I have been writing a monthly column for Project Syndicate since 2005, so my greatest debt is to him for recruiting me as a member of his team of columnists. Over all these years, Agata Sagan has brought to my attention topics that have led to columns, carried out research on which I have drawn, and made helpful comments on drafts. Project Syndicate's editors, Ken Murphy and Jonathan Stein, have shown me that even my best efforts to write clearly can be improved upon. I thank Project Syndicate for permission to reproduce the columns. Other articles come from the *New York Times,* the *Washington Post,* the *New York Daily News,* and *Free Inquiry.* A few of them are co-authored, and I acknowledge the important contributions to my thinking and writing made by my co-authors: Nick Beckstead, Teng Fei, Marc Hauser, Frances Kissling, Agata Sagan, and Matt Wage. I have updated some of the essays where that seemed desirable, but most are essentially as they first appeared.

The idea for this book came from Rob Tempio of Princeton University Press, so an especially big thank you, Rob, for conceiving the project and seeing it through to completion. Agata Sagan went through many of my shorter writings and suggested candidates for inclusion. I accepted most of these suggestions, and thank her for the important role she has played in shaping the book. I am grateful to two anonymous reviewers for the Press for their many constructive comments, to Ellen Foos, the production editor, for her efficient management of the production process, and to Jodi Beder, the copy editor, for her light touch that nevertheless did not prevent her making suggestions that have enhanced the clarity and readability of the final text.

Peter Singer
University Center for Human Values, Princeton University,
and School of Historical and Philosophical Studies,
University of Melbourne

··· Big Questions ···

THE VALUE OF A PALE BLUE DOT

THE EIGHTEENTH-CENTURY GERMAN PHILOSOPHER Immanuel Kant wrote: "Two things fill the heart with ever renewed and increasing awe and reverence, the more often and more steadily we meditate upon them: the starry firmament above and the moral law within."

This year, the 400th anniversary of Galileo's first use of a telescope, has been declared the International Year of Astronomy, so this seems a good time to ponder Kant's first source of "awe and reverence." Indeed, the goal of the commemoration—to help the world's citizens "rediscover their place in the universe"—now has the incidental benefit of distracting us from nasty things nearer to home, like swine flu and the global financial crisis.

What does astronomy tell us about "the starry firmament above"?

By expanding our grasp of the vastness of the universe, science has, if anything, increased the awe and reverence we feel when we look up on a starry night (assuming, that is, that we have got far enough away from air pollution and excessive street lighting to see the stars properly). But, at the same time, our greater knowledge surely forces us to acknowledge that our place in the universe is not particularly significant.

In his essay "Dreams and Facts," the philosopher Bertrand Russell wrote that our entire Milky Way galaxy is a tiny fragment of the universe, and within this fragment our solar system is "an infinitesimal speck," and within this speck "our planet is a microscopic dot."

Today, we don't need to rely on such verbal descriptions of our planet's insignificance against the background of our galaxy. The astronomer Carl Sagan suggested that the Voyager space probe capture an image of Earth as it reached the outer reaches of our solar system. It did so, in 1990, and Earth shows up in a grainy image as a pale blue dot. If you go to YouTube and search for "Carl Sagan—Pale Blue Dot," you can see it, and hear Sagan himself telling us that we must cherish our world because everything humans have ever valued exists only on that pale blue dot.

That is a moving experience, but what should we learn from it?

Russell sometimes wrote as if the fact that we are a mere speck in a vast universe showed that we don't really matter all that much: "On this dot, tiny lumps of impure carbon and water, of complicated structure, with somewhat unusual physical and chemical properties, crawl about for a few years, until they are dissolved again into the elements of which they are compounded."

But no such nihilistic view of our existence follows from the size of our planetary home, and Russell himself was no nihilist. He thought that it was important to confront the fact of our insignificant place in the universe, because he did not want us to live under the illusory comfort of a belief that somehow the world had been created for our sake, and that we are under the benevolent care of an all-powerful creator. "Dreams and Facts" concludes with these stirring words: "No man is liberated from fear who dare not see his place in the world as it is; no man can achieve the greatness of which he is capable until he has allowed himself to see his own littleness."

After World War II, when the world was divided into nuclear-armed camps threatening each other with mutual destruction, Russell did not take the view that our insignificance, when considered against the vastness of the universe, meant that the end of life on Earth did not matter. On the contrary, he made nuclear disarmament the chief focus of his political activity for the remainder of his life.

Sagan took a similar view. While seeing the Earth as a whole diminishes the importance of things like national boundaries that divide us, he said, it also "underscores our responsibility to deal more kindly with one another, and to preserve and cherish the pale blue dot, the only home we've ever known." Al Gore used the "pale blue dot" image at the end of his film, *An Inconvenient Truth,* suggesting that if we wreck this planet, we have nowhere else to go.

That's probably true, even though scientists are now discovering other planets outside our solar system. Perhaps one day we will find that we are not the only intelligent beings in the universe, and perhaps we will be able to discuss issues of interspecies ethics with such beings.

This brings us back to Kant's other object of reverence and awe, the moral law within. What would beings with a completely different evolutionary origin from us—perhaps not even carbon-based life forms—think of our moral law?

from Project Syndicate, May 14, 2009

DOES ANYTHING MATTER?

CAN MORAL JUDGMENTS BE TRUE OR FALSE? Or is ethics, at bottom, a purely subjective matter, for individuals to choose, or perhaps relative to the culture of the society in which one lives? We might have just found out the answer.

Among philosophers, the view that moral judgments state objective truths has been out of fashion since the 1930s, when logical positivists asserted that, because there seems to be no way of verifying the truth of moral judgments, they cannot be anything other than expressions of our feelings or attitudes. So, for example, when we say, "You ought not to hit that child," all we are really doing is expressing our disapproval of your hitting the child, or encouraging you to stop hitting the child. There is no truth to the matter of whether or not it is wrong for you to hit the child.

Although this view of ethics has often been challenged, many of the objections have come from religious thinkers who appealed to God's commands. Such arguments have limited appeal in the largely secular world of Western philosophy. Other defenses of objective truth in ethics made no appeal to religion, but could make little headway against the prevailing philosophical mood.

Last month, however, saw a major philosophical event: the publication of Derek Parfit's long-awaited book *On What Matters*. Until now, Parfit, who is Emeritus Fellow of All Souls College, Oxford, had written only one book, *Reasons and Persons*, which appeared in 1984, to great acclaim. Parfit's entirely secular arguments, and the comprehensive way in which he tackles alternative positions, have, for the first time in decades, put those who reject objectivism in ethics on the defensive.

On What Matters is a book of daunting length: two large volumes, totaling more than 1,400 pages, of densely argued text. But the core of the argument comes in the first 400 pages, which is not an insurmountable challenge for the intellectually curious—particularly given that Parfit, in the best tradition of English-language philosophy, always strives for lucidity, never using obscure words where simple ones will do. Each sentence is straightforward, the argument is clear, and Parfit often uses vivid examples to make his points. Thus, the book is an intellectual treat for anyone who wants to understand not so much "what matters" as whether anything really *can* matter, in an objective sense.

Many people assume that rationality is always instrumental: reason can tell us only how to get what we want, but our basic wants and desires are beyond the scope of reasoning. Not so, Parfit argues. Just as we can grasp the truth that $1 + 1 = 2$, so we can see that I have a reason to avoid suffering agony at some future time, regardless of whether I now care about, or have desires about, whether I will suffer agony at that time. We can also have reasons (though not always conclusive reasons) to prevent others from suffering agony. Such self-evident normative truths provide the basis for Parfit's defense of objectivity in ethics.

One major argument against objectivism in ethics is that people disagree deeply about right and wrong, and this disagreement extends to philosophers who cannot be accused of being ignorant or confused. If great thinkers like Immanuel Kant and Jeremy Bentham disagree about what we ought to do, can there really be an objectively true answer to that question?

Parfit's response to this line of argument leads him to make a claim that is perhaps even bolder than his defense of objectivism in ethics. He considers three leading theories about what we ought to do—one deriving from Kant, one from the social-contract tradition of Hobbes, Locke, Rousseau, and the contemporary philosophers John Rawls and T. M. Scanlon, and one from Bentham's utilitarianism— and argues that the Kantian and social-contract theories must be revised in order to be defensible.

Then he argues that these revised theories coincide with a particular form of consequentialism, which is a theory in the same broad family as utilitarianism. If Parfit is right, there is much less disagreement between apparently conflicting moral theories than we all thought. The defenders of each of these theories are, in Parfit's vivid phrase, "climbing the same mountain on different sides."

Readers who go to *On What Matters* seeking an answer to the question posed by its title might be disappointed. Parfit's real interest is in combating subjectivism and nihilism. Unless he can show that objectivism is true, he believes, nothing matters.

When Parfit does come to the question of "what matters," his answer might seem surprisingly obvious. He tells us, for example, that what matters most now is that "we rich people give up some of our luxuries, ceasing to overheat the Earth's atmosphere, and taking care of this planet in other ways, so that it continues to support intelligent life."

Many of us had already reached that conclusion. What we gain from Parfit's work is the possibility of defending these and other moral claims as objective truths.

from Project Syndicate, June 13, 2011

IS THERE MORAL PROGRESS?

AFTER A CENTURY THAT SAW TWO WORLD WARS, the Nazi Holocaust, Stalin's Gulag, the killing fields of Cambodia, and the atrocities in Rwanda and Darfur, the belief that we are progressing morally has become difficult to defend. Yet there is more to the question than extreme cases of moral breakdown.

This year marks the 60th anniversary of the United Nations General Assembly's adoption of the Universal Declaration of Human Rights. In response to the crimes committed during World War II, the Declaration sought to establish the principle that everyone is entitled to the same basic rights, irrespective of race, color, sex, language, religion, or other status. So, perhaps we can judge moral progress by asking how well we have done in combating racism and sexism.

Assessing the extent to which racism and sexism have actually been reduced is a daunting task. Nevertheless, recent polls by WorldPublicOpinion.org shed some indirect light on this question.

The polls, involving nearly 15,000 respondents, were conducted in 16 countries, representing 58% of the world's population: Azerbaijan, China, Egypt, France, Great Britain, India, Indonesia, Iran, Mexico, Nigeria, the Palestinian Territories, Russia, South Korea, Turkey, Ukraine, and the United States. In 11 of these countries, most people believe that, over their lifetimes, people of different races and ethnicities have come to be treated more equally.

On average, 59% say this, with only 19% thinking that people are treated less equally, and 20% saying that there has been no change. People in the United States, Indonesia, China, Iran, and Great Britain are particularly likely to perceive greater equality. Palestinians are the only people of whom a majority sees less equality for people of different racial or ethnic groups, while opinion is relatively evenly divided in Nigeria, Ukraine, Azerbaijan, and Russia.

An even stronger overall majority, 71%, regards women as having made progress toward equality, although once again, the Palestinian territories are an exception, this time joined by Nigeria. Russia, Ukraine, and Azerbaijan again have significant minorities saying that women are now treated less equally than they once were. In India, although only 53% say that women have gained greater equality, an additional 14% say that women now have more rights than men! (Presumably, they were thinking only of those females who are not aborted because prenatal testing has shown them not to be male.)

Overall, it seems likely that these opinions reflect real changes, and thus are signs of moral progress toward a world in which people are not denied rights on the basis of race, ethnicity, or sex. That view is backed up by the polls' most striking results: very widespread rejection of inequality based on race, ethnicity, or sex. On average, 90% of those asked said that equal treatment for people of different races or ethnic origins is important, and in no country were more than 13% of respondents prepared to say that equal treatment is not important.

When asked about equal rights for women, support was almost as strong, with an average of 86% rating it important. Significantly, these majorities also existed in Muslim countries. In Egypt, for example, 97% said that racial and ethnic equality is important, and 90% said that equality for women is important. In Iran, the figures were 82% and 78%, respectively.

Compared to just a decade before the Universal Declaration of Human Rights, this represents a significant change in people's views. Equal rights for women—not simply suffrage, but also working outside the home or living independently—was still a radical idea in many countries. Openly racist ideas prevailed in Germany and the American South, and much of the world's population lived in colonies ruled by European powers. Today, despite what happened in Rwanda and the former Yugoslavia—and appeared to be on the verge of happening after the recent disputed election in Kenya—no country openly accepts racist doctrines.

Unfortunately, the same cannot be said about equal rights for women. In Saudi Arabia, women are not even permitted to drive a car, let alone vote. In many other countries, too, whatever people may say about gender equality, the reality is that women are far from having equal rights.

This may mean that the surveys I have quoted indicate not widespread equality, but widespread hypocrisy. Nevertheless, hypocrisy is the tribute that vice pays to virtue, and the fact that racists and sexists must pay this tribute is an indication of some moral progress.

Words do have consequences, and what one generation says but does not really believe, the next generation may believe, and even act upon. Public acceptance of ideas is itself progress of a kind, but what really matters is that it provides leverage that can be used to bring about more concrete progress. For that reason, we should greet the poll results positively, and resolve to close the gaps that still exist between rhetoric and reality.

from Project Syndicate, April 14, 2008

GOD AND SUFFERING, AGAIN

THE CONSERVATIVE COMMENTATOR DINESH D'SOUZA is on a mission to debate atheists on the topic of the existence of god. He has been challenging all the prominent ones he can find, and has debated Daniel Dennett, Christopher Hitchens, and Michael Schermer. I accepted his invitation, and the debate took place at Biola University. The name "Biola" comes from "Bible Institute of Los Angeles," which tells you what the predominant religious orientation of the audience was.

Given that I was debating an experienced and evidently intelligent opponent, I wanted to stake my position on firm ground. So I argued that while I cannot disprove the existence of every possible kind of deity, we can be sure that we do not live in a world that was created by a god who is all-powerful, all-knowing, and all good. Christians, of course, think we do live in such a world. Yet a powerful reason for doubting this confronts us every day: the world contains a vast amount of pain and suffering. If god is all-knowing, he knows how much suffering there is. If he is all-powerful, he could have created a world without so much suffering. If he is all-good, he surely would have created a world without so much suffering.

Christians usually respond that god bestowed on us the gift of free will, and so is not responsible for the evil we do. This response fails to deal with the suffering of those who drown in floods, are burned alive in forest fires caused by lightning, or die of hunger or thirst during a drought.

Sometimes Christians attempt to explain this suffering by saying that all humans are sinners, and so deserve their fate, even if it is a horrible one. But infants and small children are just as likely to suffer and die in natural disasters as adults, and it seems impossible that they could deserve to suffer and die. Yet, according to traditional Christian doctrine, since they have descended from Eve, they inherit the original sin of their mother, who defied god's decree against eating from the tree of knowledge. This is a triply repellant idea, for it implies, firstly, that knowledge is a bad thing, secondly, that disobeying god's will is the greatest sin of all, and thirdly, that children inherit the sins of their ancestors, and may justly be punished for them.

Even if one were to accept all this, however, the problem remains unresolved. For humans are not the only victims of floods, fires, and droughts. Animals, too, suffer from these events, and since they are not descended from Adam and Eve, they cannot have inherited original sin.

In earlier times, when original sin was taken more seriously than it generally is today, the suffering of animals posed a particularly difficult problem for thoughtful Christians. The seventeenth-century French philosopher René Descartes solved it by the drastic expedient of denying that animals can suffer. They are, he maintained, merely very ingenious mechanisms, and we should not take their cries and struggles as a sign of pain any more than we take the noise of an alarm clock as a sign that it has consciousness. That claim is unlikely to convince anyone who lives with a dog or a cat.

Surprisingly, given his experience debating with atheists, D'Souza struggled to find a convincing answer to the problem. He first said that, given that humans can live forever in heaven, the suffering of this world is less important than it would be if our life in this world were the only life we have. That still fails to explain why an all-powerful and all-good god would permit it. Relatively insignificant as it may be, from the perspective of all eternity, it is still a vast amount of suffering, and the world would be better without it, or at least without most of it. (Some say that we need to have some suffering to appreciate what it is like to be happy. Maybe—but we surely don't need as much as we have.)

Next, D'Souza argued that since god gave us life, we are not in a position to complain if our life is not perfect. He used the example of being born with one limb missing. If life itself is a gift, he said, we are not wronged by being given less than we might want. In response I pointed out that we condemn mothers who cause harm to their babies by taking alcohol or cocaine when pregnant. Yet since they have given life to their children, it seems that, on D'Souza's view, there is nothing wrong with what they have done.

Finally, D'Souza fell back, as many Christians do when pressed, on the claim that we should not expect to understand god's reasons for creating the world as it is. It is as if an ant should try to understand our decisions, so puny is our intelligence in comparison to the infinite wisdom of god. (This is the answer given, in more poetic form, in *The Book of Job*.) But once we abdicate our own powers of reason in this way, we may as well believe anything at all.

Moreover, the assertion that our intelligence is puny in comparison with god's presupposes just the point that is under debate—that there is a god who is infinitely wise, as well as all-powerful and all-good. The evidence of our own eyes makes it more plausible to believe that the world is not created by a god at all. If, however, we insist on divine creation, the god who made the world cannot be all-powerful and all-good. He must either be evil or a bungler.

from Free Inquiry, *a publication of the Council for Secular Humanism, a program of the Center for Inquiry,*
October/November 2008

GODLESS MORALITY

(with Marc Hauser)

IS RELIGION NECESSARY FOR MORALITY? Many people consider it outrageous, even blasphemous, to deny the divine origin of morality. Either some divine being crafted our moral sense, or we picked it up from the teachings of organized religion. Either way, we need religion to curb nature's vices. Paraphrasing Katharine Hepburn in the movie *The African Queen*, religion allows us to rise above wicked old Mother Nature, handing us a moral compass.

Yet problems abound for the view that morality comes from God. One problem is that we cannot, without lapsing into tautology, simultaneously say that God is good, and that he gave us our sense of good and bad. For then we are simply saying that God meets God's standards.

A second problem is that there are no moral principles that are shared by all religious people, regardless of their specific beliefs, but by no agnostics and atheists. Indeed, atheists and agnostics do not behave less morally than religious believers, even if their virtuous acts rest on different principles. Non-believers often have as strong and sound a sense of right and wrong as anyone, and have worked to abolish slavery and contributed to other efforts to alleviate human suffering.

The opposite is also true. From God's command to Moses to slaughter the Midianites—men, women, boys, and non-virginal girls—through the Crusades, the Inquisition, innumerable conflicts between Sunni and Shiite Muslims, and suicide bombers convinced that martyrdom will lead them to paradise, religion has led people to commit a long litany of horrendous crimes.

The third difficulty for the view that morality is rooted in religion is that some elements of morality seem to be universal, despite sharp doctrinal differences among the world's major religions. In fact, these elements extend even to cultures like China, where religion is less significant than philosophical outlooks like Confucianism.

Perhaps a divine creator handed us these universal elements at the moment of creation. But an alternative explanation, consistent with the facts of biology and geology, is that over millions of years we have evolved a moral faculty that generates intuitions about right and wrong.

For the first time, research in the cognitive sciences, building on theoretical arguments emerging from moral philosophy, has made it possible to resolve the ancient dispute about the origin and nature of morality.

Consider the following three scenarios. For each, fill in the blank space with "obligatory," "permissible," or "forbidden."

1. A runaway boxcar is about to run over five people walking on the tracks. A railroad worker is standing next to a switch that can turn the boxcar onto a side track, killing one person, but allowing the five to survive. Flipping the switch is _____.

2. You pass by a small child drowning in a shallow pond, and you are the only one around. If you pick up the child, she will survive and your pants will be ruined. Picking up the child is _____.

3. Five people have just been rushed into a hospital in critical condition, each requiring an organ to survive. There is not enough time to

request organs from outside the hospital, but there is a healthy person in the hospital's waiting room. If the surgeon takes this person's organs, he will die, but the five in critical care will survive. Taking the healthy person's organs is _____.

If you judged case 1 as permissible, case 2 as obligatory, and case 3 as forbidden, then you are like the 1,500 subjects around the world who responded to these dilemmas on our web-based moral sense test (http://moral.wjh.harvard.edu). If morality is God's word, atheists should judge these cases differently from religious people, and their responses should rely on different justifications.

For example, because atheists supposedly lack a moral compass, they should be guided by pure self-interest and walk by the drowning child. But there were no statistically significant differences between subjects with or without religious backgrounds, with approximately 90% of subjects saying that it is permissible to flip the switch on the boxcar, 97% saying that it is obligatory to rescue the baby, and 97% saying that is forbidden to remove the healthy person's organs.

When asked to justify why some cases are permissible and others forbidden, subjects are either clueless or offer explanations that cannot account for the relevant differences. Importantly, those with a religious background are as clueless or incoherent as atheists.

These studies provide empirical support for the idea that, like other psychological faculties of the mind, including language and mathematics, we are endowed with a moral faculty that guides our intuitive judgments of right and wrong. These intuitions reflect the outcome of millions of years in which our ancestors have lived as social mammals, and are part of our common inheritance.

Our evolved intuitions do not necessarily give us the right or consistent answers to moral dilemmas. What was good for our ancestors may not be good today. But insights into the changing moral landscape, in which issues like animal rights, abortion, euthanasia, and international aid have come to the fore, have not come from religion, but from careful reflection on humanity and what we consider a life well lived.

In this respect, it is important for us to be aware of the universal set of moral intuitions so that we can reflect on them and, if we choose, act contrary to them. We can do this without blasphemy, because it is our own nature, not God, that is the source of our morality.

from Project Syndicate, January 4, 2006

ARE WE READY FOR A "MORALITY PILL"?

(with Agata Sagan)

LAST OCTOBER, IN FOSHAN, CHINA, a two-year-old girl was run over by a van. The driver did not stop. Over the next seven minutes, more than a dozen people walked or bicycled past the injured child. A second truck ran over her. Eventually, a woman pulled her to the side, and her mother arrived. The child died in a hospital. The entire scene was captured on video and caused an uproar when it was shown by a television station and posted online. A similar event occurred in London in 2004, as have others, far from the lens of a video camera.

Yet people can, and often do, behave in very different ways.

A news search for the words "hero saves" will routinely turn up stories of bystanders braving oncoming trains, swift currents, and raging fires to save strangers from harm. Acts of extreme kindness, responsibility, and compassion are, like their opposites, nearly universal.

Why are some people prepared to risk their lives to help a stranger when others won't even stop to dial an emergency number?

Scientists have been exploring questions like this for decades. In the 1960s and early '70s, famous experiments by Stanley Milgram and Philip Zimbardo suggested that most of us would, under specific circumstances, voluntarily do great harm to innocent people. During the same period, John

Darley and C. Daniel Batson showed that even some semi-nary students on their way to give a lecture about the para-ble of the Good Samaritan would, if told that they were running late, walk past a stranger lying moaning beside the path. More recent research has told us a lot about what hap-pens in the brain when people make moral decisions. But are we getting any closer to understanding what drives our moral behavior?

Here's what much of the discussion of all these experi-ments missed: some people did the right thing. A recent ex-periment (about which we have some ethical reservations) at the University of Chicago seems to shed new light on why.

Researchers there took two rats who shared a cage and trapped one of them in a tube that could be opened only from the outside. The free rat usually tried to open the door, eventually succeeding. Even when the free rats could eat up all of a quantity of chocolate before freeing the trapped rat, they mostly preferred to free their cage-mate. The experi-menters interpret their findings as demonstrating empathy in rats. But if that is the case, they have also demonstrated that individual rats vary, for only 23 of 30 rats freed their trapped companions.

The causes of the difference in their behavior must lie in the rats themselves. It seems plausible that humans, like rats, are spread along a continuum of readiness to help others. There has been considerable research on abnormal people, like psychopaths, but we need to know more about relatively stable differences (perhaps rooted in our genes) in the great majority of people as well.

Undoubtedly, situational factors can make a huge differ-ence, and perhaps moral beliefs do as well, but if humans are just different in their predispositions to act morally, we also need to know more about these differences. Only then will we gain a proper understanding of our moral behavior, including why it varies so much from person to person and whether there is anything we can do about it.

If continuing brain research does in fact show biochemical differences between the brains of those who help others and the brains of those who do not, could this lead to a "morality pill"—a drug that makes us more likely to help? Given the many other studies linking biochemical conditions to mood and behavior, and the proliferation of drugs to modify them that have followed, the idea is not farfetched. If so, would people choose to take it? Could criminals be given the option, as an alternative to prison, of a drug-releasing implant that would make them less likely to harm others? Might governments begin screening people to discover those most likely to commit crimes? Those who are at much greater risk of committing a crime might be offered the morality pill; if they refused, they might be required to wear a tracking device that would show where they had been at any given time, so that they would know that if they did commit a crime, they would be detected.

Fifty years ago, Anthony Burgess wrote *A Clockwork Orange*, a futuristic novel about a vicious gang leader who undergoes a procedure that makes him incapable of violence. Stanley Kubrick's 1971 movie version sparked a discussion in which many argued that we could never be justified in depriving someone of his free will, no matter how gruesome the violence that would thereby be prevented. No doubt any proposal to develop a morality pill would encounter the same objection.

But if our brain's chemistry does affect our moral behavior, the question of whether that balance is set in a natural way or by medical intervention will make no difference in how freely we act. If there are already biochemical differences between us that can be used to predict how ethically we will act, then either such differences are compatible with free will, or they are evidence that at least as far as some of our ethical actions are concerned, none of us have ever had free will anyway. In any case, whether or not we have free will, we may soon face new choices about the ways in which we are willing to influence behavior for the better.

from The New York Times, *January 28, 2012*

THE QUALITY OF MERCY

THE RECENT RELEASE OF ABDEL BASSET ALI AL-MEGRAHI, the only person convicted of blowing up Pan Am Flight 103 over Lockerbie, Scotland, in 1988, sparked outrage. Around the same time, the Philadelphia Eagles, an American football team, offered a second chance to former star Michael Vick, who was convicted of running a dog-fighting operation in which unsuccessful fighters were tortured and killed. And William Calley, who commanded the platoon that massacred hundreds of Vietnamese civilians at the village of My Lai in 1968, has now broken his media silence and apologized for his actions.

When should we forgive or show mercy to wrongdoers? Many societies treat crimes involving cruelty to animals far too lightly, but Vick's penalty—23 months in prison—was substantial. In addition to imprisonment, he missed two years of his playing career, and millions of dollars in earnings. If Vick were never to play football again, he would suffer punishment well beyond that imposed by the court.

Vick has expressed remorse. Perhaps more importantly, he has turned words into deeds, volunteering at an animal shelter and working with the Humane Society of the United States to oppose dog fighting. It is hard to see what good would come from not allowing him to complete his rehabilitation and return to doing what he does best.

Megrahi was convicted of murdering 270 people, and sentenced to life imprisonment. He had served only seven years when Kenny MacAskill, the Scottish Justice Minister, released him on compassionate grounds, based on a medical report that Megrahi has terminal cancer, and only three months to live. The question of remorse has not arisen, because Megrahi has never admitted guilt, and did not drop an appeal against his conviction until just before his release.

Doubts have been raised about whether Megrahi is really near death. Only the prison doctor, it seems, was prepared to say that he did not have more than three months to live, while four specialists refused to say how long he might have.[1] There has also been speculation that Megrahi's release was related to negotiations over oil contracts between Britain and Libya. Finally, some question whether Megrahi really was the perpetrator of the crime, and this may have played a role in MacAskill's decision (although, if so, that would have been better left to the courts to resolve).

But let us leave such questions aside for the moment. Assuming that Megrahi was guilty, and that he was released because he has only a short time to live, does a prisoner's terminal illness justify compassionate release?

The answer might depend on the nature of the crime, the length of the sentence, and the proportion of it that remains to be served. For a pickpocket who has served half of a two-year sentence, it would be excessively harsh to insist on the sentence being served in full if that meant that he would die in prison, rather than with his family. But to release a man who served only seven years of a life sentence for mass murder is a very different matter. As the victims' relatives point out, in planning his crime, Megrahi showed no compassion. Why, they ask, should we show compassion to him?

---

[1] He lived until May 2012, nearly three years after his release.

MacAskill, in a statement to the Scottish Parliament defending his decision, refrained from quoting from the best-known speech on mercy in the English language—that of Portia in Shakespeare's *The Merchant of Venice*—but Portia's words would have fitted the core of his statement. Portia acknowledges that Shylock is under no obligation to show mercy to Antonio, who is in breach of his agreement to him. "The quality of mercy is not strained"—that is, constrained, or obligatory—she tells Shylock, but rather something that falls freely, like rain. MacAskill acknowledged that Megrahi himself showed no compassion, but rightly points out that this alone is not a reason to deny him compassion in his final days. He then appeals to the values of humanity, compassion, and mercy as "the beliefs we seek to live by" and frames his decision as being true to Scottish values.

We can reasonably disagree with MacAskill's decision, but we should acknowledge that—unless there is more going on than appears on the surface—he was motivated by some of the finest values we are capable of exercising. And, if we believe that Megrahi was not sufficiently punished for his crime, what are we to make of the treatment of former lieutenant William Calley?

In 1971, Calley was convicted of the murder of "no less than 22 Vietnamese civilians of undetermined age and sex." He was also convicted of assault with intent to murder a Vietnamese child. Yet three days—yes, days—after his conviction, President Richard Nixon ordered that he be released from prison and allowed to serve his sentence in a comfortable two-bedroom house. There he lived with a female companion and a staff to assist him. After three years, he was released even from this form of detention.

Calley always claimed that he was following orders. Captain Ernest Medina, his commanding officer, ordered him to burn the village down and pollute its wells, but there is no clear evidence that the order included killing non-combatants—and of course if such an order were issued, it should not have been obeyed. (Medina was acquitted of murder.)

After decades of refusing to speak publicly, Calley, who is now 66, recently said that "not a day goes by" when he does not feel remorse "for what happened that day in My Lai." One wonders if the relatives of those murdered at My Lai are more ready to forgive Calley than the relatives of those killed at Lockerbie are to forgive Megrahi.

from Project Syndicate, August 31, 2009

THINKING ABOUT THE DEAD

I HAVE JUST PUBLISHED A BOOK about my maternal grandfather, David Oppenheim.[1] A Viennese of Jewish descent, he was a member first of Sigmund Freud's circle, and later of that of Alfred Adler. But despite his abiding interest in exploring human psychology, he underestimated the Nazi threat, and did not leave quickly enough after the Nazi annexation of Austria. Deported to the overcrowded, underfed ghetto of Theresienstadt, he soon died. Fortunately my parents left Vienna in time. They were able to go to Australia where, after the war, I was born.

Many of my grandfather's letters and papers have survived. One of them asks: What is a good life? Since David Oppenheim was a classical scholar, he discusses this question in the context of a classical text: the passage from the first book of Herodotus describing the visit of Solon, the wise lawgiver of Athens, to Croesus, the fabulously wealthy king of Lydia. After entertaining Solon and hearing about his travels, Croesus asks him: "Who is the happiest man you have ever seen?" Croesus expects to hear that he, Croesus, is the happiest of all—for who is richer, or rules over a greater and more numerous people, than he? Solon dashes Croesus's expectation by naming an Athenian called Tellus. Taken aback, Croesus demands to know the reason for this choice,

[1] Peter Singer, *Pushing Time Away: My Grandfather and the Tragedy of Jewish Vienna* (New York: Ecco, 2003).

and so Solon describes the key points of Tellus's life. He lived in a prosperous city, had fine sons, and lived to see each of them have children. He had wealth enough. And he had a glorious death, falling in battle just as the enemy were being routed. The Athenians paid him the high honor of a public funeral on the spot where he fell.

From this story my grandfather distils Solon's conception of a happy life as consisting in ten elements:

1. A period of peaceful prosperity for his country.
2. A life that stretches out far into the third generation.
3. One does not lose the complete vigor of a valiant man.
4. A comfortable income.
5. Well-brought-up children.
6. Assurance of the continuation of one's line through numerous thriving grandchildren.
7. A quick death.
8. Victorious confirmation of one's own strength.
9. The highest funeral honors.
10. The preservation of one's own name through glorious commemoration by the citizens.

As we can see from the last two points, Solon believed that what happens to people after they die—what kind of funeral they have, and how their name is remembered—makes a difference to how good their lives were. This was not because Solon imagined that, after you died, you could look down from somewhere and see what kind of a funeral you were given. There is no suggestion that Solon believed in any kind of afterlife, and certainly I don't. But does skepticism about a life after death force one to conclude that what happens after you die cannot make a difference to how well your life has gone?

In thinking about this issue, I vacillate between two incompatible positions: that something can only matter to you if it has an impact on your awareness, that is, if you experience it in some way; and that what matters is that your preferences be satisfied, whether or not you know of it, and indeed whether or not you are alive at the time when they are satisfied. The former view, held by classical utilitarians like Jeremy Bentham, is more straightforward, and in some ways easier to defend, philosophically. But imagine the following situation. A year ago a colleague of yours in the university department in which you work was told that she had cancer, and could not expect to live more than a year or so. On hearing the news, she took leave without pay and spent the year writing a book that drew together ideas that she had been working on during the ten years you had known her. The task exhausted her, but now it is done. Close to death, she calls you to her home and presents you with a typescript. "This," she tells you, "is what I want to be remembered by. Please find a publisher for it." You congratulate your friend on finishing the work. She is weak and tired, but evidently satisfied just with having put it in your hands. You say your farewells. The next day you receive a phone call telling you that your colleague died in her sleep shortly after you left her house. You read her typescript. It is undoubtedly publishable, but not ground-breaking work. "What's the point?" you think to yourself, "We don't really need another book on these topics. She's dead, and she'll never know if her book appears anyway." Instead of sending the typescript to a publisher, you drop it in a recycling bin.

Did you do something wrong? More specifically, did you wrong your colleague? Did you in some way make her life less good than it would have been if you had taken the book to a publisher, and it had appeared, gaining as much and as little attention as many other worthy but not ground-breaking academic works? If we answer that question affirmatively, then what we do after a person dies can make a difference to how well their life went.

Writing about my grandfather has forced me to think about whether it makes sense to believe that, in reading my grandfather's works and bringing his life and thought to a larger audience, I am doing something *for him*, and in some way mitigating, however slightly, the wrong that the Nazis did to him. It is easy to imagine that a grandfather would like to be remembered by his grandchildren, and that a scholar and author would like to be read after his death. Perhaps this is especially so when he dies a victim of persecution by a dictatorship that sought to suppress the liberal, cosmopolitan ideas my grandfather favored, and to exterminate all members of his tribe. Do I have here an example of how, as Solon said, what happens after one dies does make a difference to how well one's life goes? I don't think you have to believe in an afterlife to give this question an affirmative answer.

from Free Inquiry, *a publication of the Council for Secular Humanism, a program of the Center for Inquiry, Summer 2003*

SHOULD THIS BE THE LAST GENERATION?

HAVE YOU EVER THOUGHT ABOUT WHETHER to have a child? If so, what factors entered into your decision? Was it whether having children would be good for you, your partner, and others close to the possible child, such as children you may already have, or perhaps your parents? For most people contemplating reproduction, those are the dominant questions. Some may also think about the desirability of adding to the strain that the nearly seven billion people already here are putting on our planet's environment. But very few ask whether coming into existence is a good thing for the child itself. Most of those who consider that question probably do so because they have some reason to fear that the child's life would be especially difficult—for example, if they have a family history of a devastating illness, physical or mental, that cannot yet be detected prenatally.

All this suggests that we think it is wrong to bring into the world a child whose prospects for a happy, healthy life are poor, but we don't usually think the fact that a child is likely to have a happy, healthy life is a reason for bringing the child into existence. This has come to be known among philosophers as "the asymmetry," and it is not easy to justify. But rather than go into the explanations usually proffered—and why they fail—I want to raise a related problem. How good does life have to be to make it reasonable to bring a child into the world? Is the standard of life experienced by most people in developed nations today good enough to make this decision unproblematic, in the absence of specific knowledge that the child will have a severe genetic disease or other problem?

The nineteenth-century German philosopher Arthur Schopenhauer held that even the best life possible for humans is one in which we strive for ends that, once achieved, bring only fleeting satisfaction. New desires then lead us on to further futile struggle, and the cycle repeats itself.

Schopenhauer's pessimism has had few defenders over the past two centuries, but one has recently emerged, in the South African philosopher David Benatar, author of a fine book with an arresting title: *Better Never to Have Been: The Harm of Coming into Existence.* One of Benatar's arguments trades on something like the asymmetry noted earlier. To bring into existence someone who will suffer is, Benatar argues, to harm that person, but to bring into existence someone who will have a good life is not to benefit him or her. Few of us would think it right to inflict severe suffering on an innocent child, even if that were the only way in which we could bring many other children into the world. Yet everyone will suffer to some extent, and if our species continues to reproduce, we can be sure that some future children will suffer severely. Hence continued reproduction will harm some children severely, and benefit none.

Benatar also argues that human lives are, in general, much less good than we think they are. We spend most of our lives with unfulfilled desires, and the occasional satisfactions that are all most of us can achieve are insufficient to outweigh these prolonged negative states. If we think that this is a tolerable state of affairs it is because we are, in Benatar's view, victims of the illusion of pollyannaism. This illusion may have evolved because it helped our ancestors survive, but it is an illusion nonetheless. If we could see our lives objectively, we would see that they are not something we should inflict on anyone.

Here is a thought experiment to test our attitudes to this view. Most thoughtful people are extremely concerned about climate change. Some stop eating meat, or flying abroad on vacation, in order to reduce their carbon footprint. But the people who will be most severely harmed by climate change have not yet been conceived. If there were to be no future generations, there would be much less for us to feel guilty about.

So why don't we make ourselves the last generation on Earth? If we would all agree to have ourselves sterilized then no sacrifices would be required—we could party our way into extinction!

Of course, it would be impossible to get agreement on universal sterilization, but just imagine that we could. Then is there anything wrong with this scenario? Even if we take a less pessimistic view of human existence than Benatar, we could still defend it, because it makes us better off—for one thing, we can get rid of all that guilt about what we are doing to future generations—and it doesn't make anyone worse off, because there won't be anyone else to be worse off.

Is a world with people in it better than one without? Put aside what we do to other species—that's a different issue. Let's assume that the choice is between a world like ours and one with no sentient beings in it at all. And assume, too—here we have to get fictitious, as philosophers often do—that if we choose to bring about the world with no sentient beings at all, everyone will agree to do that. No one's rights will be violated—at least, not the rights of any existing people. Can non-existent people have a right to come into existence?

I do think it would be wrong to choose the non-sentient universe. In my judgment, for most people, life is worth living. Even if that is not yet the case, I am enough of an optimist to believe that, should humans survive for another century or two, we will learn from our past mistakes and bring about a world in which there is far less suffering than there is now. But justifying that choice forces us to reconsider the deep issues with which I began. Is life worth living? Are the interests of a future child a reason for bringing that child into existence? And is the continuance of our species justifiable in the face of our knowledge that it will certainly bring suffering to innocent future human beings?

from The New York Times, *June 6, 2010*

PHILOSOPHY ON TOP

LAST YEAR, A REPORT FROM HARVARD UNIVERSITY set off alarm bells, because it showed that the proportion of students in the United States completing bachelor's degrees in the humanities fell from 14 to 7 percent. Even elite universities like Harvard itself have experienced a similar decrease. Moreover, the decline seems to have become steeper in recent years. There is talk of a crisis in the humanities.

I don't know enough about the humanities as a whole to comment on what is causing enrollments to fall. Perhaps many humanities disciplines are not seen as likely to lead to fulfilling careers, or to any careers at all. Maybe that is because some disciplines are failing to communicate to outsiders what they do and why it matters. Or, difficult as it may be to accept, maybe it is not just a matter of communication: perhaps some humanities disciplines really *have* become less relevant to the exciting and fast-changing world in which we live.

I state these possibilities without reaching a judgment about any of them. What I do know something about, however, is my own discipline, philosophy, which, through its practical side, ethics, makes a vital contribution to the most urgent debates that we can have.

I am a philosopher, so you would be justified in suspecting bias in my view. Fortunately, I can draw on an independent report by the Gottlieb Duttweiler Institute (GDI), a Swiss think tank, to support my claim.

GDI recently released a ranked list of the top 100 Global Thought Leaders for 2013. The ranking includes economists, psychologists, authors, political scientists, physicists, anthropologists, information scientists, biologists, entrepreneurs, theologians, physicians, and people from several other disciplines. Yet three of the top five global thinkers are philosophers: Slavoj Žižek, Daniel Dennett, and me. GDI classifies a fourth, Jürgen Habermas, as a sociologist, but the report acknowledges that he, too, is arguably a philosopher.

The only Global Thought Leader in the top five not involved in philosophy is Al Gore. There are more economists in the top 100 than thinkers from any other single discipline, but the top-ranking economist, Nicholas Stern, ranks tenth overall.

Can it really be true that four of the world's five most influential thinkers come from the humanities, and three or four from philosophy? To answer that question, we have to ask what GDI measures when it compiles its ranking of Global Thought Leaders.

GDI aims to identify "the thinkers and ideas that resonate with the global infosphere as a whole." The infosphere from which the data are drawn may be global, but it is also English-language only, which may explain why no Chinese thinker is represented in the top 100. There are three eligibility requirements: one has to be working primarily as a thinker; one must be known beyond one's own discipline; and one must be influential.

The ranking is an amalgam of many different measurements, including how widely the thinkers are watched and followed on YouTube and Twitter, and how prominently they feature in blogs and in the wikisphere. The outcome indicates each thinker's relevance across countries and subject areas, and the ranking selects those thinkers who are most talked about and who are triggering wider debate.

The rankings will no doubt vary from year to year. But we have to conclude that in 2013 a handful of philosophers were particularly influential in the world of ideas.

That would not have been news to the Athenian leaders who considered what Socrates was doing to be sufficiently disturbing to put him to death for "corrupting the youth." Nor will it be news to anyone familiar with the many successful efforts to bring philosophy to a broader market.

There is, for example, the magazine *Philosophy Now,* and equivalents in other languages. There are the Philosophy Bites podcasts, many blogs, and free online courses, which are attracting tens of thousands of students.

Perhaps the growing interest in reflecting on the universe and our lives is the result of the fact that, for at least a billion people on our planet, the problems of food, shelter, and personal security have largely been solved. That leads us to ask what else we want, or should want, from life, and that is a starting point for many lines of philosophical inquiry.

Doing philosophy—thinking and arguing about it, not just passively reading it—develops our critical reasoning abilities, and so equips us for many of the challenges of a rapidly changing world. Perhaps that is why many employers are now keen to hire graduates who have done well in philosophy courses.

More surprising, and possibly even more significant than the benefits of doing philosophy for general reasoning abilities, is the way in which taking a philosophy class can change a person's life. I know from my own experience that taking a course in philosophy can lead students to turn vegan, pursue careers that enable them to give half their income to effective charities, and even donate a kidney to a stranger. How many other disciplines can say that?

from Project Syndicate, April 9, 2014

... Animals ...

Animals

FORTY YEARS AGO, I STOOD WITH A FEW OTHER STUDENTS in a busy Oxford street handing out leaflets protesting the use of battery cages to hold hens. Most of those who took the leaflets did not know that their eggs came from hens kept in cages so small that even one bird—the cages normally housed four—would be unable to fully stretch and flap her wings. The hens could never walk around freely, or lay eggs in a nest.

Many people applauded our youthful idealism, but told us that we had no hope of ever changing a major industry. They were wrong.

On the first day of 2012, keeping hens in such cages became illegal, not only in the United Kingdom, but in all 27 countries of the European Union. Hens can still be kept in cages, but they must have more space, and the cages must have nest boxes and a scratching post. Last month, members of the British Hen Welfare Trust provided a new home for a hen they named "Liberty." She was, they said, among the last hens in Britain still living in the type of cages we had opposed.

In the early 1970s, when the modern animal liberation movement began, no major organization was campaigning against the battery cage. The Royal Society for the Prevention of Cruelty to Animals, the mother of all animal-protection organizations, had lost its early radicalism long before. It focused on isolated cases of abuse, and failed to challenge well-established ways of mistreating animals on farms or in laboratories. It took a concerted effort by the new animal radicals of the 1970s to stir the RSPCA from its complacency toward the battery cage and other forms of intensive animal rearing.

Eventually, the new animal-rights movement managed to reach the broader public. Consumers responded by buying eggs from free-ranging hens. Some supermarket chains even ceased to carry eggs from battery hens.

In Britain and some European countries, animal welfare became politically salient, and pressure on parliamentary representatives mounted. The European Union established a scientific committee to investigate animal-welfare issues on farms, and the committee recommended banning the battery cage, along with some other forms of close confinement of pigs and calves. A ban on battery cages in the EU was eventually adopted in 1999, but, to ensure that producers would have plenty of time to phase out the equipment in which they had invested, its implementation was delayed until January 1, 2012.

To its credit, the British egg industry accepted the situation, and developed new and less cruel methods of keeping hens. Not all countries are equally ready, however, and it has been estimated that up to 80 million hens may still be in illegal battery cages. But at least 300 million hens who would have lived miserable lives in standard battery cages are now in significantly better conditions, and there is great pressure on the EU bureaucracy to enforce the ban everywhere—not least from egg producers who are already complying with it.

With the ban on battery cages, Europe confirms its place as the world leader in animal welfare, a position also reflected in its restrictions on the use of animals to test cosmetics. But why is Europe so far ahead of other countries in its concern for animals?

In the United States, there are no federal laws about how egg producers house their hens. But, when the issue was put to California voters in 2008, they overwhelmingly supported a proposition requiring that all farm animals have room to stretch their limbs fully and turn around without touching other animals or the sides of their cage. That suggests that the problem may not be with US citizens' attitudes, but rather that, at the federal level, the US political system allows industries with large campaign chests too much power to thwart the wishes of popular majorities.

In China, which, along with the US, confines the largest number of hens in cages, an animal welfare movement is only just beginning to emerge. For the sake of the welfare of billions of farmed animals, we should wish it rapid growth and success.

The start of this year is a moment to celebrate a major advance in animal welfare, and, therefore, for Europe, a step toward becoming a more civilized and humane society—one that shows its concern for all beings capable of suffering. It is also an occasion for celebrating the effectiveness of democracy, and the power of an ethical idea.

The anthropologist Margaret Mead is reported to have said: "Never doubt that a small group of thoughtful, committed citizens can change the world. Indeed, it is the only thing that ever has." The last part may not be true, but the first part surely is. The end of the battery cage in Europe is a less dramatic development than the Arab Spring, but, like that popular uprising, it began with a small group of thoughtful and committed people.

from Project Syndicate, January 17, 2012

IF FISH COULD SCREAM

WHEN I WAS A CHILD, my father used to take me for walks, often along a river or by the sea. We would pass people fishing, perhaps reeling in their lines with struggling fish hooked at the end of them. Once I saw a man take a small fish out of a bucket and impale it, still wriggling, on an empty hook to use as bait.

Another time, when our path took us by a tranquil stream, I saw a man sitting and watching his line, seemingly at peace with the world, while next to him, fish he had already caught were flapping helplessly and gasping in the air. My father told me that he could not understand how anyone could enjoy an afternoon spent taking fish out of the water and letting them die slowly.

These childhood memories flooded back when I read *Worse Things Happen at Sea: The Welfare of Wild-Caught Fish*, a breakthrough report released last month on fishcount. org.uk. In most of the world, it is accepted that if animals are to be killed for food, they should be killed without suffering. Regulations for slaughter generally require that animals be rendered instantly unconscious before they are killed, or death should be brought about instantaneously, or, in the case of ritual slaughter, as close to instantaneously as the religious doctrine allows.

Not for fish. There is no humane slaughter requirement for wild fish caught and killed at sea, nor, in most places, for farmed fish. Fish caught in nets by trawlers are dumped on board the ship and allowed to suffocate. In the commercial fishing technique known as longline fishing, trawlers let out lines that can be 50–100 kilometers long, with hundreds or even thousands of baited hooks. Fish taking the bait are likely to remain fully conscious while they are dragged around for many hours by hooks through their mouths, until eventually the line is hauled in.

Likewise, commercial fishing frequently depends on gill nets—walls of fine netting in which fish become snared, often by the gills. They may suffocate in the net, because, with their gills constricted, they cannot breathe. If not, they may remain trapped for many hours before the nets are pulled in.

The most startling revelation in the report, however, is the staggering number of fish on which humans inflict these deaths. By using the reported tonnages of the various species of fish caught, and dividing by the estimated average weight for each species, Alison Mood, the report's author, has put together what may well be the first-ever systematic estimate of the size of the annual global capture of wild fish. It is, she calculates, in the order of *one trillion*, although it could be as high as 2.7 trillion.

To put this in perspective, the United Nations Food and Agriculture Organization estimates that 60 billion vertebrate land animals are killed each year for human consumption— the equivalent of about nine animals for each human being on the planet. If we take Mood's lower estimate of one trillion, the comparable figure for fish is 150. This does not include billions of fish caught illegally nor unwanted fish accidentally caught and discarded, nor does it count the live fish impaled on hooks as bait in longline fishing.

Many of these fish are consumed indirectly—ground up and fed to factory-farmed chicken or fish. A typical salmon farm churns through 3–4 kilograms of wild fish for every kilogram of salmon that it produces.

Let's assume that all this fishing is sustainable, though of course it is not. It would then be reassuring to believe that killing on such a vast scale does not matter, because fish do not feel pain. But the nervous systems of fish are sufficiently similar to those of birds and mammals to suggest that they do. When fish experience something that would cause other animals physical pain, they behave in ways suggestive of pain, and the change in behavior may last several hours. (It is a myth that fish have short memories.) Fish learn to avoid unpleasant experiences, like electric shocks. And pain-killers reduce the symptoms of pain that they would otherwise show.

Victoria Braithwaite, a professor of fisheries and biology at Pennsylvania State University, has probably spent more time investigating this issue than any other scientist. Her recent book *Do Fish Feel Pain?* shows that fish not only are capable of feeling pain, but also are a lot smarter than most people believe. Last year, a scientific panel to the European Union concluded that the preponderance of the evidence indicates that fish do feel pain.

Why are fish the forgotten victims on our plate? Is it because they are cold-blooded and covered in scales? Is it because they cannot give voice to their pain? Whatever the explanation, the evidence is now accumulating that commercial fishing inflicts an unimaginable amount of pain and suffering. We need to learn how to capture and kill wild fish humanely—or, if that is not possible, to find less cruel and more sustainable alternatives to eating them.

from Project Syndicate, September 13, 2010

CULTURAL BIAS AGAINST WHALING?

THIRTY YEARS AGO, AUSTRALIAN VESSELS WERE, with government blessing, killing sperm whales off the West Australian coast. Last month, Australia led international protests against Japan's plan to kill 50 humpback whales, and Japan, under pressure, announced that it would suspend the plan for a year or two. The change in public opinion about whaling has been dramatic, and not only in Australia.

Greenpeace began the protests against Australian whaling. The government appointed Sydney Frost, a retired judge, to head an inquiry into whaling. As a concerned Australian and a philosophy professor working on the ethics of our treatment of animals, I made a submission.

I did not argue that whaling should stop because whales are endangered. I knew that there were many expert ecologists and marine biologists who would put forward that claim. Instead I argued that whales are social mammals with big brains, capable of enjoying life and of feeling pain—and not only physical pain, but very likely also distress at the loss of one of their group. Whales cannot be humanely killed—they are too large, and even with an explosive harpoon, it is difficult to hit the whale in the right spot. Moreover, whalers do not want to use a large amount of explosive, because that will blow the whale to pieces, and the whole point of whaling is to recover valuable oil or flesh from the whale. Hence harpooned whales typically die slowly and painfully.

These facts raise a big ethical question mark over whaling. If there were some life-or-death need that humans could only meet by killing whales, perhaps the ethical case against it could be met. But there is no essential human need that requires us to kill whales. Everything we get from whales can be obtained without cruelty. Causing suffering to innocent beings without an extremely weighty reason for doing so is wrong, and hence whaling is unethical.

Frost agreed. He said that there could be no doubt that the methods used to kill whales were inhumane—he even described them as "most horrible." He also mentioned "the real possibility that we are dealing with a creature which has a remarkably developed brain and a high degree of intelligence." He recommended that whaling be stopped, and the conservative government, led by Prime Minister Malcolm Fraser, accepted the recommendation. Australia soon became an anti-whaling nation.

Despite the suspension of the plan to kill humpback whales, the Japanese whaling fleet will still kill about 1,000 other whales, mostly smaller minke whales. It justifies its whaling as "research" because a provision in the rules of the International Whaling Commission allows member nations to kill whales for research purposes. But the research seems to be largely directed to building a scientific case for a resumption of commercial whaling, so if whaling is unethical, then the research is itself both unnecessary and unethical.

Japan says that it wants the discussion of whaling to be carried out calmly, on the basis of scientific evidence, without "emotion." They think that the evidence will show that humpback whale numbers have increased sufficiently for the killing of 50 to pose no danger to the species. On this narrow point, they could be right. But no amount of science can tell us whether or not to kill whales. "Emotion" is just as much behind the Japanese desire to continue to kill whales as it is behind the opposition of environmentalists to that killing. Eating whales is not necessary for the health or better nutrition of the Japanese. It is a tradition that they wish to continue, presumably because some Japanese are emotionally attached to it.

The Japanese do have one argument that is not so easily dismissed. They claim that Western countries object to Japanese whaling because for them whales are a special kind of animals, as cows are for Hindus. Western nations should not, the Japanese say, try to impose their cultural beliefs on them.

The best response to this argument is that the wrongness of causing needless suffering to sentient beings is not a culturally specific value. It is, for example, one of the first precepts of one of Japan's major ethical traditions, Buddhism. But Western nations are in a weak position to make this response, because they themselves inflict so much unnecessary suffering on animals. The Australian government, which has come out so strongly against whaling, permits the killing of millions of kangaroos each year, a slaughter that involves a great deal of animal suffering. The same can be said of various forms of hunting in other countries, not to mention the vast quantities of animal suffering caused by factory farms.

Whaling should stop because it brings needless suffering to social, intelligent animals capable of enjoying their own lives. But against the Japanese charge of cultural bias, Western nations will have little defense until they do much more about the needless animal suffering in their own countries.

from Project Syndicate, January 14, 2008

A CASE FOR VEGANISM

CAN WE DEFEND THE THINGS WE DO TO ANIMALS? Christians, Jews, and Muslims may appeal to scripture to justify their dominion over animals. Once we move beyond a religious outlook, we have to face "the animal question" without any prior assumption that animals were created for our benefit or that our use of them has divine sanction. If we are just one species among others that have evolved on this planet, and if the other species include billions of nonhuman animals who can also suffer, or conversely can enjoy their lives, should our interests always count for more than theirs?

Of all the ways in which we affect animals, the one most in need of justification today is raising them for food. Far more animals are affected by this than by any other human activity. In the United States alone, the number of animals raised and killed for food every year is now nearly ten billion.[1] All of this is, strictly speaking, unnecessary. In developed countries, where we have a wide choice of foods, no one needs to eat meat. Many studies show that we can live as healthily, or more healthily, without it. We can also live well on a vegan diet, consuming no animal products at all. (Vitamin B12 is the only essential nutrient not available from plant foods, and it is easy to take a supplement obtained from vegan sources.)

[1] Surprisingly, the number of farm animals killed in the US peaked around the time this article was written, and has subsequently fallen to 9.1 billion.

Ask people what the main ethical problem about eating animals is, and most will refer to killing. That is an issue, of course, but at least as far as modern industrial animal productions is concerned, there is a more straightforward objection. Even if there were nothing wrong with killing animals because we like the taste of their flesh, we would still be supporting a system of agriculture that inflicts prolonged suffering on animals.

Chickens raised for meat are kept in sheds that hold more than 20,000 birds. The level of ammonia in the air from their accumulated droppings stings the eyes and hurts the lungs. Today's chickens have been bred to gain weight as fast as possible; the result is that they reach market weight at only 42 days, but their immature bones can hardly bear the weight of their bodies. Some collapse and, unable to reach food or water, soon die, their fate irrelevant to the economics of the enterprise as a whole. Catching, transport, and slaughter are brutal processes in which the economic incentives all favor speed, and the welfare of the birds plays no role at all.

Laying hens are crammed into wire cages so small that even if there were just one per cage, she would be unable to stretch her wings. But there are usually at least four hens per cage, and often more. Under such crowded conditions, the more dominant, aggressive birds are likely to peck to death the weaker hens in the cage. To prevent this, producers sear off the beaks of all the birds with a hot blade. A hen's beak is full of nerve tissue—it is her principal means of relating to her environment—but no anesthetic or analgesic is used to relieve the pain.

Pigs may be the most intelligent and sensitive of the animals we commonly eat. In today's factory farms, pregnant sows are kept in crates so narrow that they cannot turn around, or even walk more than a step forward or backward.

They lie on concrete without straw or any other form of bedding. They have no way of satisfying their instinct to build a nest just before giving birth. The piglets are taken from the sow as soon as possible, so that she can be made pregnant again, but they too are kept indoors, on concrete, until they are taken to slaughter.

Beef cattle spend the last six months of their lives in feedlots, on bare dirt, eating grain that is not suitable for their digestion, fed steroids to make them put on more muscle, and antibiotics to keep them alive. They have no shade from the blazing summer sun, or shelter from winter blizzards.

But what, you may ask, is wrong with milk and other dairy products? Don't the cows have a good life, grazing on the fields? And we don't have to kill them to get milk. But most dairy cows are now kept inside, and do not have access to pasture. Like human females, they do not give milk unless they have recently had a baby, and so dairy cows are made pregnant every year. The calf is taken away from its mother just hours after birth, so that it will not drink the milk intended for humans. If it is male, it may be killed immediately, or raised for veal, or perhaps for hamburger beef. The bond between a cow and her calf is strong, and she will often call for the calf for several days after it is taken away.

In addition to the ethical question of our treatment of animals, there is now a powerful new argument for a vegan diet. Ever since Frances Moore Lappé published *Diet for a Small Planet* in 1971, we have known that modern industrial animal production is extremely wasteful. Pig farms use six pounds of grain for every pound of boneless meat they produce. For beef cattle in feedlots, the ratio is 13:1. Even for chickens, the least inefficient factory-farmed meat, the ratio is 3:1.

Lappé was concerned about the waste of food and the extra pressure on arable land this involves, since we could be eating the grain and soybeans directly, and feeding ourselves just as well from much less land. Now global warming sharpens the problem. Most Americans think that the best thing they could do to cut their personal contribution to global warming would be to swap their family car for a fuel-efficient hybrid like the Toyota Prius. Gidon Eshel and Pamela Martin, researchers at the University of Chicago, have calculated that while this would indeed lead to a reduction in emissions of about 1 ton of carbon dioxide per driver, switching from the typical US diet to a vegan diet would save the equivalent of almost 1.5 tons of carbon dioxide per person. Vegans are therefore doing significantly less damage to our climate than those who eat animal products.[2]

Is there an ethical way of eating animal products? It is possible to obtain meat, eggs, and dairy products from animals who have been treated less cruelly, and allowed to eat grass rather than grain or soy. Limiting one's consumption of animal products to these sources also avoids some of the greenhouse gas emissions, although cows kept on grass still emit substantial amounts of methane, a particularly potent contributor to global warming. So *if* there is no serious ethical objection to killing animals, as long as they have had good lives, then being selective about the animal products you eat could provide an ethically defensible diet. It needs care,

[2] Gidon Eshel and Pamela Martin, "Diet, Energy and Global Warming," *Earth Interactions* 10 (2006):1–17.

however. "Organic," for instance, says little about animal welfare, and hens not kept in cages may still be crowded into a large shed. Going vegan is a simpler choice that sets a clear-cut example for others to follow.

from Free Inquiry, *a publication of the Council for Secular Humanism, a program of the Center for Inquiry,*
April/May 2007

CONSIDER THE TURKEY: THOUGHTS
FOR THANKSGIVING

WHEN I TEACH PRACTICAL ETHICS, I encourage my students to take the arguments we discuss outside the classroom and talk to friends and family about them. For Americans, there is no better occasion for a conversation about the ethics of what we eat than Thanksgiving, the holiday at which, more than any other, families come together around a meal. With that in mind, I arrange the topics in my course so that issues about food and ethics arise just before Thanksgiving.

The traditional centerpiece of the Thanksgiving meal is a turkey, so that is the obvious place to start the conversation. According to the National Turkey Federation, about 46 million turkeys are killed for Thanksgiving each year, a substantial part of the 300 million turkeys Americans eat annually. The vast majority of them—at least 99 percent—are raised on factory farms. In many respects, their lives are like those of factory-farmed chickens. The newly hatched turkeys are raised in incubators and then, before they are sent to the producers to be raised, at a time when chickens are debeaked, the young turkeys undergo that too, and also have their talons cut off, and for male turkeys, their snood—the fleshy erectile protuberance that grows from the forehead of a male turkey. All this is done without anesthetic, despite the pain it clearly causes. The beak, for example, is not just a horny substance like a fingernail. It is full of nerves that enable a free-living turkey to peck at the ground and distinguish something edible from something that is not.

The reason for these mutilations is that the birds are about to be placed in dim, poorly ventilated sheds, where they will live out the rest of their lives crowded together with thousands of other birds. The air reeks of ammonia from the birds' droppings, which accumulate for the four or five months that the turkeys are in the sheds. In these unnatural and stressful conditions, turkeys will peck or claw at other birds, and cannibalism can occur. The snood is removed because it is often a target for pecking from other birds.

When the birds reach market weight, they are deprived of food and water, rounded up, often in a very rough manner (undercover videos show turkeys being picked up and thrown into shipping crates) and transported to slaughter. Each year, hundreds of thousands don't even make it to slaughter—they die from the stress of the journey. If they do make it, then, again like chickens, they are still not guaranteed a humane death, because the US Department of Agriculture interprets the Humane Slaughter Act as not applying to birds.

One difference between turkeys and chickens is that turkeys have been drastically altered by breeding designed to enlarge the breast, which is considered the most desirable part of the turkey to eat. This process has gone so far that the standard American turkey, the descriptively named Broad Breasted White, is incapable of mating because the male's big breast gets in the way. Here, I tell my students, is an interesting question to drop into a lull in conversation around the Thanksgiving dinner table. Point to the turkey on the table and ask: if turkeys can't mate, how was that turkey produced?

Some years ago, I teamed up with Jim Mason, who grew up on a farm in Missouri, to write a book called *The Ethics of*

What We Eat. Jim decided to see for himself how all the hundreds of millions of sexually disabled turkeys are produced. He saw that Butterball, a large industrial producer and processor of turkeys, was advertising for workers for its artificial insemination crew in Carthage, Missouri. No prior experience was required. Jim passed a drug test and was put to work. His first role was to catch the male turkeys by the legs and hold them upside down so that another worker could masturbate them. When the semen flowed out, the worker used a vacuum pump to collect it in a syringe. This was done with one bird after another until the semen, diluted with an "extender," filled the syringe, which was then taken to the hen house.

Jim also had a spell working in the hen house, which he found worse than working with the males. Here is his account:

> You grab a hen by the legs, trying to cross both "ankles" in order to hold her feet and legs with one hand. The hens weigh 20 to 30 pounds and are terrified, beating their wings and struggling in panic. They go through this every week for more than a year, and they don't like it. Once you have grabbed her with one hand, you flop her down, chest first, on the edge of the pit with the tail end sticking up. You put your free hand over the vent and tail and pull the rump and tail feathers upward. At the same time, you pull the hand holding the feet downward, thus "breaking" the hen so that her rear is straight up and her vent open. The inseminator sticks his thumb right under the vent and pushes, which opens it further until the end of the oviduct is exposed. Into this, he inserts a straw of semen connected to the end of a tube from an air compressor and pulls a trigger, releasing a shot of compressed air that blows the semen solution from the straw and into the hen's oviduct. Then you let go of the hen and she flops away.

Jim was supposed to "break" one hen every 12 seconds, 300
an hour, for 10 hours a day. He had to dodge spurting shit
from panicked birds, and torrents of verbal abuse from the
foreman if he didn't keep up the pace. It was, he told me, "the
hardest, fastest, dirtiest, most disgusting, worst-paid work I
have ever done."

Back to the Thanksgiving table. Now that the family un-
derstands exactly how the bird they are eating came into existence, and what kind of a life and death it has had, I suggest
to my students that they canvass opinions on whether it is
ethical to support this way of treating animals. If the answer
is no, then something needs to be changed for next year's
Thanksgiving, because our willingness to purchase industri-
ally produced turkeys is the only incentive the turkey industry needs to continue to treat turkeys with so little respect
for their interests.

There are other options. A heritage turkey, of a breed able
to mate, raised on pasture and not mutilated, will cost you
about four times as much, pound for pound, as a factory-
farmed one, but at least you will know that the bird had a
good life. Or will you? There have been allegations of fraud
against producers who keep a few hundred turkeys in humane conditions outdoors, but sell several times that many
turkeys, most of them birds who never go outside. If you
really want to ensure your bird was raised outdoors, you
have some work ahead of you checking the veracity of the
producer.

The alternative, of course, is a plant-based Thanksgiving
meal, which, as well as avoiding complicity in cruelty to animals, is better for the environment and for you too. Search
for "vegetarian Thanksgiving" on the *New York Times* website and you'll find plenty of delicious seasonal recipes suited

for the occasion. Or if you don't want to cook, you can always buy a tofurkey.

People will say that turkey is traditional at Thanksgiving. In fact it isn't clear if the pilgrims ate wild turkey at that first Thanksgiving in 1621, but one thing is sure: they didn't eat a factory-farmed Broad Breasted White.

Not previously published

IN VITRO MEAT

EIGHTY YEARS AGO, WINSTON CHURCHILL looked forward to the day when "we shall escape the absurdity of growing a whole chicken in order to eat the breast or wing, by growing these parts separately under a suitable medium." Churchill thought this would take only 50 years. We are still not there, but today we will reach a milestone on the road to the future that Churchill envisaged: the first public tasting of in vitro meat.

The scientist behind this historic event is Dr. Mark Post, of the University of Maastricht, in the Netherlands. The idea is simple: take some muscle tissue from a single cow and grow it in a nutrient solution. It will multiply and eventually we will have something that really is meat, cell for cell. In practice, however, there are many obstacles to overcome. We aren't even close to growing chicken breasts, or a steak. The first objective is to produce a hamburger, and this week's tasting is intended to demonstrate that it can be done. The hamburger will consist of real bovine muscle tissue, but it was never part of a cow that suffered, or belched methane as it digested its food.

Should beef producers look for some other line of work? Eventually, perhaps, but not quite yet; the cost of producing the piece of hamburger that will be tasted exceeds £200,000.

Still, once the researchers have found ways of overcoming the initial obstacles, there is no reason in vitro meat should not be competitive in price with meat from animals. Most of the meat sold today comes from animals that have been fed on grain or soybeans. Those crops had to be grown and transported to the animals, who then use part of the nutrients from their food to produce bone or other body parts that we do not eat. It ought to be possible to make considerable savings by going directly from the nutrients to the meat.

There are important ethical reasons why we should replace animal meat with in vitro meat, if we can do it at reasonable cost. The first is to reduce animal suffering. Just as the cruelty inflicted on working horses, so movingly depicted in Anna Sewell's *Black Beauty*, was eventually eliminated by the efficiency of the internal combustion engine, so the vastly greater quantity of suffering that is inflicted on tens of billions of animals in today's factory farms could be eliminated by a more efficient way of producing meat.

You would have to have a heart of stone not to applaud such an outcome. But it needn't be simply an emotional response. Among philosophers who discuss the ethics of our treatment of animals there is a remarkable degree of consensus that factory farming violates basic ethical principles that extend beyond the boundary of our own species. Even a staunch conservative such as Roger Scruton, who vigorously defended hunting foxes with hounds, has written that a true morality of animal welfare ought to begin from the premise that factory farming is wrong.

The second reason for replacing animal meat is environmental. Using meat from animals, especially ruminants, is heating the planet and contributing to a future in which hundreds of millions of people become climate refugees. Much of the emissions from livestock is methane, an extremely potent greenhouse gas emitted by ruminant animals as they digest their food. In vitro meat won't belch or fart methane. Nor will it defecate, and as a result, the vast cesspools that intensive farms require to handle manure will become un-necessary. With that single change, the world's production of nitrous oxide, another powerful contributor to climate change, will be slashed by two-thirds.

The United Nations Food and Agriculture Organization has acknowledged that greenhouse gas emissions from livestock exceed those from all forms of transport—cars, trucks, planes, and ships—combined. On some calculations, livestock emissions in countries with large populations of cattle and sheep can make up as much as half of the country's total greenhouse gas emissions. If they are right, replacing coal and other fossil fuels with clean sources of energy is not going to be enough. We have to reduce the number of cattle on the planet.

Some vegetarians and vegans may object to in vitro meat, because they don't see the need for meat at all. That's fine for them, and of course they are free to remain vegetarians and vegans, and choose not to eat in vitro meat. My own view is that being a vegetarian or vegan is not an end in itself, but a means toward reducing both human and animal suffering, and leaving a habitable planet to future generations. I haven't eaten meat for 40 years, but if in vitro meat becomes commercially available, I will be pleased to try it.

from The Guardian, *August 5, 2013*

CHIMPANZEES ARE PEOPLE, TOO

TOMMY IS 26 YEARS OLD. He is being held in solitary confinement in a wire cage. He has never been convicted of any crime, or even accused of one. He is not in Guantanamo, but in upstate Gloversville, New York. How is this possible? Because Tommy is a chimpanzee.

Now the Nonhuman Rights Project has invoked the ancient legal procedure of *habeas corpus* (Latin for "you have the body") to bring Tommy's imprisonment before a state appeals court.

The writ is typically used to get a court to consider whether the detention of a prisoner or perhaps someone confined to a mental institution is lawful. The court is being asked to send Tommy to a sanctuary in Florida, where he can live with other chimps on a three-acre island in a lake.

Five appellate judges listened attentively this month as Nonhuman Rights Project founder Steve Wise presented the case for Tommy. The judges asked sensible questions, including the obvious one: isn't legal personhood just for human beings?

Wise cited legal precedents to show that it is not. In civil law, to be a person is to count as an entity in one's own right. A corporation can be a legal person, and so, too, can a river, a holy book, and a mosque.

The judges have the power to declare Tommy a legal person. That is what they should do, and not only because it is cruel to keep a chimpanzee in solitary confinement. The real reason for recognizing Tommy as a legal person is that he *is* a person, in the proper and the philosophical sense of that term.

What is a person? We can trace the term back to Roman times, and show that it was never limited to human beings. Early Christian theologians debated the doctrine of the Trinity—that God is "three persons in one." If "person" meant "human being," that doctrine would be plainly contrary to Christian belief, for Christians hold that only one of those "persons" was ever a human being.

In more contemporary usage, in science fiction movies, we have no difficulty in grasping that aliens like the extra-terrestrial in *E.T.*, or the Na'vi in *Avatar*, are persons, even though they are not members of the species *Homo sapiens*.

In reading the work of scientists like Jane Goodall or Dian Fossey, we have no difficulty in recognizing that the great apes they describe are persons.

They have close and complex personal relationships with others in their group. They grieve for lost loved ones. They are self-aware beings, capable of thought. Their foresight and anticipation enable them to plan ahead. We can even recognize the rudiments of ethics in the way they respond to other apes who fail to return a favor.

Contrary to the caricatures of some opponents of this lawsuit, declaring a chimpanzee a person doesn't mean giving him or her the right to vote, attend school, or sue for defamation. It simply means giving him or her the most basic, fundamental right of having legal standing, rather than being considered a mere object.

Over the past 30 years, European laboratories have, in recognition of the special nature of chimpanzees, freed them from research labs. That left only the United States still using chimpanzees in medical research, and last year the National

Institutes of Health announced that it was retiring almost all of the chimpanzees utilized in testing and sending them to a sanctuary.

If the nation's leading medical research agency has decided that, except possibly in very unusual circumstances, it will not use chimpanzees as research subjects, why are we allowing individuals to lock them up for no good reason at all?

It is time for the courts to recognize that the way we treat chimpanzees is indefensible. They are persons and we should end their wrongful imprisonment.[1]

from New York Daily News, *October 21, 2014*

[1] The New York State Appellate Court, Third Judicial Department, rejected the Nonhuman Rights Project's application on behalf of Tommy, and subsequently the New York State Court of Appeals refused to grant leave to appeal. As this book goes to press, the Project is seeking other avenues for taking the case further.

THE COW WHO . . .

LAST MONTH, A STEER ESCAPED FROM A SLAUGHTERHOUSE in the New York City borough of Queens. Video of the animal trotting down a busy street was soon featured on many media outlets. For those who care about animals, the story has a happy ending: the steer was captured and taken to a sanctuary, where he will live out the remainder of his natural life.

To me, however, the most interesting aspect of the story was the language that the media used to refer to the animal. The *New York Times* had a headline that read: "Cow Who Escaped New York Slaughterhouse Finds Sanctuary." Animal advocates have long struggled against the convention of reserving "who" for people, and using "that" or "which" for animals. Not all languages make this distinction, but in English, to refer to "the cow that escaped" seems to deny the animal's agency. We would all say "the prisoner who escaped" but "the rock that rolled down the hill."

It would be premature to conclude that the *New York Times* article indicates a shift in usage. Rather, it seems to show uncertainty, for the first line of the article refers to "A cow that was captured by police."

I asked Philip Corbett, the standards editor for the *New York Times*, if the use of "cow who" reflected a change of policy. He told me that the *Times* style manual, like that of the Associated Press, suggested using "who" only for a named or personified animal. The manual gives the example "The dog, which was lost, howled" and contrasts this with "Adelaide, who was lost, howled."

Corbett added that the editors may have been caught between the two examples. The cow, or rather steer, did not have a name at the time of the escape, but was given one—Freddie—by Mike Stura, the founder of Freddie's new home, Skylands Animal Sanctuary and Rescue.

Among media reporting the story, some used "who" and others "that." A little searching on Google also shows mixed usage. Put in "cow who" and you get nearly 400,000 hits, compared to nearly 600,000 for "cow that." If you substitute "dog" for "cow," the numbers get closer—more than eight million for "dog who" and over ten million for "dog that."

This could be because most of the dog stories are about people's pets, who have names. Yet, if Google is any indication, chimpanzees, who are rarely pets, are referred to as "who" almost twice as often as they are referred to as "that." Their similarity to us, and their undeniable individuality, must be playing a role. For gorillas and orangutans, too, "who" is more common than "that."

Google Ngram, which charts the frequencies of words or phrases in printed sources in different years, provides another interesting perspective. Whereas there were more than ten references to "cow that" for every reference to "cow who" in 1920, by 2000 the ratio had dropped to less than five to one. It seems that we are personifying cows more, despite the fact that many family-run dairy farms, in which the farmer knows every cow, have been replaced by corporate-run factory farms with thousands of nameless animals.

More surprising, perhaps, is that using "who" apparently is becoming more acceptable even for animals who are not pets and are less likely than great apes to be thought of as individuals. It's hard to connect canned tuna with an individual fish, let alone to think of that fish as a person, but the writer Sean Thomason recently tweeted about "the tuna who died to get put in a can that wound up in the back of my cabinet until past expiration and which I just threw away."

Many social movements recognize that language matters because it both reflects and reinforces injustices that need to be remedied. Feminists have provided evidence that the supposedly gender-neutral use of "man" and "he" to include females has the effect of making women invisible.

Several remedies have been proposed, the most successful of which may be the use of the plural "they" in contexts like "Each person should collect their belongings." Terms used for members of racial minorities, and for people with disabilities, have also been challenged, to such an extent that it can be hard to keep up with the terms preferred by those in these categories.

The use of "who" for animals ranks alongside these other linguistic reforms. In most legal systems today, animals are property, just as tables and chairs are. They may be protected under animal welfare legislation, but that is not enough to prevent them being things, because antiquities and areas of natural beauty are also protected. English usage should change to make it clear that animals are fundamentally more like us than they are like tables and chairs, paintings and mountains.

The law is starting to show signs of change. In 1992, Switzerland became the first country to include a statement about protecting the dignity of animals in its constitution; Germany followed ten years later. In 2009, the European Union amended its fundamental treaty to include a statement that because animals are sentient beings, the EU and its member states must, in formulating policies for agriculture, fisheries, research, and several other areas, "pay full regard to the welfare requirements of animals."

In a language like English, which implicitly categorizes animals as things rather than persons, adopting the personal pronoun would embody the same recognition—and remind us who animals really are.

from Project Syndicate, February 2016

... Beyond the Ethic of the
Sanctity of Life ...

THE REAL ABORTION TRAGEDY

IN THE DOMINICAN REPUBLIC LAST MONTH, a pregnant teenager suffering from leukemia had her chemotherapy delayed, because doctors feared that the treatment could terminate her pregnancy and therefore violate the nation's strict anti-abortion law. After consultations between doctors, lawyers, and the girl's family, chemotherapy eventually was begun, but not before attention had again been focused on the rigidity of many developing countries' abortion laws.

Abortion receives extensive media coverage in developed countries, especially in the United States, where Republicans have used opposition to it to rally voters. Recently, President Barack Obama's re-election campaign counterattacked, releasing a television advertisement in which a woman says that it is "a scary time to be a woman," because Mitt Romney has said that he supports outlawing abortion.

But much less attention is given to the 86 percent of all abortions that occur in the developing world. Although a majority of countries in Africa and Latin America have laws prohibiting abortion in most circumstances, official bans do not prevent high abortion rates.

In Africa, there are 29 abortions per 1,000 women per year, and 32 per 1,000 in Latin America. The comparable figure for Western Europe, where abortion is generally permitted in most circumstances, is 12. According to a recent report by the World Health Organization, unsafe abortions lead to the death of 47,000 women every year, with almost all of these deaths occurring in developing countries. A further five million women are injured each year, sometimes permanently.

Almost all of these deaths and injuries could be prevented, the WHO says, by meeting the need for sex education and information about family planning and contraception, and by providing safe, legal induced abortion, as well as follow-up care to prevent or treat medical complications. An estimated 220 million women in the developing world say that they want to prevent pregnancy, but lack either knowledge of, or access to, effective contraception.

That is a huge tragedy for individuals and for the future of our already very heavily populated planet. Last month, the London Summit on Family Planning, hosted by the British government's Department for International Development and the Gates Foundation, announced commitments to reach 120 million of these women by 2020.

The Vatican newspaper responded by criticizing Melinda Gates, whose efforts in organizing and partly funding this initiative will, it is estimated, lead to nearly three million fewer babies dying in their first year of life, and to 50 million fewer abortions. One would have thought that Roman Catholics would see these outcomes as desirable. (Gates is herself a practicing Catholic who has seen what happens when women cannot feed their children, or are maimed by unsafe abortions.)

Restricting access to legal abortion leads many poor women to seek abortion from unsafe providers. The legalization of abortion on request in South Africa in 1998 saw abortion-related deaths drop by 91 percent. And the development of the drugs misoprostol and mifepristone, which can be provided by pharmacists, makes relatively safe and inexpensive abortion possible in developing countries.

Opponents will respond that abortion is, by its very nature, unsafe—for the fetus. They point out that abortion kills a unique, living human individual. That claim is difficult to deny, at least if by "human" we mean "member of the species *Homo sapiens*."

It is also true that we cannot simply invoke a woman's "right to choose" in order to avoid the ethical issue of the moral status of the fetus. If the fetus really did have the moral status of any other human being, it would be difficult to argue that a pregnant woman's right to choose includes the right to bring about the death of the fetus, except perhaps when the woman's life is at stake.

The fallacy in the anti-abortion argument lies in the shift from the scientifically accurate claim that the fetus is a living individual of the species *Homo sapiens* to the ethical claim that the fetus therefore has the same right to life as any other human being. Membership of the species *Homo sapiens* is not enough to confer a right to life on a being. Nor can something like self-awareness or rationality warrant greater protection for the fetus than for, say, a cow, because the fetus has mental capacities that are inferior to those of cows. Yet "pro-life" groups that picket abortion clinics are rarely seen picketing slaughterhouses.

We can plausibly argue that we ought not to kill, against their will, self-aware beings who want to continue to live. We can see this as a violation of their autonomy, or a thwarting of their preferences. But why should a being's potential to become rationally self-aware make it wrong to end its life before it actually has the capacity for rationality or self-awareness?

We have no obligation to allow every being with the potential to become a rational being to realize that potential. If it comes to a clash between the supposed interests of potentially rational but not yet even conscious beings and the vital interests of actually rational women, we should give preference to the women every time.

from Project Syndicate, August 13, 2012

TREATING (OR NOT) THE TINIEST BABIES

IN FEBRUARY, NEWSPAPERS HAILED THE "MIRACLE BABY" Amillia Taylor, claiming that she is the most prematurely born surviving baby ever recorded. Born in October with a gestational age of just 21 weeks and six days, she weighed only 280 grams, or 10 ounces, at birth. Previously no baby born at less than 23 weeks had been known to survive, so doctors did not expect Amillia to live. But after nearly four months in a neonatal intensive care unit in a Miami hospital, and having grown to a weight of 1800 grams, or 4 pounds, doctors judged her ready to go home.

There was a certain amount of hype in all this. Amillia was conceived by in vitro fertilization, so the day on which conception took place could be known precisely. Usually this is not possible, and gestational age is calculated from the first day of the mother's last menstrual period. Since babies are usually conceived around the middle of the menstrual cycle, this adds about two weeks to the date of conception, and Amillia should therefore have been regarded as being born in the 23rd week of pregnancy. It is not uncommon for such babies to survive. Nevertheless, Amillia was certainly a very premature, and very tiny baby (according to one source, the fourth-smallest baby to survive). We can, of course, be delighted for Amillia's parents that their much-wanted daughter has done so remarkably well. But the use of all the resources of modern medicine to save smaller and smaller babies raises issues that need to be discussed.

In an article published in last November's issue of the *Medical Journal of Australia,* Dr. Kei Lui, director of the department for newborn care at Sydney's Royal Hospital for Women, and colleagues at several other hospitals, reported on the outcome of a workshop involving 112 professionals from each of the ten units offering the highest level of intensive care to newborn infants in New South Wales, Australia's most populous state, and the Australian Capital Territory, the district surrounding Canberra.

The workshop included not merely medical specialists in the relevant disciplines, but also midwives, neonatal nurses, and parent and community advocates. Before considering any proposals, the participants were given the results of a study of the outcome of births of babies at less than 26 weeks' gestation in the region between 1998 and 2000. The study showed that no babies born at less than 23 weeks survived. Between 23 and 25 weeks, the percentage surviving improved from 29 to 65 percent.

The survivors were followed up and examined when they were between two and three years old. Among those born at 23 weeks, two-thirds had some form of functional disability, and in one-third of all assessed survivors at this gestational age, the disability was rated as "severe." That meant either a severe developmental delay, or blindness, or that, because of cerebral palsy, the children were unable to walk even with the assistance of aids. On the other hand, of those born at 25 weeks, only one third had any form of functional disability, and only 13 percent had a severe disability. Clearly, two additional weeks inside the mother's womb makes a huge difference to the child's chances of survival without disability.

In these circumstances, what should doctors—and society—do? Should they treat all children as best they can? Should they draw a line, say at 24 weeks, and say that no child born prior to that cutoff should be treated? A policy of not treating babies born earlier than 24 weeks would save the community the considerable expense of medical treatment that is likely to prove futile, as well as the need to support severely disabled children who do survive. But it would also be harsh on couples who have had difficulty in conceiving, and whose premature infant represents perhaps their last chance of having a child. Amillia's parents may have been in that category. If the parents understand the situation, and are ready to welcome a severely disabled child into their family and give that child all the love and care they can, should a comparatively wealthy industrialized country simply say "No, your child was born too early"?

Bearing these possibilities in mind, instead of trying to set a rigid cutoff line, the workshop defined a "gray zone" within which treatment might or might not be given, depending on the wishes of the parents. If the parents of an infant born at 23 weeks did not want their baby treated, every participant would accept that request, and there was consensus that, although the possibility of active treatment could be discussed, it would be discouraged. Even at 25 weeks, 72 percent of the participants would not initiate treatment if the parents did not want it. By 26 weeks, however, the consensus was that the infant should be treated, except in unusual circumstances.

In the United States, although the American Academy of Pediatrics states that babies born at less than 23 weeks and weighing less than 400 grams are not considered viable, it can be difficult to challenge the prevailing rhetoric that every possible effort must be made to save every human life. Instead of openly discussing the options with parents, some doctors will say that treatment is "futile" and "nothing can be done." In fact, in these cases active treatment would often prolong life, but with a high probability of severe disability.

In this situation, to say that treatment is "futile" is to make the ethical judgment that life with such a high level of disability is either not worth living, or not worth the effort required by the parents and the community to make it possible for the child to live.

Other doctors believe that all human life is of infinite value, and it is their duty to do everything possible to save every baby, irrespective of the likelihood that the baby will be severely disabled.

In neither of these situations are parents given the chance to participate in the decision about their child. While that may relieve them of the heavy burden of responsibility, it also denies them the opportunity to say how precious this child is to them, and whether or not they could love and welcome into their home a child with a severe disability. That is why, in making life-and-death decisions for premature infants born in the "gray zone" where survival is uncertain and the risk of serious disability is high, parents' views should play a major role in the decision to provide life-prolonging treatment.

Amillia's survival has stretched the boundaries of that "gray zone" but has not eliminated it. We do not yet know if her extremely premature birth will lead to any long-term disabilities, but whether or not it does, other parents may reasonably decide that they don't want to take that risk, or put the public to the considerable expense of doing everything possible to ensure the survival of their tiny newborn.

from Free Inquiry, *a publication of the Council for Secular Humanism, a program of the Center for Inquiry, June/July 2007*

PULLING BACK THE CURTAIN ON THE MERCY KILLING OF NEWBORNS

IN THURSDAY'S *NEW ENGLAND JOURNAL OF MEDICINE*, two doctors from the University Medical Center Groningen in the Netherlands outline the circumstances in which doctors in their hospital have, in 22 cases over seven years, carried out euthanasia on newborn infants. All of these cases were reported to a district attorney's office in the Netherlands. None of the doctors were prosecuted.

Eduard Verhagen and Pieter Sauer divide into three groups the newborns for whom decisions about ending life might be made.

The first consists of infants who would die soon after birth even if all existing medical resources were employed to prolong their lives.

In the second group are infants who require intensive care, such as a respirator, to keep them alive, and for whom the expectations regarding their future are "very grim." These are infants with severe brain damage. If they can survive beyond intensive care, they will still have a very poor quality of life.

The third group includes infants with a "hopeless prognosis" and who also are victims of "unbearable suffering." For example, in the third group was "a child with the most serious form of spina bifida," the failure of the spinal cord to form and close properly. Yet infants in group three may no longer be dependent on intensive care.

It is this third group that creates the controversy, because their lives cannot be ended simply by withdrawing intensive care. Instead, at the University Medical Center Groningen, if suffering cannot be relieved and no improvement can be expected, the physicians will discuss with the parents whether this is a case in which death "would be more humane than continued life." If the parents agree that this is the case, and the team of physicians also agrees—as well as an independent physician not otherwise associated with the patient—the infant's life may be ended.

American "pro-life" groups will no doubt say that this is just another example of the slippery slope that the Netherlands began to slide down once it permitted voluntary euthanasia 20 years ago. But before they begin denouncing the Groningen doctors, they should take a look at what is happening in the United States.

One thing is undisputed: infants with severe problems are allowed to die in the United States. These are infants in the first two of the three groups identified by Verhagen and Sauer. Some of them—those in the second group—can live for many years if intensive care is continued. Nevertheless, US doctors, usually in consultation with parents, make decisions to withdraw intensive care. This happens openly, in Catholic as well as non-Catholic hospitals.

I have taken my Princeton students to St. Peter's University Hospital, a Catholic facility in New Brunswick, NJ, that has a major neonatal intensive care unit, where Dr. Mark Hiatt, the unit director, has described cases in which he has withdrawn intensive care from infants with severe brain damage.

Among neonatologists in the United States and the Netherlands, there is widespread agreement that sometimes it is ethically acceptable to end the life of a newborn infant with severe medical problems. Even the Roman Catholic Church accepts that it is not always required to use "extraordinary" means of life support and that a respirator can be considered "extraordinary."

The only serious dispute is whether it is acceptable to end the life of infants in Verhagen and Sauer's third group, that is, infants who are no longer dependent on intensive care for survival. To put this another way: the dispute is no longer about whether it is justifiable to end an infant's life if it won't be worth living but whether that end may be brought about by active means, or only by the withdrawal of treatment.

I believe the Groningen protocol to be based on the sound ethical perception that the means by which death occurs is less significant, ethically, than the decision that it is better that an infant's life should end. If it is sometimes acceptable to end the lives of infants in group two—and virtually no one denies this—then it is also sometimes acceptable to end the lives of infants in group three.

And, on the basis of comments made to me by some physicians, I am sure that the lives of infants in group three are sometimes ended in the United States. But this is never reported or publicly discussed, for fear of prosecution. That means that standards governing when such actions are justified cannot be appropriately debated, let alone agreed upon.

In the Netherlands, on the other hand, as Verhagen and Sauer write, "obligatory reporting with the aid of a protocol and subsequent assessment of euthanasia in newborns help us to clarify the decision-making process." There are many who will think that the existence of 22 cases of infant euthanasia over seven years at one hospital in the Netherlands shows that it is a society that has less respect for human life than the United States. But I'd suggest that they take a look at the difference in infant mortality rates between the two countries.

The CIA World Factbook shows that the United States has an infant mortality rate of 6.63 per 1,000 live births, the Netherlands 5.11. If the US had infant mortality rates as low as the Netherlands, there would be 6,296 fewer infant deaths nationwide each year.

Building a healthcare system in the United States as good as that in the Netherlands—as measured by infant mortality—is far more worthy of the attention of those who value human life than the deaths of 22 tragically afflicted infants.

from The Los Angeles Times, *March 11, 2005*

NO DISEASES FOR OLD MEN

PNEUMONIA USED TO BE CALLED "the old man's friend" because it often brought a swift and relatively painless end to a life that was already of poor quality and would otherwise have continued to decline. Now a study of severely demented patients in US nursing homes around Boston, Massachusetts, shows that the "friend" is often being fought with antibiotics. Are doctors routinely treating illnesses because they can, rather than because doing so is in the best interests of the patient?

The study, carried out by Erika D'Agata and Susan Mitchell and published in the *Archives of Internal Medicine*, showed that over 18 months, two-thirds of 214 severely demented patients in nursing homes were treated with antibiotics. The mean age of these patients was 85. On a standard test for severe impairment, where scores can range from 0 to 24, with the lower scores indicating more severe impairment, three-quarters of these patients scored 0. Their ability to communicate verbally ranged from nil to minimal.

It isn't clear that using antibiotics in these circumstances prolongs life, but even if it did, how many people want their lives to be prolonged if they are incontinent, need to be fed by others, can no longer walk, and their mental capacities have irreversibly deteriorated so that they can neither speak nor recognize their children?

The interests of patients should come first, and I doubt that longer life was in the interests of these patients. Moreover, when there is no way of finding out what the patients wants, and it is very doubtful that continued treatment is in the interests of a patient, it is reasonable to take account of other factors, including the views of the family, and the cost to the community. Medicare costs for people with Alzheimer's disease amounted to $91 billion in 2005, and are expected to increase to $160 billion by 2010. For comparison, in 2005 United States foreign aid totaled $27 billion. Even if we consider only the Medicare budget, however, there are higher spending priorities than prolonging the lives of elderly nursing home patients with severe dementia.

D'Agata and Mitchell point out that the use of so many antibiotics by these patients carries with it a different kind of cost for the community: it exacerbates the increasing problem of antibiotic-resistant bacteria. When a dementia patient is transferred to a hospital to deal with an acute medical problem, these resistant bacteria can spread and may prove fatal to patients who otherwise would have made a good recovery and had many years of normal life ahead of them.

One may suspect that a misguided belief in the sanctity of all human life plays some role in decisions to prolong human life beyond the point where it benefits the person whose life it is. Yet on this, some religions are more reasonable than others. The Roman Catholic Church, for instance, holds that there is no obligation to provide care that is disproportionate to the benefit it produces, or unduly burdensome to the patient. In my experience, many Catholic theologians would accept a decision to withhold antibiotics from severely demented elderly patients who develop pneumonia.

Other religions are more rigid. Pneumonia has been unable to play its traditional friendly role for Samuel Golubchuk, an 84-year-old man from Winnipeg, Canada. Golubchuk suffered a brain injury some years ago, and ever since has had limited physical and mental capacities. When he developed pneumonia and was hospitalized, his doctors proposed withdrawing life support. His children, however, said that discontinuing life support would be contrary to their Orthodox Jewish beliefs. They obtained an interim court order compelling the doctors to maintain life support.

Since November 2007, Golubchuk has been kept alive, with a tube down his throat to help him breathe, and another into his stomach to feed him. He does not speak, nor get out of bed. His case will now go to trial, and—at the time of writing, March 2008—it is still unclear when a verdict will be reached.

Normally, when patients are unable to make decisions about their treatment, the wishes of the family should be given great weight. But doctors have an ethical responsibility to act in the best interests of their patient, and the family's wishes should not override that. One relevant fact, therefore, is how much awareness Golubchuk has. This is in dispute. The family believes that he can interact with them, but this isn't clear. In any case, he is unable to give any opinion on whether he wants to be kept alive.

For the family, establishing their father's awareness could be double-edged sword, since it could also mean that keeping him alive is pointless torture. It seems likely that it is in his best interests to be allowed to die peacefully. But that, of course, is not the issue for his family. The issue is what, in their view, God commands them to do.

From a public policy perspective, the central issue raised by the Golubchuk case is how far a publicly funded healthcare system has to go to satisfy the wishes of the family, when these wishes clash with what, in the view of the doctors, is in the best interests of the patient. There has to be a limit to what a family can demand from the public purse, because to spend more money on long-term care for a patient with no prospect of recovery means that there is less money for other patients with better prospects.

In the case of a family seeking treatment that, in the professional judgment of the physicians, is futile, there is no requirement to provide expensive long-term care. If Golubchuk's children wish their father to remain on life support—and if they can show that keeping him alive is not causing him to suffer—they should be told that they are free to arrange for such care, at their own expense. What the court should not do is order the hospital to continue to care for Golubchuk, at its own expense, and against the better judgment of its health-care professionals. Canadian taxpayers are not required to go that far in order to support the religious beliefs of their fellow citizens.

from Project Syndicate, March 14, 2008

WHEN DOCTORS KILL

OF ALL THE ARGUMENTS AGAINST voluntary euthanasia, the most influential is the "slippery slope": once we allow doctors to kill patients, we will not be able to limit the killing to those who want to die.

There is no evidence for this claim, even after many years of legal physician-assisted suicide or voluntary euthanasia in the Netherlands, Belgium, Luxembourg, Switzerland, and the American state of Oregon. But recent revelations about what took place in a New Orleans hospital after Hurricane Katrina point to a genuine danger from a different source.

When New Orleans was flooded in August 2005, the rising water cut off Memorial Medical Center, a community hospital that was holding more than 200 patients. Three days after the hurricane hit, the hospital had no electricity, the water supply had failed, and toilets could no longer be flushed. Some patients who were dependent on ventilators died.

In stifling heat, doctors and nurses were hard-pressed to care for surviving patients lying on soiled beds. Adding to the anxiety were fears that law and order had broken down in the city, and that the hospital itself might be a target for armed bandits.

Helicopters were called in to evacuate patients. Priority was given to those who were in better health, and could walk. State police arrived and told staff that because of the civil unrest, everybody had to be out of the hospital by 5 p.m.

On the eighth floor, Jannie Burgess, a 79-year-old woman with advanced cancer, was on a morphine drip and close to death. To evacuate her, she would have to be carried down six flights of stairs, and would require the attention of nurses who were needed elsewhere. But if she were left unattended, she might come out of her sedation, and be in pain. Ewing Cook, one of the physicians present, instructed the nurse to increase the morphine, "giving her enough until she goes." It was, he later told Sheri Fink, who recently published an account of these events in the *New York Times*, a "no-brainer."

According to Fink, Anna Pou, another physician, told nursing staff that several patients on the seventh floor were also too ill to survive. She injected them with morphine and another drug that slowed their breathing until they died.

At least one of the patients injected with this lethal combination of drugs appears to have otherwise been in little danger of imminent death. Emmett Everett was a 61-year-old man who had been paralyzed in an accident several years earlier, and was in the hospital for surgery to relieve a bowel obstruction. When others from his ward were evacuated, he asked not to be left behind.

But he weighed 380 pounds (173 kilograms), and it would have been extremely difficult to carry him down the stairs and then up again to where the helicopters were landing. He was told the injection he was being given would help with the dizziness from which he suffered.

In 1957, a group of doctors asked Pope Pius XII whether it is permissible to use narcotics to suppress pain and consciousness "if one foresees that the use of narcotics will shorten life." The Pope said that it was. In its *Declaration on Euthanasia*, issued in 1980, the Vatican reaffirmed that view.

The Vatican's position is an application of what is known as "the doctrine of double effect." An action that has two effects, one good and the other bad, may be permissible if the good effect is the one that is intended and the bad effect is merely an unwanted consequence of achieving the good effect. Significantly, neither the Pope's remarks, nor the *Declaration on Euthanasia*, place any emphasis on the importance of obtaining the voluntary and informed consent of patients, where possible, before shortening their lives.

According to the doctrine of double effect, two doctors may, to all outward appearances, do exactly the same thing: that is, they may give patients in identical conditions an identical dose of morphine, knowing that this dose will shorten the patient's life. Yet one doctor, who intends to relieve the patient's pain, acts in accordance with good medical practice, whereas the other, who intends to shorten the patient's life, commits murder.

Dr. Cook had little time for such subtleties. Only "a very naïve doctor" would think that giving a person a lot of morphine was not "prematurely sending them to their grave," he told Fink, and then bluntly added: "We kill 'em." In Cook's opinion, the line between something ethical and something illegal is "so fine as to be imperceivable."

At Memorial Medical Center, physicians and nurses found themselves under great pressure. Exhausted after 72 hours with little sleep, and struggling to care for their patients, they were not in the best position to make difficult ethical decisions. The doctrine of double effect, properly understood, does not justify what the doctors did; but, by inuring them to the practice of shortening patients' lives without obtaining consent, it seems to have paved the way for intentional killing.

Roman Catholic thinkers have been among the most vocal in invoking the "slippery slope" argument against the legalization of voluntary euthanasia and physician-assisted dying. They would do well to examine the consequences of their own doctrines.

from Project Syndicate, November 13, 2009

CHOOSING DEATH

"I WILL TAKE MY LIFE TODAY AROUND NOON. IT IS TIME."

With these words, posted online, Gillian Bennett, an 85-year-old New Zealander living in Canada, began her explanation of her decision to end her life. Bennett had known for three years that she was suffering from dementia. By August, the dementia had progressed to the point at which, as she put it, "I have nearly lost *me*."

"I want out," Bennett wrote, "before the day when I can no longer assess my situation, or take action to bring my life to an end." Her husband, Jonathan Bennett, a retired philosophy professor, and her children supported her decision, but she refused to allow them to assist her suicide in any way, as doing so would have exposed them to the risk of a 14-year prison sentence. She therefore had to take the final steps while she was still competent to do so.

For most of us, fortunately, life is precious. We want to go on living because we have things to look forward to, or because, overall, we find it enjoyable, interesting, or stimulating. Sometimes we want to go on living because there are things that we want to achieve, or people close to us whom we want to help. Bennett was a great-grandmother; if all had been well with her, she would have wanted to see the next generation grow up.

Bennett's developing dementia deprived her of all of the reasons for wanting to continue to live. That makes it hard to deny that her decision was both rational and ethical. By committing suicide, she was giving up nothing that she wanted, or could reasonably value. "All I lose is an indefinite number of years of being a vegetable in a hospital setting, eating up the country's money but having not the faintest idea of who I am."

Bennett's decision was also ethical because, as the reference to "the country's money" suggests, she was not thinking only of herself. Opponents of legal voluntary euthanasia or physician-assisted suicide sometimes say that if the laws were changed, patients would feel pressured to end their lives in order to avoid being a burden to others.

Baroness Mary Warnock, the moral philosopher who chaired the British government committee responsible for the 1984 "Warnock Report," which established the framework for her country's pioneering legislation on in vitro fertilization and embryo research, does not see this as a reason against allowing patients to choose to end their lives. She has suggested that there is nothing wrong with feeling that you ought to die for the sake of others as well as for yourself. In an interview published in 2008 in the Church of Scotland's magazine *Life and Work*, she supported the right of those suffering intolerably to end their lives. "If somebody absolutely, desperately wants to die because they're a burden to their family, or the state," she argued, "then I think they too should be allowed to die."

Because Canada's public health service provides care for people with dementia who are unable to care for themselves, Bennett knew that she would not have to be a burden on her family; nonetheless, she was concerned about the burden that she would impose upon the public purse. In a hospital, she might survive for another ten years in a vegetative state, at a cost she conservatively estimated to be around $50,000–$75,000 per year.

As Bennett would not benefit from remaining alive, she regarded this as a waste. She was concerned, too, about the health-care workers who would have to care for her: "Nurses, who thought they were embarked on a career that had great meaning, find themselves perpetually changing my diapers and reporting on the physical changes of an empty husk." Such a situation is, in her words, "ludicrous, wasteful and unfair."

Some will object to the description of a person with advanced dementia as an "empty husk." But, having seen this condition overtake my mother and my aunt—both vibrant, intelligent women, who were reduced to lying, unresponsive, in a bed for months or (in my aunt's case) years—it seems to me entirely accurate. Beyond a certain stage of dementia, the person we knew is gone.

If the person did not want to live in that condition, what is the point of maintaining the body? In any health-care system, resources are limited and should be used for care that is wanted by the patient, or from which the patient will benefit.

For people who do not want to live on when their mind has gone, deciding when to die is difficult. In 1990, Janet Adkins, who was suffering from Alzheimer's disease, traveled to Michigan to end her life with the assistance of Dr. Jack Kevorkian, who was widely criticized for helping her to die, because at the time of her death she was still well enough to play tennis. She chose to die nonetheless, because she could have lost control over her decision if she had delayed it.

Bennett, in her eloquent statement, looked forward to the day when the law would allow a physician to act not only on a prior "living will" that bars life-prolonging treatment, but also on one that requests a lethal dose when the patient becomes incapacitated to a specified extent. Such a change would remove the anxiety that some patients with progressive dementia have that they will go on too long and miss the opportunity to end their life at all. The legislation Bennett suggests would enable people in her condition to live as long as they want—but not longer than that.

from Project Syndicate, September 9, 2014

DYING IN COURT

GLORIA TAYLOR, A CANADIAN, has amyotrophic lateral sclerosis (ALS), also known as Lou Gehrig's disease. Over a period of a few years, her muscles will weaken until she can no longer walk, use her hands, chew, swallow, speak, and, ultimately, breathe. Then she will die. Taylor does not want to go through all of that. She wants to die at a time of her own choosing.

Suicide is not a crime in Canada, so, as Taylor put it, "I simply cannot understand why the law holds that the able-bodied who are terminally ill are allowed to shoot themselves when they have had enough because they are able to hold a gun steady, but because my illness affects my ability to move and control my body, I cannot be allowed compassionate help to allow me to commit an equivalent act using lethal medication."

Taylor sees the law as offering her a cruel choice: either end her life when she still finds it enjoyable, but is capable of killing herself, or give up the right that others have to end their lives when they choose. She went to court, arguing that the provisions of the Criminal Code that prevent her from receiving assistance in dying are inconsistent with the Canadian Charter of Rights and Freedoms, which gives Canadians rights to life, liberty, personal security, and equality.

The court hearing was remarkable for the thoroughness with which Justice Lynn Smith examined the ethical questions before her. She received expert opinions from leading figures on both sides of the issue, not only Canadians, but also authorities in Australia, Belgium, the Netherlands, New Zealand, Switzerland, the United Kingdom, and the United States. The range of expertise included general medicine, palliative care, neurology, disability studies, gerontology, psychiatry, psychology, law, philosophy, and bioethics.

Many of these experts were cross-examined in court. Along with Taylor's right to die, decades of debate about assistance in dying came under scrutiny.

Last month, Smith issued her judgment. The case, *Carter v. Canada*, could serve as a textbook on the facts, law, and ethics of assistance in dying.

For example, there has been much debate about the difference between the accepted practice of withholding life support or some other treatment, knowing that the patient is likely to die without it, and the contested practice of actively helping a patient to die. Smith's ruling finds that "a bright-line ethical distinction is elusive," and that the view that there is no such ethical distinction is "persuasive." She considers, and accepts, an argument advanced by Wayne Sumner, a distinguished Canadian philosopher: if the patient's circumstances are such that suicide would be ethically permissible were the patient able to do it, then it is also ethically permissible for the physician to provide the means for the patient to do it.

Smith also had to assess whether there are public-policy considerations that count against the legalization of physician assistance in dying. Her decision focuses mainly on the risk that vulnerable people—for example, the aged or those with disabilities—will be pressured into accepting assistance in dying when they do not really want it.

There are conflicting views about whether legalization of voluntary euthanasia in the Netherlands, and of physician assistance in dying in Oregon, has led to an increase in the number of vulnerable people being killed or assisted in dying without their full, informed consent. For many years, Herbert Hendin, a psychiatrist and suicide expert, has asserted that the safeguards incorporated in these laws fail to protect the vulnerable. He gave evidence at the trial.

So, too, on the other side, did Hans van Delden, a Dutch nursing home physician and bioethicist who for the past 20 years has been involved in all of the major empirical studies of end-of-life decisions in his country. Peggy Battin, the most prominent American bioethicist working on assisted dying and euthanasia, also took the stand.

In this dispute, Smith comes down firmly on the side of van Delden and Battin, finding that "the empirical evidence gathered in the two jurisdictions does not support the hypothesis that physician-assisted death has imposed a particular risk to socially vulnerable populations." Instead, she says, "The evidence does support Dr. van Delden's position that it is possible for a state to design a system that both permits some individuals to access physician-assisted death and socially protects vulnerable individuals and groups." (The most recent Dutch report, released after Smith handed down her judgment, confirms that there has been no dramatic increase in euthanasia cases in the Netherlands.)

Smith then declared, after considering the applicable law, that the provisions of the Criminal Code preventing physician assistance in dying violate disabled people's right not only to equality, but also to life, liberty, and security. She thus opened the door for physician assistance in dying for any grievously and irremediably ill competent adult, under conditions not very different from those that apply in other jurisdictions where physician assistance in dying is legal.

from Project Syndicate, July 16, 2012

Postscript: In October 2012 Gloria Taylor died peacefully, without assistance in dying, as the result of a severe infection. Meanwhile Justice Lynn Smith's decision was appealed, initially to the Court of Appeal for British Columbia, which in 2013, by a 2–1 majority, overturned the decision. An appeal was then made to the Supreme Court of Canada. In February 2015 the Supreme Court unanimously ruled that the prohibition of assisted suicide is contrary to the Canadian Charter of Rights and Freedoms, and hence unconstitutional. In 2016, the Canadian parliament implemented this decision by making physician-assisted suicide legal in Canada.

··· Bioethics and Public Health ···

THE HUMAN GENOME AND THE GENETIC SUPERMARKET

FOR A SCIENTIFIC DISCOVERY TO BE ANNOUNCED jointly by the president of the United States and the prime minister of the United Kingdom, it has to be something special. The completion of a "rough draft" of the human genome, announced on June 26th, is undoubtedly an important scientific milestone, but since this "most wondrous map ever produced by humankind," as President Clinton called it, does not tell us what the genes actually do, nothing much will follow from it, at least in the short run. It is as if we had learned how to read the alphabet of a foreign language, without understanding what most of the words mean. In a few years what has been done so far will be seen simply as a stepping stone on the way to the really important goal, that of understanding which aspects of human nature are genetically controlled, and by which genes. Nevertheless, the publicity accorded to gaining the stepping stone can be turned to advantage, for it may make us more ready to think seriously about the kinds of changes that could occur when we attain the further goal, a decade or two from now.

The official line is, of course, that knowing all about the human genome will enable us to discover the origins of many major diseases, and to cure them in a way that was never before possible, not by treating the symptoms, as we do now, but by eliminating the real cause—the genetic fault that gives rise to the disease or enables it to take hold of us. This will indeed be possible for some diseases. But it would be naive to think that our new knowledge of the human genome will not be put to any other use.

One indication of the kind of use to which such knowledge could be put can be seen from the advertisements that have been appearing in the last year or two in student newspapers in some of America's most prestigious universities, offering up to $50,000 for an egg from a donor who has scored extremely well in scholastic aptitude tests, and is at least 5'10" tall. Unless there are some remarkably ignorant rich people around, this sum is being offered in the knowledge that the randomness of natural human reproduction means that tall intelligent women sometimes have short stupid children. How much would people be prepared to pay for a method that, by screening embryos, eliminated the genetic lottery, and ensured that their child would have the genetic basis for above-average intelligence, height, athletic ability, or some other desired trait?

Once this becomes technically possible, there will be pressure to prohibit it, on the grounds that it will lead to a resurgence of eugenics. But for most parents, giving their child the best possible start in life is extremely important. The desire to do so sells millions of books telling parents how to help their child achieve her or his potential; it causes couples to move out to suburbs where the schools are better, even though they then have to spend time in daily commuting; and it stimulates saving so that later the child will be able to go to a good college. Selecting the "best" genes may well benefit one's child more effectively than any of these techniques. Combine the well-known American resistance to government regulation with the fact that genetic screening could be an effective route to so widely held a goal and it seems unlikely that the US Congress will prohibit it, or if it does, that the ban will be effective.

Like it or not, then, we face a future in which eugenics will once again become an issue. Unlike earlier eugenic movements, however, it will not be state-sponsored and it will not work by coercive sterilization of the "unfit," much less by genocide. It will, instead, come about in the way that so much change comes about in America, by consumer choice, in the marketplace. That is, of course, vastly preferable to coercive eugenics, but it still raises many questions about the future of our society. Among the most troubling is: what will happen to those who cannot afford to shop at the genetic supermarket? Will their children be predestined to mediocrity? Will this be the end of the great American myth of equality of opportunity? If we do not want this to happen, we had better start thinking hard what we can do about it.

from Free Inquiry, *a publication of the Council for Secular Humanism, a program of the Center for Inquiry, Winter 2001*

THE YEAR OF THE CLONE?

IN JANUARY PANOS ZAVOS, a professor of reproductive physiology at the University of Kentucky, announced that he was teaming up with Italian gynecologist Severino Antinori to try to produce the first cloned human being within the next year or two. To those who have followed Antinori's career, this should not come as a great surprise. Back in October 1998, Antinori said that he wanted to be the first scientist to clone a human being. Knowledgeable people then were doubtful that anything would happen soon. Today, they are still skeptical that Antinori will be able to pull off the feat in the foreseeable future.

Zavos and Antinori are not the only ones trying to clone a human being at the moment. The Raelians, a sect whose founder claims to have had contact with aliens, are working with an American couple whose baby died in infancy, to help them have a genetic carbon copy of their lost child.

Graeme Bulfield, chief executive of the Roslin Institute, where Dolly the sheep was cloned, has said that he would be "absolutely flabbergasted" if human cloning were done in his lifetime. Flabbergasted he may yet be. Let's leave the Raelians out of it, and focus on the scientists with proven credentials in reproductive medicine. Antinori has a record of pushing the boundaries back in the area of reproductive medicine. In 1994, he helped a 62-year-old woman become the oldest woman recorded to have a child, as a result of the use of new reproductive technology. But that was, technically speaking, a relatively simple task compared to cloning a human being. Until Ian Wilmut and his colleagues produced Dolly the sheep, the consensus was that it was impossible to produce a clone from an adult mammal. ("Cloning" in the sense of splitting an embryo, thus creating twins, happens in nature and can be done in the laboratory too—but it does not raise the same issues as cloning in the sense of making a genetic carbon copy of a more developed human being.)

Now we know that cloning from an adult mammal can be done, but the question is whether anyone would have enough human volunteers to succeed in pulling it off. Bulfield has estimated that it would take 400 eggs and 50 surrogate mothers to produce a cloned human being—not to mention about $150 million. It seems doubtful that Zavos and Antinori can assemble such resources, both human and financial. (The Raelians claim that they have 50 women volunteering to act as egg donors and surrogate mothers, but their budget is nowhere near $150 million.)

Suppose, though, that someone did manage to produce a cloned human child. They would, of course, achieve headlines for themselves, an accomplishment at which Antinori and the Raelians have already demonstrated considerable skill. But would they have harmed anyone? Would anything significant really have changed? Let's take these two questions separately.

If a human being were cloned, who would be harmed? The most obvious answer is: the being who was cloned. There are real questions about the likely health of a clone. There have been suggestions that Dolly's cells are in some respects not behaving like the cells of a four-year-old sheep, but rather like the cells of a sheep that is six years older—the age of the sheep from which Dolly was cloned. If that were the case, then a human being cloned from, say, a 50-year-old adult would have a sadly diminished life expectancy. It now seems that this may not be the case, but other concerns have emerged. At the University of Hawaii, Dr. Ryuzo Yanagimachi cloned mice and found that some of them became extremely obese, despite not being given any more food than normal mice. Other abnormalities have also been detected. Cows cloned at Texas A & M University have had abnormal hearts and lungs. If these problems are also likely to occur in humans, it would be ethically irresponsible to go ahead with a human clone.

Suppose, however, that these fears turn out to be groundless, and it is possible to clone humans without any higher-level abnormalities. Then would the life of a cloned human be significantly worse than the life of the rest of us? Only, I imagine, in the constant media attention. Otherwise, being a clone of, say, a child who had died, and who the grieving parents were wishing to "recreate," would not be very different from being one of a pair of identical twins, one of whom had died (although one would, evidently, have parents with a rather unusual attachment to a dead child).

Even if it could be argued that a cloned child would face psychological burdens, how serious would these be? Given that if cloning were prohibited, this particular child would not have existed at all, would the burdens be so terrible that he or she would wish that cloning had been prohibited? That seems very unlikely. If not, then it is not possible to argue that cloning ought to be prohibited *for the sake of the cloned child.*

If not for the child, then for whose sake would we be acting, if we were to prohibit cloning? Obviously not for the sake of the couple who wanted to have the cloned child, and not for the sake of the scientists willing to assist them. Does society need protecting from clones? Yes, if we are talking about whole armies of clones of popular rock stars or sporting heroes. That could lead to a worrying loss of genetic diversity. But no, if only a small number of people will want to have children who are clones. That is much the most likely prospect, especially as long as cloning remains a very expensive and complicated procedure, with a higher than normal risk of abnormalities. Since that seems bound to be the case for a long time to come, we do not need to waste too much thought on how to deal with the would-be cloners. If they can assure us of their ability to produce normal human beings, then let them go ahead. In the larger scheme of things, it will not make all that much difference to the shape of human society in the twenty-first century.

from Free Inquiry, *a publication of the Council for*
Secular Humanism, a program of the Center
for Inquiry, Summer 2001

KIDNEYS FOR SALE?

THE ARREST IN NEW YORK LAST MONTH of Levy-Izhak Rosenbaum, a Brooklyn businessman whom police allege tried to broker a deal to buy a kidney for $160,000, coincided with the passage of a law in Singapore that some say will open the way for organ trading there.

Last year, Singapore retail magnate Tang Wee Sung was sentenced to one day in jail for agreeing to buy a kidney illegally. He subsequently received a kidney from the body of an executed murderer—which, though legal, is arguably more ethically dubious than buying a kidney, since it creates an incentive for convicting and executing those accused of capital crimes.

Now Singapore has legalized payments to organ donors. Officially, these payments are only for reimbursement of costs; payment of an amount that is an "undue inducement" remains prohibited. But what constitutes an "undue inducement" is left vague.

Both these developments raise again the question as to whether selling organs should be a crime at all. In the United States alone, 100,000 people seek an organ transplant each year, but only 23,000 are successful. Some 6,000 people die before receiving an organ.

In New York, patients wait nine years on average to receive a kidney. At the same time, many poor people are willing to sell a kidney for far less than $160,000. Although buying and selling human organs is illegal almost every-where, the World Health Organization estimates that world-wide about 10 percent of all kidneys transplanted are bought on the black market.

The most common objection to organ trading is that it ex-ploits the poor. That view received support from a 2002 study of 350 Indians who illegally sold a kidney. Most told the researchers that they were motivated by a desire to pay off their debts, but six years later, three-quarters of them were still in debt, and regretted having sold their kidney.

Some free-market advocates reject the view that govern-ment should decide for individuals what body parts they can sell—hair, for instance, and in the United States, sperm and eggs—and what they cannot sell. When the television pro-gram *Taboo* covered the sale of body parts, it showed a slum dweller in Manila who sold his kidney so that he could buy a motorized tricycle taxi to provide income for his family. After the operation, the donor was shown driving around in his shiny new taxi, beaming happily.

Should he have been prevented from making that choice? The program also showed unhappy sellers, but there are un-happy sellers in, say, the housing market as well.

To those who argue that legalizing organ sales would help the poor, Nancy Scheper-Hughes, founder of Organ Watch, pointedly replies: "Perhaps we should look for better ways of helping the destitute than dismantling them." No doubt we should, but we don't: our assistance to the poor is woefully inadequate, and leaves more than a billion people living in extreme poverty.

In an ideal world, there would be no destitute people, and there would be enough altruistic donors so that no one would die while waiting to receive a kidney. Zell Kravinsky, an

American who has given a kidney to a stranger, points out that donating a kidney can save a life, while the risk of dying as a result of the donation is only 1 in 4,000. Not donating a kidney, he says, thus means valuing your own life at 4,000 times that of a stranger—a ratio he describes as "obscene." But most of us still have two kidneys, and the need for more kidneys persists, along with the poverty of those we do not help.

We must make policies for the real world, not an ideal one. Could a legal market in kidneys be regulated to ensure that sellers were fully informed about what they were doing, including the risks to their health? Would the demand for kidneys then be met? Would this produce an acceptable outcome for the seller?

To seek an answer, we can turn to a country that we do not usually think of as a leader in either market deregulation or social experimentation: Iran. Since 1988, Iran has had a government-funded, regulated system for purchasing kidneys. A charitable association of patients arranges the transaction, for a set price, and no one except the seller profits from it.

According to a study published in 2006 by Iranian kidney specialists, the scheme has eliminated the waiting list for kidneys in that country, without giving rise to ethical problems. A 2006 BBC television program showed many potential donors turned away because they did not meet strict age criteria, and others who were required to visit a psychologist.

A more systematic study of the Iranian system is still needed. Meanwhile, developments in Singapore will be watched with interest, as will the outcome of the allegations against Levy-Izhak Rosenbaum.

from Project Syndicate, August 14, 2009

Postscript: Levy-Izhak Rosenbaum pleaded guilty to the sale of three kidneys. He was sentenced to two and a half years in prison, and served more than two years before his release. Singapore's rate of organ donation did not increase significantly after it legalized the payment of reimbursement of donors' costs.

THE MANY CRISES OF HEALTH CARE

PRESIDENT BARACK OBAMA'S ADMINISTRATION spent much of 2009 preoccupied domestically with the political fight over extending health insurance to the tens of millions of Americans who have none. People living in other industrialized countries find this difficult to understand. They have a right to health care, and even conservative governments do not attempt to take that right away.

The difficulties that some Americans have with healthcare reform tell us more about American hostility to government than they do about health care in general. But the debate in the United States highlights an underlying issue that will worry almost every developed country in 2010 and beyond: the struggle to control health-care costs.

Health care now accounts for about one dollar in every six of all US spending—private as well as public—and is on track to double by 2035. That is a greater share than anywhere else in the world, but rising health-care costs are also a problem in countries that spend far less.

There are many places where savings can be made. Encouraging people to exercise, to avoid smoking, to use alcohol only in moderation, and to eat less red meat would help to reduce health-care costs. But, given developed countries' aging populations, the cost of caring for the elderly is bound to rise. So we will have to find other ways to save money.

Here it makes sense to start at the end. Treating dying patients who do not want to go on living is a waste, yet only a few countries allow physicians actively to assist a patient who requests aid in dying. In the United States, about 27 percent of Medicare's budget goes toward care in the last year of life. While some of that is spent in the hope that the patient will have many years to live, it is not unusual for hospitals to provide treatments costing tens of thousands of dollars to patients who have no hope of living more than a week or two—and often under sedation or barely conscious.

One factor in such decisions is fear on the part of doctors or hospitals that they will be sued by the family for letting their loved one die. So, for example, patients close to death are resuscitated, against the doctor's better judgment, because they have not specifically stated that they do not want to be resuscitated in such circumstances.

The system by which doctors and hospitals are paid is another factor in providing expensive treatment that is of little benefit to the patient. When Intermountain Healthcare, a network of hospitals in Utah and Idaho, improved its treatment for premature babies, it reduced the time they spent in intensive care, thereby slashing the costs of treating them. But, because hospitals are paid a fee for each service they provide, and better care meant that the babies needed fewer services, the change cost the hospital network $329,000 a year.

Even if such perverse incentives are removed, tougher questions about controlling costs need to be faced. One is the cost of new drugs. Development costs of $800 million are not unusual for a drug, and we can expect to see more of a new type of drug—biopharmaceuticals made from living cells—which cost even more.

Development costs have to be passed on in drug prices, which may be exceptionally high when a drug benefits only a relatively small number of patients. Gaucher's disease, for example, is a rare crippling genetic condition that, in its more severe forms, usually killed its victims in childhood. Now those with the disease can lead an almost normal life, thanks to a drug called Cerezyme—but it costs $175,000 a year.

New medical devices pose equally difficult dilemmas. The artificial heart machine, also known as a left ventricular assist device, or LVAD, has been used to keep patients alive until they receive a heart transplant. But there is a shortage of hearts for transplantation, and in the United States, LVADs are now being implanted as a long-term treatment for heart failure, just as a dialysis machine replaces a kidney.

According to Manoj Jain of Emory University, every year 200,000 US patients could be kept alive a little longer with an LVAD, at a cost of $200,000 per patient, or $40 billion. Is that a sensible use of resources in a country in which there are officially 39 million people below the poverty line, which for a family of four is $22,000?

In countries that provide free health care to their citizens, it is extraordinarily difficult for officials to tell anyone that the government will not pay for the only drug or medical device that can save their life—or their child's life. But eventually the point will come when such things must be said.

No one likes putting a dollar value on a human life, but the fact is that we already do, implicitly, by failing to give enough support to organizations working in developing countries. GiveWell, which evaluates organizations working to save the lives of the world's poor, has identified several that can save a life for under $5,000.

The World Health Organization estimates that its immunization programs in developing countries cost about $300 per life saved—lives that are saved not for a year, but usually for a lifetime. Similarly, the World Bank's Disease Control Priorities Report tells us that a program to treat tuberculosis in the developing world, promoted by the Stop TB Partnership, gives people an extra year of life at a cost ranging from $5 to $50.

Against that background, spending $200,000 to give a patient in an affluent country a relatively short period of extra life becomes more than financially dubious. It is morally wrong.

from Project Syndicate, December 7, 2009

PUBLIC HEALTH VERSUS PRIVATE FREEDOM?

IN CONTRASTING DECISIONS LAST MONTH, a United States Court of Appeals struck down a US Food and Drug Administration requirement that cigarettes be sold in packs with graphic health warnings, while Australia's highest court upheld a law that goes much further. The Australian law requires not only health warnings and images of the physical damage that smoking causes, but also that the packs themselves be plain, with brand names in small generic type, no logos, and no color other than a drab olive-brown.

The US decision was based on America's constitutional protection of free speech. The court accepted that the government may require factually accurate health warnings, but the majority, in a split decision, said that it could not go as far as requiring images. In Australia, the issue was whether the law implied uncompensated expropriation—in this case, of the tobacco companies' intellectual property in their brands. The High Court ruled that it did not.

Underlying these differences, however, is the larger issue: who decides the proper balance between public health and freedom of expression? In the US, courts make that decision, essentially by interpreting a 225-year-old text, and if that deprives the government of some techniques that might reduce the death toll from cigarettes—currently estimated at 443,000 Americans every year—so be it. In Australia, where freedom of expression is not given explicit constitutional protection, courts are much more likely to respect the right of democratically elected governments to strike the proper balance.

There is widespread agreement that governments ought to prohibit the sale of at least some dangerous products. Countless food additives are either banned or permitted only in limited quantities, as are children's toys painted with substances that could be harmful if ingested. New York City has banned trans fats from restaurants and is now limiting the permitted serving size of sugary drinks. Many countries prohibit the sale of unsafe tools, such as power saws without safety guards.

Although there are arguments for prohibiting a variety of different dangerous products, cigarettes are unique, because no other product, legal or illegal, comes close to killing the same number of people—more than traffic accidents, malaria, and AIDS combined. Cigarettes are also highly addictive. Moreover, wherever health-care costs are paid by everyone—including the US, with its public health-care programs for the poor and the elderly—everyone pays the cost of efforts to treat the diseases caused by cigarettes.

Whether to prohibit cigarettes altogether is another question, because doing so would no doubt create a new revenue source for organized crime. It seems odd, however, to hold that the state may, in principle, prohibit the sale of a product, but may not permit it to be sold only in packs that carry graphic images of the damage it causes to human health.

The tobacco industry will now take its battle against Australia's legislation to the World Trade Organization. The industry fears that the law could be copied in much larger markets, like India and China. That is, after all, where such legislation is most needed.

Indeed, only about 15 percent of Australians and 20 percent of Americans smoke, but in 14 low and middle-income countries covered in a survey recently published in *The Lancet,* an average of 41 percent of men smoked, with an increasing number of young women taking up the habit. The World Health Organization estimates that about 100 million people died from smoking in the twentieth century, but smoking will kill up to one billion people in the twenty-first century.

Discussions of how far the state may go in promoting the health of its population often start with John Stuart Mill's principle of limiting the state's coercive power to acts that prevent harm to others. Mill could have accepted requirements for health warnings on cigarette packs, and even graphic photos of diseased lungs, if that helps people to understand the choice that they are making; but he would have rejected a ban.

Mill's defense of individual liberty, however, assumes that individuals are the best judges and guardians of their own interests—an idea that today verges on naiveté. The development of modern advertising techniques marks an important difference between Mill's era and ours. Corporations have learned how to sell us unhealthy products by appealing to our unconscious desires for status, attractiveness, and social acceptance. As a result, we find ourselves drawn to a product without quite knowing why. And cigarette makers have learned how to manipulate the properties of their product to make it maximally addictive.

Graphic images of the damage that smoking causes can counterbalance the power of these appeals to the unconscious, thereby facilitating more deliberative decision-making and making it easier for people to stick to a resolution to quit smoking. Instead of rejecting such laws as restricting freedom, therefore, we should defend them as ways to level the playing field between individuals and giant corporations that make no pretense of appealing to our capacities for reasoning and reflection. Requiring that cigarettes be sold in plain packs with health warnings and graphic images is equal-opportunity legislation for the rational beings inside us.

from Project Syndicate, September 6, 2012

WEIGH MORE, PAY MORE

WE ARE GETTING FATTER. In Australia, the United States, and many other countries, it has become commonplace to see people so fat that they waddle rather than walk. The rise in obesity is steepest in rich nations, but is happening in middle-income and poor nations as well. Is a person's weight his or her own business? Should we simply become more accepting of diverse body shapes? I don't think so. Obesity is an ethical issue, because an increase in weight by some imposes costs on others.

I am writing this at an airport. A slight Asian woman has checked in with, I'd guess, about 40 kg of suitcases and boxes. She pays extra for being over the limit. A man who must weigh at least 40 kg more than she does, but whose baggage is under the limit, pays nothing. Yet for the jet engines, it is all the same whether the weight is baggage or body fat.

Tony Webber, a former chief economist for Qantas, has pointed out that since 2000 the average weight of adult passengers carried by the Australian airline has increased by 2 kg. For a large modern aircraft like the Airbus A380 flying from Sydney to London, that means an extra US$472 of fuel has to be burned, and if the airline flies that route in both directions three times a day, over a year that will add up to a million dollars' worth of fuel, or, on current margins, about 13 percent of the airline's profit operating that route.

Webber suggests that airlines set a standard passenger weight, say 75 kg. If a passenger weighs 100 kg, then a surcharge would be charged to cover the extra fuel costs. For a passenger who is 25 kg overweight, on a Sydney-London return ticket, the surcharge would be AUD$29. A passenger weighing just 50 kg would get a discount of the same amount. Another way to do this would be to set a standard for passenger and luggage, and then ask people to get on the scales with their luggage. That would have the advantage of avoiding embarrassment for those who do not wish to reveal their weight.

Friends with whom I discuss this proposal often say that many fat people can't help being overweight—they just have a different metabolism from the rest of us. But the point of charging for weight is not to punish for sin, whether the charge is levied on your baggage or on your body weight. It is a way of recouping the true cost of flying you to your destination from you, rather than imposing it on your fellow passengers. Flying is different from, say, health care. It is not a human right.

An increase in the use of jet fuel isn't just a matter of cost; it also means greater greenhouse gas emissions, and thus exacerbates the problem of global warming. It is a minor example of how the size of our fellow citizens affects us all. When people get larger and heavier, fewer of them fit onto a bus or train, which increases the costs of public transport. Hospitals now have to order stronger beds and operating tables, build extra-large toilets, and even order extra-large refrigerators for their mortuaries—all adding to their costs. But a far more significant cost of excess weight is that it leads to a greater need for health care. Last year the Society of Actuaries estimated that in the United States and Canada, people who are overweight or obese accounted for $127 billion in additional health-care expenditures. That adds hundreds of dollars to annual health-care costs for taxpayers and for those who pay for private health insurance. The same study indicated that the costs of lost productivity, both among those still working and among those unable to work at all because of obesity, amounted to $115 billion.

These facts are enough to justify public policies that discourage weight gain. Taxing foods that are disproportionately implicated in obesity, especially foods of no nutritive value like sugary drinks, would help. The revenue raised could then be used to offset the extra costs that overweight people impose on others. If the increased cost of these foods also acted as a disincentive for people to buy them, that would help those who are at risk of obesity, which is second only to tobacco as a leading cause of preventable death.

Many of us are rightly concerned about whether our planet can support a human population that has passed seven billion. We should think of the size of the human population not just in numbers, but as the product of the number of people and the average weight of those people. If we value both sustainable human well-being and the natural environment of our planet, "my weight is my own business" just isn't true.

from Project Syndicate, March 12, 2012

SHOULD WE LIVE TO 1,000?

ON WHICH PROBLEMS SHOULD WE FOCUS research in medicine and the biological sciences? There is a strong argument for tackling the diseases that kill the most people—diseases like malaria, measles, and diarrhea, which kill millions in developing countries, but very few in the developed world.

Developed countries, however, devote most of their research funds to the diseases from which their citizens suffer, and that seems likely to continue for the foreseeable future. Given that constraint, which medical breakthrough would do the most to improve our lives?

If your first thought is "a cure for cancer" or "a cure for heart disease," think again. Aubrey de Grey, Chief Science Officer of SENS Foundation and the world's most prominent advocate of anti-aging research, argues that it makes no sense to spend the vast majority of our medical resources on trying to combat the diseases of aging without tackling aging itself. If we cure one of these diseases, those who would have died from it can expect to succumb to another in a few years. The benefit is therefore modest.

In developed countries, aging is the ultimate cause of 90 percent of all human deaths; thus, treating aging is a form of preventive medicine for all of the diseases of old age. Moreover, even before aging leads to our death, it reduces our capacity to enjoy our own lives and to contribute positively to the lives of others. So, instead of targeting specific diseases that are much more likely to occur when people have reached a certain age, wouldn't a better strategy be to attempt to forestall or repair the damage done to our bodies by the aging process?

De Grey believes that even modest progress in this area over the coming decade could lead to a dramatic extension of the human lifespan. All we need to do is reach what he calls "longevity escape velocity"—that is, the point at which we can extend life sufficiently to allow time for further scientific progress to permit additional extensions, and thus further progress and greater longevity. Speaking recently at Princeton University, de Grey said: "We don't know how old the first person who will live to 150 is today, but the first person to live to 1,000 is almost certainly less than 20 years younger."

What most attracts de Grey about this prospect is not living forever, but rather the extension of healthy, youthful life that would come with a degree of control over the process of aging. In developed countries, enabling those who are young or middle-aged to remain youthful longer would attenuate the looming demographic problem of an historically unprecedented proportion of the population reaching advanced age—and often becoming dependent on younger people.

On the other hand, we still need to pose the ethical question: Are we being selfish in seeking to extend our lives so dramatically? And, if we succeed, will the outcome be good for some but unfair to others?

People in rich countries already can expect to live about 30 years longer than people in the poorest countries. If we discover how to slow aging, we might have a world in which the poor majority must face death at a time when members of the rich minority are only one-tenth of the way through their expected lifespans.

That disparity is one reason to believe that overcoming aging will increase the stock of injustice in the world. Another is that if people continue to be born, while others do not die, the planet's population will increase at an even faster rate than it does now, which will likewise make life for some much worse than it would have been otherwise.

Whether we can overcome these objections depends on our degree of optimism about future technological and economic advances. De Grey's response to the first objection is that, while anti-aging treatment may be expensive initially, the price is likely to drop, as it has for so many other innovations, from computers to the drugs that prevent the development of AIDS. If the world can continue to develop economically and technologically, people will become wealthier, and, in the long run, anti-aging treatment will benefit everyone. So why not get started and make it a priority now?

As for the second objection, contrary to what most people assume, success in overcoming aging could itself give us breathing space to find solutions to the population problem, because it would also delay or eliminate menopause, enabling women to have their first children much later than they can now. If economic development continues, fertility rates in developing countries will fall, as they have in developed countries. In the end, technology, too, may help to overcome the population objection, by providing new sources of energy that do not increase our carbon footprint.

The population objection raises a deeper philosophical question. If our planet has a finite capacity to support human life, is it better to have fewer people living longer lives, or more people living shorter lives? One reason for thinking it better to have fewer people living longer lives is that only those who are born know what death deprives them of; those who do not exist cannot know what they are missing.

De Grey has set up the SENS Foundation to promote research into anti-aging. By most standards, his fundraising efforts have been successful, for the foundation now has an annual budget of around $4 million. But that is still pitifully small by the standards of medical research foundations. De Grey might be mistaken, but if there is only a small chance that he is right, the huge payoffs make anti-aging research a better bet than areas of medical research that are currently far better funded.

from Project Syndicate, December 10, 2012

POPULATION AND THE POPE

As Pope Francis was returning to Rome from the Philippines last month, he told journalists about a woman who had had seven children by caesarean section and was now pregnant again. This was, he said, "tempting God." He asked her if she wanted to leave seven orphans. Catholics have approved ways of regulating births, he continued, and should practice "responsible parenthood" rather than breeding "like rabbits."

Francis's "rabbit" comment was widely covered in the media, but fewer reported that he had also said that no outside institution should impose its views about regulating family size on the developing world. "Every people," he insisted, should be able to maintain its identity without being "ideologically colonized."

The irony of this remark is that in the Philippines, a country of more than 100 million people, of whom four out of five are Roman Catholic, it is precisely the Church that has been the ideological colonizer. It is the Church, after all, that has vigorously sought to impose its opposition to contraception on the population, opposing even the provision of contraceptives by the government to the rural poor.

Meanwhile, surveys have repeatedly shown that most Filipinos favor making contraceptives available, which is not surprising, given that the Church-approved birth-control methods mentioned by Francis are demonstrably less reliable than modern alternatives. It is hard to believe that if the

Philippines had been colonized by, say, Protestant Britain rather than Catholic Spain, the use of contraception would be an issue there today.

The larger issue that Francis raised, however, is whether it is legitimate for outside agencies to promote family planning in developing countries. There are several reasons why it is. First, leaving aside the "ideological" question of whether family planning is a right, there is overwhelming evidence to show that a lack of access to contraception is bad for women's health.

Frequent pregnancies, especially in countries without universal modern health care, are associated with high maternal mortality. Aid by outside agencies to help developing countries reduce premature deaths in women is surely not "ideological colonization."

Second, when births are more widely spaced, children do better, both physically and in terms of educational attainment. We should all agree that it is desirable for aid organizations to promote the health and education of children in developing countries.

The broader and more controversial reason for promoting family planning, however, is that making it available to all who want it is in the interest of the world's seven billion people and the generations that, barring disaster, should be able to inhabit the planet for untold millennia to come. And here, the relationship between climate change and birth control needs to be brought into focus.

The key facts about climate change are well known. Our planet's atmosphere has already absorbed such a large quantity of human-produced greenhouse gases that global warming is underway, with more extreme heat waves, droughts, and floods than ever before. Arctic sea ice is melting, and rising sea levels are threatening to inundate low-lying densely populated coastal regions in several countries. If rainfall patterns change, hundreds of millions of people could become climate refugees.

Moreover, an overwhelming majority of scientists in the relevant fields believe that we are on track to exceed the level of global warming at which feedback mechanisms will kick in and climate change will become uncontrollable, with unpredictable and possibly catastrophic consequences.

It is often pointed out that it is the affluent countries that have caused the problem, owing to their higher greenhouse gas emissions over the past two centuries. They continue to have the highest levels of per capita emissions, and they can reduce emissions with the least hardship. There is no doubt that, ethically, the world's developed countries should be taking the lead in reducing emissions.

What is not so often mentioned, however, is the extent to which continuing global population growth would undermine the impact of whatever emission reductions affluent countries can be persuaded to make.

Four factors influence the level of emissions: economic output per capita; the units of energy used to generate each unit of economic output; greenhouse gases emitted per unit of energy; and total population. A reduction in any three of these factors will be offset by an increase in the fourth. In the "Summary for Policymakers" of its 2014 *Fifth Assessment Report*, the Intergovernmental Panel on Climate Change stated that, globally, economic and population growth continue to be "the most important drivers" of increases in CO_2 emissions from fossil-fuel combustion.

According to the World Health Organization, an estimated 222 million women in developing countries do not want to have children now, but lack the means to ensure that they do not conceive. Providing them with access to contraception would help them plan their lives as they wish, weaken demand for abortion, reduce maternal deaths, give children a better start in life, *and* contribute to slowing population growth and greenhouse gas emissions, thus benefiting us all.

Who could oppose such an obvious win-win proposition? The only naysayers, we may suspect, are those in the grip of a religious ideology that they seek to impose on others, no matter what the consequences for women, children, and the rest of the world, now and for centuries to come.

from Project Syndicate, February 11, 2015

... Sex and Gender ...

SHOULD ADULT SIBLING INCEST BE A CRIME?

LAST MONTH, THE GERMAN ETHICS COUNCIL, a statutory body that reports to the Bundestag, recommended that sexual intercourse between adult siblings should cease to be a crime. The recommendation follows a 2012 decision by the European Court of Human Rights upholding the conviction of a Leipzig man for having a sexual relationship with his sister. The man has served several years in prison, owing to his refusal to abandon the relationship. (His sister was judged to be less responsible and was not jailed.)

Incest between adults is not a crime in all jurisdictions. In France, the offense was abolished when Napoleon introduced his new penal code in 1810. Consensual adult incest is also not a crime in Belgium, the Netherlands, Portugal, Spain, Russia, China, Japan, South Korea, Turkey, Côte d'Ivoire, Brazil, Argentina, and several other Latin American countries.

The Ethics Council took its investigation seriously. Its report (currently available only in German) begins with testimony from those in a forbidden relationship, particularly half-brothers and sisters who came to know each other only as adults. These couples describe the difficulties created by the criminalization of their relationship, including extortion demands and the threat of loss of custody of a child from a previous relationship.

The report does not attempt to provide a definitive assessment of the ethics of consensual sexual relationships between siblings. Instead, it asks whether there is an adequate basis for the criminal law to prohibit such relationships. It points out that in no other situation are voluntary sexual relationships between people capable of self-determination prohibited. There is, the report argues, a need for a clear and convincing justification for intruding into this core area of private life.

The report examines the grounds on which it might be claimed that this burden of justification has been met. The risk of genetically abnormal children is one such reason; but, even if it were sufficient, it would justify only a prohibition that was both narrower and wider than the current prohibition on incest.

The prohibition would be narrower, because it would apply only when children are possible: the Leipzig man whose case brought the issue to attention had a vasectomy in 2004, but that did not affect his criminal liability. And the goal of avoiding genetic abnormalities would justify widening the prohibition to sexual relationships between *all* couples who are at high risk of having abnormal offspring. Given Germany's Nazi past, it is difficult for Germans today to treat that goal as anything but permitting the state to determine who may reproduce.

The Council also considered the need to protect family relationships. The report notes that few families are threatened by incest between siblings, not because it is a crime, but because being brought up together in a family or family-like environment (including Israeli kibbutzim that rear unrelated children collectively) tends to negate sexual attraction. Incest between siblings is therefore a rare occurrence.

The report does recognize the legitimacy of the objective of protecting the family, however, and makes use of it to limit the scope of its recommendation to sexual relations between adult siblings. Sexual relations between other close relatives, such as parents and their adult children, are, the report argues, in a different category because of the different power relations between generations, and the greater potential for damage to other family relationships.

The taboo against incest runs deep, as the social psychologist Jonathan Haidt demonstrated when he told experimental subjects about Julie and Mark, adult siblings who take a holiday together and decide to have sex, just to see what it would be like. In the story, Julie is already on the Pill, but Mark uses a condom, just to be safe. They both enjoy the experience, but decide not to do it again. It remains a secret that brings them even closer.

Haidt then asked his subjects whether it was okay for Julie and Mark to have sex. Most said that it was not, but when Haidt asked them why, they offered reasons that were already excluded by the story—for example, the dangers of inbreeding, or the risk that their relationship would suffer. When Haidt pointed out to his subjects that the reasons they had offered did not apply to the case, they often responded: "I can't explain it, I just know it's wrong." Haidt refers to this as "moral dumbfounding."

Perhaps not coincidentally, when a spokesperson for German Chancellor Angela Merkel's Christian Democrats was asked to comment on the Ethics Council's recommendation, she also said something completely beside the point, referring to the need to protect children. The report, however, made no recommendations about incest involving children, and some of those caught by the criminal law did not even know each other as children.

In the case of the incest taboo, our response has an obvious evolutionary explanation. But should we allow our judgment of what is a crime to be determined by feelings of repugnance that may have strengthened the evolutionary fitness of ancestors who lacked effective contraception?

Even discussing that question has proved controversial. In Poland, a comment presenting the views of the German Ethics Council was posted online by Jan Hartman, a philosophy professor at the Jagiellonian University in Krakow. The university authorities described Hartman's statement as "undermining the dignity of the profession of a university teacher" and referred the matter to a disciplinary commission.

In so quickly forgetting that the profession's dignity requires freedom of expression, a renowned university appears to have succumbed to instinct. That does not augur well for a rational debate about whether incest between adult siblings should remain a crime.

from Project Syndicate, October 8, 2014

Postscript: The German government has not acted on the recommendation of its Ethics Council. Professor Hartman was interrogated twice by the disciplinary officer of his university, but after he provided evidence in support of the factual elements in his statements, the proceedings were discontinued.

HOMOSEXUALITY IS NOT IMMORAL

IN RECENT YEARS, THE NETHERLANDS, Belgium, Canada, and Spain have recognized marriages between people of the same sex. Several other countries recognize civil unions with similar legal effect. An even wider range of countries have laws against discrimination on the basis of a person's sexual orientation, in areas like housing and employment. Yet in the world's largest democracy, India, sex between two men remains a crime punishable, according to statute, by imprisonment for life.

India is not, of course, the only nation to retain severe punishments for homosexuality. In some Islamic nations—Afghanistan, Iran, Iraq, Saudi Arabia, and Yemen, for instance—sodomy is a crime for which the maximum penalty is death. But the retention of such laws is easier to understand in the case of countries that incorporate religious teachings into their criminal law—no matter how much others may regret it—than in a secular democracy like India.

Anyone who has visited India and seen the sexually explicit temple carvings that are common there will know that the Hindu tradition has a less prudish attitude to sex than Christianity. India's prohibition of homosexuality dates back to 1861, when the British ruled the subcontinent and imposed Victorian morality upon it. It is ironic, therefore, that Britain has long ago repealed its own similar prohibition, while India retains its law as a colonial relic.

Fortunately, the prohibition of sodomy in India is not enforced. Yet it provides a basis for blackmail and harassment of homosexuals, and has made it more difficult for groups that educate people about HIV and AIDS to carry out their work.

Vikram Seth, the author of *A Suitable Boy* and other fine novels, recently published an open letter to the government of India calling for a repeal of the law that makes homosexuality a crime. Many other notable Indians signed the letter, while still others, including the Nobel laureate Amartya Sen, have given it their support. A legal challenge to the law is currently before the high court in Delhi.

Around the time when India's prohibition of sodomy was enacted, John Stuart Mill was writing his celebrated essay *On Liberty*, in which he put forward the following principle:

> . . . the only purpose for which power can be rightfully exercised over any member of a civilized community, against his will, is to prevent harm to others. His own good, either physical or moral, is not sufficient warrant. . . . Over himself, over his own body and mind, the individual is sovereign.

Mill's principle is not universally accepted. The distinguished twentieth-century British philosopher of law, H.L.A. Hart, argued for a partial version of Mill's principle. Where Mill says that the good of the individual, "either physical or moral," is "not sufficient warrant" for state interference, Hart says that the individual's physical good *is* sufficient warrant, if individuals are likely to neglect their own best interests and the interference with their liberty is slight. For example, the state may require us to wear a seat belt when driving, or a helmet when riding a motorcycle.

But Hart sharply distinguished such legal paternalism from legal moralism. He rejected the prohibition on moral grounds of actions that do not lead to physical harm. The state may not, on his view, make homosexuality criminal on the grounds that it is immoral.

The problem with this argument is that it is not easy to see why legal paternalism is justified but legal moralism is not. Defenders of the distinction often claim that the state should be neutral between competing moral ideals, but is such neutrality really possible? If I were a proponent of legal moralism, I would argue that it is, after all, a moral judgment—if a widely shared one—that the value of riding my motorbike with my hair flowing free is outweighed by the risk of head injuries if I crash.

The stronger objection to the prohibition of homosexuality is to deny the claim that lies at its core: that sexual acts between consenting people of the same sex are immoral. Sometimes it is claimed that homosexuality is wrong because it is "unnatural," and even a "perversion of our sexual capacity," which supposedly exists for the purpose of reproduction. But we might just as well say that using artificial sweeteners is a "perversion of our sense of taste," which exists so that we can detect nourishing food. We should beware of equating "natural" with "good."

Does the fact that homosexual acts cannot lead to reproduction make them immoral? That would be a particularly bizarre ground for prohibiting sodomy in a densely populated country like India, which encourages contraception and sterilization. If a form of sexual activity brings satisfaction to those who take part in it, and harms no one, what can be immoral about it?

The underlying problem with prohibiting homosexual acts, then, is not that the state is using the law to enforce private morality. It is that the law is based on the mistaken view that homosexuality is immoral.

from Project Syndicate, October 16, 2006

VIRTUAL VICES

IN A POPULAR INTERNET ROLE-PLAYING GAME called Second Life, people can create a virtual identity for themselves, choosing such things as their age, sex, and appearance. These virtual characters then do things that people in the real world do, such as having sex. Depending on your preferences, you can have sex with someone who is older or younger than you—perhaps much older or younger. In fact, if your virtual character is an adult, you can have sex with a virtual character who is a child.

If you did that in the real world, most of us would agree that you did something seriously wrong. But is it seriously wrong to have virtual sex with a virtual child?

Some Second Life players say that it is, and have vowed to expose those who do it. Meanwhile, the manufacturers, Linden Labs, have said they will modify the game to prevent virtual children from having sex. German prosecutors have also become involved, although their concern appears to be the use of the game to spread child pornography, rather than whether people have virtual sex with virtual children.

Laws against child pornography in other countries may also have the effect of prohibiting games that permit virtual sex with virtual children. In Australia, Connor O'Brien, chair of the criminal law section of the Law Institute of Victoria, recently told the Melbourne newspaper *The Age* that he thought the manufacturer of Second Life could be prosecuted for publishing images of children in a sexual context.

The law is on solid ground when it protects children from being exploited for sexual purposes. It becomes ethically questionable when it interferes with sexual acts between consenting adults. What adults choose to do in the bedroom, many thoughtful people believe, is their own business, and the state ought not to pry into it.

If you get aroused by having your adult partner dress up as a schoolchild before you have sex, and he or she is happy to enter into that fantasy, your behavior may be abhorrent to most people, but as long as it is done in private, few would think that it makes you a criminal.

Nor should it make any difference if you invite a few adult friends over, and in the privacy of your own home they all choose to take part in a larger-scale sexual fantasy of the same kind. Are computers linked via the Internet—again, assuming that only consenting adults are involved—so different from a group fantasy of this kind?

When someone proposes making something a criminal offense, we should always ask: who is harmed? If it can be shown that the opportunity to act out a fantasy by having virtual sex with a virtual child makes people more likely to engage in real pedophilia, then real children will be harmed, and the case for prohibiting virtual pedophilia becomes stronger.

But looking at the question in this way raises another, and perhaps more significant, issue about virtual activities: video game violence.

Those who play violent video games are often at an impressionable age. Doom, a popular violent video game, was a favorite of Eric Harris and Dylan Klebold, the teenage Columbine High School murderers. In a chilling videotape they made before the massacre, Harris says, "It's going to be like fucking Doom. . . . That fucking shotgun [he kisses his gun] is straight out of Doom!"

There are other cases in which aficionados of violent video games have become killers, but they do not prove cause and effect. More weight, however, should be given to the growing number of scientific studies, both in the laboratory and in the field, of the effect of such games. In *Violent Video Game Effects on Children and Adults*, Craig Anderson, Douglas Gentile, and Katherine Buckley, of the Department of Psychology at Iowa State University, draw these studies together to argue that violent video games increase aggressive behavior.

If criminal prosecution is too blunt an instrument to use against violent video games, there is a case for awarding damages to the victims, or families of the victims, of violent crimes committed by people who play violent video games. To date, such lawsuits have been dismissed, at least in part on the grounds that the manufacturers could not foresee that their products would cause people to commit crimes. But the evidence that Anderson, Gentile, and Buckley provide has weakened that defense.

André Peschke, editor-in-chief of Krawall.de, one of Germany's leading online computer and video game magazines, informs me that in ten years in the video game industry, he has never seen any serious debate within the industry on the ethics of producing violent games. The manufacturers fall back on the simplistic assertion that there is no scientific proof that violent video games lead to violent acts. But sometimes we cannot wait for proof. This seems to be one of those cases: the risks are great, and outweigh whatever benefits violent video games may have. The evidence may not be conclusive, but it is too strong to be ignored any longer.

The burst of publicity about virtual pedophilia in Second Life may have focused on the wrong target. Video games are properly subject to legal controls, not when they enable people to do things that, if real, would be crimes, but when there is evidence on the basis of which we can reasonably conclude that they are likely to increase serious crime in the real world. At present, the evidence for that is stronger for games involving violence than it is for virtual realities that permit pedophilia.

from Project Syndicate, July 17, 2007

A PRIVATE AFFAIR?

CAN A PUBLIC FIGURE HAVE A PRIVATE LIFE? Recent events in three countries have highlighted the importance of this question.

In the French presidential election, both candidates tried to keep their domestic life separate from their campaign. Ségolène Royal is not married to François Hollande, the father of her four children. When asked whether they were a couple, Royal replied, "Our lives belong to us." Similarly, in response to rumors that President-elect Nicolas Sarkozy's wife had left him, a spokesman for Sarkozy said, "That's a private matter."

The French have a long tradition of respecting the privacy of their politicians' personal lives, and French public opinion is more broad-minded than in the United States, where an unwed mother of four would have no chance of being nominated for the presidency by a major party. Indeed, last month, Randall Tobias, the top foreign aid adviser in the US State Department, resigned after acknowledging that he had used an escort service described as providing "high-end erotic fantasy"—although Tobias said he only had a massage.

In Britain, Lord John Browne, the chief executive who transformed BP from a second-tier European oil company into a global giant, resigned after admitting he had lied in court about the circumstances in which he had met a gay companion (apparently, he met him through a male escort agency). In resigning, he said that he had always regarded his sexuality as a personal matter, and he was disappointed that a newspaper—*The Mail on Sunday*—had made it public.

Candidates for public office, and those holding high administrative or corporate positions, should be judged on their policies and performance, not on private acts that are irrelevant to how well they carry out, or will carry out, their public duties. Sometimes, of course, the two overlap. *The Mail on Sunday* and its sister paper, *The Daily Mail,* justified their publication of revelations by Browne's former companion on the grounds that they include allegations that Browne had allowed him to use corporate resources for the benefit of his own private business. The company denied that there was any substance to these allegations.

As the administrator of the US Agency for International Development, Tobias implemented the Bush administration's policy that requires organizations working against HIV/AIDS to condemn prostitution if they are to be eligible for US assistance. That policy has been criticized for making it more difficult to assist sex workers who are at high risk of contracting and spreading HIV/AIDS. Arguably, the public has an interest in knowing if those who implement such policies are themselves paying for sexual services.

Where there is no suggestion that a matter of personal morality has had an impact on the performance of a business executive or government official, we should respect that person's privacy. But what about candidates for political leadership?

Since politicians ask us to entrust them with sweeping powers, it can be argued that we should know as much as possible about their morality. For example, we might reasonably ask whether they pay their fair share of taxes, or inquire about their charitable donations. Such things tell us something about their concern for the public good. Similarly, the revelation three years ago that Mark Latham, at the time the Australian opposition leader and aspiring prime minister, had assaulted a taxi driver and broken his arm in a dispute about a fare was relevant for those who believe that a nation's leader should be slow to anger.

But does the legitimate interest in knowing more about a politician extend to details about personal relations? It is hard to draw a line of principle around any area and determine if knowledge of it will provide relevant information about a politician's moral character. The problem is that the media have an interest in publishing information that increases their audience, and personal information, especially of a sexual nature, will often do just that.

Even so, whether people choose to marry or not, whether they are heterosexual or homosexual, even whether they pay to fulfill their erotic fantasies or have fantasies they can fulfill at no cost, tells us little about whether they are good people who can be trusted with high office—unless, of course, they say one thing while doing another. If we can cultivate a wider tolerance of human diversity, politicians, business leaders, and administrators would be less fearful of "exposure," because they would realize that they have done nothing that they must hide.

Prostitution is illegal in most of the United States, including Washington, DC, and this could be one reason why Tobias had to resign. But when New Jersey Governor John Corzine was involved in a serious road accident last month, it became known that he violated his own state's law by not wearing his seat belt. By any sensible measure, Corzine's violation of the law was more serious than that of Tobias. Laws requiring the wearing of seat belts save many lives. Laws prohibiting prostitution do no evident good at all, and may well do harm. Yet no one suggested that Corzine should resign because of his foolish and illegal act. In the United States, at least, breaching sexual norms still brings with it a moral opprobrium that is unrelated to any real harm it may do.

from Project Syndicate, May 14, 2007

HOW MUCH SHOULD SEX MATTER?

(with Agata Sagan)

JENNA TALACKOVA REACHED THE FINALS OF Miss Universe Canada last month, before being disqualified because she was not a "natural born" female. The tall, beautiful blonde told the media that she had considered herself a female since she was four years old, had begun hormone treatment at 14, and had sex reassignment surgery at 19. Her disqualification raises the question of what it really means to be a "Miss."

A question of broader significance was raised by the case of an eight-year-old Los Angeles child who is anatomically female, but dresses as, and wants to be considered, a boy. His mother tried unsuccessfully to enroll him in a private school as a boy. Is it really essential that every human being be labeled "male" or "female" in accordance with his or her biological sex?

People who cross gender boundaries suffer clear discrimination. Last year, the National Center for Transgender Equality and the National Gay and Lesbian Task Force published a survey that suggested that the unemployment rate among transgender people is double that of other people. In addition, of those respondents who were employed, 90 percent reported some form of mistreatment at work, such as harassment, ridicule, inappropriate sharing of information about them by supervisors or co-workers, or trouble with access to toilets.

Moreover, transgender people can be subject to physical violence and sexual assault as a result of their sexual identity. According to Trans Murder Monitoring, at least 11 people were murdered in the United States last year for this reason.

Children who do not identify with the sex assigned to them at birth are in an especially awkward position, and their parents face a difficult choice. We do not yet have the means to turn young girls into biologically normal boys, or vice versa. Even if we could do it, specialists warn against taking irreversible steps to turn them into the sex with which they identify.

Many children display cross-gender behavior or express a wish to be of the opposite sex, but when given the option of sex reassignment, only a tiny fraction undergo the full procedure. The use of hormone blocking agents to delay puberty seems a reasonable option, as it offers both parents and children more time to make up their minds about this life-changing decision.

But the broader problem remains that people who are uncertain about their gender identification, move between genders, or have both female and male sexual organs do not fit into the standard male/female dichotomy.

Last year, the Australian government addressed this problem by providing passports with three categories: male, female, and indeterminate. The new system also allows people to choose their gender identity, which need not match the sex assigned to them at birth. This break with the usual rigid categorization shows respect for all individuals, and, if it becomes widely adopted in other countries, will save many people from the hassle of explaining to immigration officials a discrepancy between their appearance and their sex as recorded in their passport.

Nevertheless, one may wonder whether it is really necessary for us to ask people as often as we do what sex they are. On the Internet, we frequently interact with people without knowing their gender. Some people place high value on controlling what information about them is made public, so why do we force them, in so many situations, to say if they are male or female?

Is the desire for such information a residue of an era in which women were excluded from a wide range of roles and positions, and thus denied the privileges that go with them? Perhaps eliminating the occasions on which this question is asked for no good reason would not only make life easier for those who can't be squeezed into strict categories, but would also help to reduce inequality for women. It could also prevent injustices that occasionally arise for men, for example, in the provision of parental leave.

Imagine further how, wherever homosexual relationships are lawful, the obstacles to gay and lesbian marriage would vanish if the state did not require the spouses to state their sex. The same would apply to adoption. (In fact, there is some evidence that having two lesbians as parents gives a child a better start in life than any other combination.)

Some parents are already resisting the traditional "boy or girl" question by not disclosing the sex of their child after birth. One couple from Sweden explained that they want to avoid their child being forced into "a specific gender mold," saying that it is cruel "to bring a child into the world with a blue or pink stamp on their forehead." A Canadian couple wondered why "the whole world must know what is between the baby's legs."

Jane McCreedie, the author of *Making Girls and Boys: Inside the Science of Sex*, criticizes these couples for going too far. In the world as it is today, she has a point, because concealing a child's sex will only draw more attention to it. But if such behavior became more common—or even somehow became the norm—would there be anything wrong with it?

from Project Syndicate, April 13, 2012

GOD AND WOMAN IN IRAN

MY GRANDMOTHER WAS ONE OF THE FIRST WOMEN to study mathematics and physics at the University of Vienna. When she graduated, in 1905, the university nominated her for its highest distinction, an award marked by the presentation of a ring engraved with the initials of the emperor. But no woman had previously been nominated for such an honor, and Emperor Franz Joseph refused to bestow the award upon one.

More than a century later, one might have thought that by now we would have overcome the belief that women are not suited to the highest levels of education, in any area of study. So it is disturbing news that more than 30 Iranian universities have banned women from more than 70 courses, ranging from engineering, nuclear physics, and computer science to English literature, archaeology, and business. According to Shirin Ebadi, the Iranian lawyer, human-rights activist, and winner of the Nobel Peace Prize, the restrictions are part of a government policy to limit women's opportunities outside the home.

The bans are especially ironic, given that, according to UNESCO, Iran has the highest rate of female to male undergraduates in the world. Last year, women made up 60 percent of all students passing university exams, and women have done well in traditionally male-dominated disciplines like engineering.

It may well be female students' very success—and the role of educated women in opposing Iran's theocracy—that led the government to seek to reverse the trend. Now, women like Noushin, a student from Esfahan who told the BBC that she wanted to be a mechanical engineer, are unable to achieve their ambitions, despite getting high scores on their entrance exams.

Some claim that the ideal of sexual equality represents a particular cultural viewpoint, and that we Westerners should not seek to impose our values on other cultures. It is true that Islamic texts assert in various ways the superiority of men to women. But the same can be said of Jewish and Christian texts; and the right to education, without discrimination, is guaranteed in several international declarations and covenants, such as the Universal Declaration of Human Rights, to which almost all countries, including Iran, have agreed.

Discrimination against women is part of a broader pattern of official bias in Iran, especially against those who are neither Muslim nor members of one of the three minority religions—Zoroastrianism, Judaism, and Christianity—recognized in the Iranian Constitution. To enroll in a university, for example, one must declare oneself to be a believer in one of the four recognized religions. Atheists, agnostics, or members of Iran's Bahá'i community are not accepted.

Imagine how we would react if someone tried to excuse racial discrimination by arguing that it is wrong to impose one's culture on others. It was, after all, for many years the "culture" of some parts of the United States that people of African descent should sit at the back of the bus and go to separate schools, hospitals, and universities. It was the "culture" of apartheid South Africa that blacks should live apart from whites and have separate, and inferior, educational opportunities. Or, to put it more accurately, it was the culture of the whites who held power in these places at that time.

The same is true in Iran. The country's rulers are all male and Muslim. Supreme Leader Ayatollah Ali Khamenei's call in 2009 for the "Islamization" of universities led to courses being changed and the replacement of some academic staff by more conservative figures. Two months ago, Khamenei said that Iranians should return to traditional values and have more children—which would have obvious implications for the role of women, quite apart from the environmental impact.

The international sanctions against Iran that are currently in place seek to prevent the regime from building nuclear weapons, not to persuade it to end discrimination against women or on religious grounds. There are no widespread boycotts of Iran's universities, or of its other products, as there were against apartheid South Africa. It seems that we still take sexual and religious discrimination less seriously than we take racial and ethnic discrimination.

Perhaps we are more ready to accept that the biological differences between men and women are relevant to the roles they play in society. There are such differences, and they are not purely physical. So we should not leap to the conclusion that if most engineers are men, there must be discrimination against women. It may be that more men than women want to be engineers.

That, however, is a completely different question from whether women who do want to become engineers and are qualified to study engineering should be denied the opportunity to achieve their ambition. By explicitly preventing women from enrolling in courses open to men, Iran has taken a step that is as indefensible as racial discrimination, and that should be condemned just as forcefully.

from Project Syndicate, October 11, 2012

... Doing Good ...

...Doing Good...

THE ONE-PERCENT SOLUTION

MORE THAN A BILLION PEOPLE now live on less, per day, than the purchasing power equivalent, in their country, of one US dollar. In the year 2000, Americans made private donations for foreign aid of all kinds totaling about $4 per person, or roughly $20 per family. Through their government, they gave another $10 per person, or $50 per family. That makes a total of $70 per family.

In comparison, in the aftermath of the destruction of the World Trade Center, the American Red Cross received so much money that it abandoned any attempt to examine how much help potential recipients needed. It drew a line across lower Manhattan and offered anyone living below that line the equivalent of three months' rent (or, if they owned their own apartment, three months' mortgage and maintenance payments). If recipients claimed to have been affected by the destruction of the Twin Towers, they received money for utilities and groceries as well.

Most residents of the area below the line were not displaced or evacuated, but they were offered mortgage or rent assistance nonetheless. Red Cross volunteers set up card tables in the lobbies of expensive apartment buildings where financial analysts, lawyers, and rock stars live, to inform residents of the offer. The higher the rent people paid, the more money they got. New Yorkers, wealthy or not, living in lower Manhattan on September 11, 2001, were able to receive an average of $5,300 per family.

The difference between $70 and $5,300 may be a solid indication of the relative weight that Americans give to the interests of their fellow citizens compared with what they give to people elsewhere. Even that underestimates the difference, since the Americans who received the money generally had less need of it than the world's poorest people.

At the UN Millennium Summit, the nations of the world committed themselves to a set of targets, prominent among which was halving the number of people living in poverty by 2015. The World Bank estimated the cost of meeting these targets to be an additional $40–$60 billion per year. So far the money has not been forthcoming.

Although described as "ambitious," the Millennium goals are modest, for to halve the number of people living in poverty, all that is required—over 15 years—is to reach the better-off half of the world's poorest people, and move them marginally above the poverty line. That could, in theory, leave the worst-off 500 million people in poverty just as dire as they are now experiencing. Moreover, during every day of those 15 years, thousands of children will die from poverty-related causes.

How much would it require, per person, to raise the necessary $40–$60 billion? There are about 900 million people in the developed world, 600 million of them adults. A donation of about $100 per adult per year for the next 15 years could achieve the Millennium goals. For someone earning $27,500 per annum, the average salary in the developed world, this is less than 0.4% of annual income, or less than 1 cent out of every $2 that they earn.

Of course, not all residents of rich countries have income to spare after meeting their basic needs. But there are hundreds of millions of rich people who live in poor countries, and they could also give. We could, therefore, advocate that everyone with income to spare, after meeting their family's basic needs, should contribute a minimum of 0.4% of their income to organizations working to help the world's poorest people, and that would probably be enough to meet the Millennium goals.

A more useful symbolic figure than 0.4% would be 1%, and this, added to existing levels of government aid (which in every country of the world except Denmark fall below 1% of GNP, and in the United States is only 0.1%), might be closer to what it would take to eliminate, rather than halve, global poverty.

We tend to think of charity as something that is "morally optional"—good to do, but not wrong to fail to do. As long as one does not kill, maim, steal, cheat, and so on, one can be a morally virtuous citizen, even if one spends lavishly and gives nothing to charity. But those who have enough to spend on luxuries, yet fail to share even a tiny fraction of their income with the poor, must bear some responsibility for the deaths they could have prevented. Those who do not meet even the minimal 1% standard should be seen as doing something that is morally wrong.

Anyone who thinks about their ethical obligations will rightly decide that—since, no matter what we do, not everyone will give even 1%—they should do more. I have in the past advocated giving much larger sums. But if, in order to change our standards in a manner that stands a realistic chance of success, we focus on what we can expect everyone to do, there is something to be said for setting a donation of 1% of annual income to overcome world poverty as the bare minimum that one *must* do to lead a morally decent life.

To give that amount requires no moral heroics. To fail to give it shows indifference to the continuation of dire poverty and avoidable, poverty-related deaths.

from Project Syndicate, June 21, 2002

Postscript: Good news! The number of people living in extreme poverty (now defined by the World Bank as living on less than $1.90 per day) has fallen steadily since this column was written, and by the end of 2015 had dropped to 702 million. This is the first time that fewer than 10 percent of the world's population has been in extreme poverty.

HOLDING CHARITIES ACCOUNTABLE

SUPPOSE YOU ARE CONCERNED ABOUT children in Africa dying from preventable diseases. You want to donate money to a charity that is working to reduce the toll. But there are many charities doing that. How do you choose?

The first thing that many people ask about charities is, "How much of my donation is spent on administration?" In the United States, that figure is readily available from Charity Navigator, a website that has five million users. But the information is taken from forms that the charities themselves complete and send to the tax authorities. No one checks the forms, and the proportions allocated to administration and program expenses are easily massaged with a little creative accounting.

Worse still, that figure, even if accurate, tells you nothing about the charity's impact. The pressure to keep administrative expenses low can make an organization less effective. If, for example, an agency working to reduce poverty in Africa cuts staff with expert knowledge, it is more likely to end up funding projects that fail. It may not even know which of its projects fail, because evaluating them, and learning from mistakes, requires staff—and that adds to administrative costs.

In 2006, Holden Karnofsky and Elie Hassenfeld faced the question of which charity would make the best use of their money. They were in their mid-twenties, earning six-figure incomes at an investment company—more than they needed—and were thinking about donating money to help make the world a better place. As investment advisers, they would never recommend investing in a company without detailed information about how well it was achieving its goals. They wanted to make similarly well-informed choices about the charities to which they contributed.

So Karnofsky and Hassenfeld got together with six friends who also worked in finance and divided up the field to find out which charities could be shown to be effective. They contacted organizations and received lots of attractive marketing material, but nothing that answered basic questions: what do the charities do with their money, and what evidence do they have that their activities help? They called many charities, but eventually realized something that seemed extraordinary: the information was just not there.

Some foundations said that information on their work's effectiveness was confidential. This, Karnofsky and Hassenfeld thought, is not a good way to go about charitable work. Why should information about how to help people be secret? The fact that charities were unprepared for such questions indicated to Karnofsky and Hassenfeld that other donors and foundations give more or less blindly, without the information needed to make sound decisions about whom to support.

Karnofsky and Hassenfeld now had a new goal: to obtain and publicize the information. To that end, they founded an organization called GiveWell so that other donors would not have as hard a time extracting it as they had had.

However, it soon became apparent that the task required more than part-time attention, and the following year, after raising $300,000 from their colleagues, Karnofsky and Hassenfeld left their jobs and began working full-time for

GiveWell and its associated grant-making body, The Clear Fund. They invited charities to apply for grants of $25,000 in five broad humanitarian categories, with the application process demanding the kind of information that they had been seeking. In this way, a substantial part of the money they had raised would go to the most effective charity in each category, while simultaneously encouraging transparency and rigorous evaluation.

The first report on which organizations are most effective at saving or transforming lives in Africa is now available on GiveWell's website. Population Services International, which promotes and sells items like condoms, to prevent HIV infection, and bed nets, to prevent malaria, came out on top, followed by Partners in Health, an organization that provides health care to poor rural populations. The third-ranked organization was Interplast, which is more narrowly focused on correcting deformities like cleft palate.

Evaluating charities can be more difficult than making investment decisions. Investors are interested in financial returns, so there is no problem about measuring distinct values—in the end it all comes down to money. It is more difficult to compare the reduction of suffering brought about by correcting a facial deformity with saving a life. There is no single unit of value.

In other ways, too, evaluating charities takes time, and can be expensive. Perhaps for this reason, many organizations, including some of the best-known anti-poverty organizations working in Africa, did not respond to GiveWell's request for information. No doubt they calculated that a chance to get a $25,000 grant wasn't worth it. But if donors start to follow GiveWell's recommendations, then a high ranking from GiveWell could be worth far more than the value of the grant.

This is why the potential of GiveWell is revolutionary. In the United States, individual donors give about $200 billion to charities each year. No one knows how effective that vast sum is in achieving the goals that donors intend to support. By giving charities an incentive to become more transparent and more focused on being demonstrably effective, GiveWell could make our charitable donations do much more good than ever before.

from Project Syndicate, February 14, 2008

Postscript: In the years since this column was written, GiveWell has thrived, increasing its staff to enable it to do more research. In 2015, GiveWell tracked approximately $100 million dollars in donations going to its recommended charities as a result of its research. The current list of its top-ranked charities is available at www.givewell.org.

BLATANT BENEVOLENCE

JESUS SAID THAT WE SHOULD GIVE ALMS in private rather than when others are watching. That fits with the common-sense idea that if people only do good in public, they may be motivated by a desire to gain a reputation for generosity. Perhaps when no one is looking, they are not generous at all.

That thought may lead us to disdain the kind of philanthropic graffiti that leads to donors' names being prominently displayed on concert halls, art museums, and college buildings. Often, names are stuck not only over the entire building, but also on as many constituent parts of it as fundraisers and architects can manage.

According to evolutionary psychologists, such displays of blatant benevolence are the human equivalent of the male peacock's tail. Just as the peacock signals his strength and fitness by displaying his enormous tail—a sheer waste of resources from a practical point of view—so costly public acts of benevolence signal to potential mates that one possesses enough resources to give so much away.

From an ethical perspective, however, should we care so much about the purity of the motive with which the gift was made? Surely, what matters is that something was given to a good cause. We may well look askance at a lavish new concert hall, but not because the donor's name is chiseled into the marble façade. Rather, we should question whether, in a world in which 25,000 impoverished children die unnecessarily every day, another concert hall is what the world needs.

A substantial body of current psychological research points against Jesus's advice. One of the most significant factors determining whether people give to charity is their beliefs about what others are doing. Those who make it known that they give to charity increase the likelihood that others will do the same. Perhaps we will eventually reach a tipping point at which giving a significant amount to help the world's poorest becomes sufficiently widespread to eliminate the majority of those 25,000 needless daily deaths.

That is what Chris and Anne Ellinger hope their website, www.boldergiving.org, will achieve. The website tells the story of more than 50 members of the 50 Percent League—people who have given away either 50 percent of their assets or 50 percent of their income in each of the last three years. Members of the league want to change expectations about what is a "normal" or "reasonable" amount to give.

They are a diverse group of people. Tom White ran a big construction company, and started giving millions to Paul Farmer's efforts to bring health services to Haiti's rural poor. Tom Hsieh and his wife, Bree, made a commitment to live on less than the national median income, currently $46,000 a year. As Hsieh, who is 36, earned more, they gave away more, mostly to organizations helping the poor in developing countries. Hal Taussig and his wife have given away about $3 million, amounting to 90 percent of their assets, and now live happily on their social security checks.

Most donors see giving as personally rewarding. Hsieh says that whether or not his giving has saved the lives of others, it has saved his own: "I could easily have lived a life that was boring and inconsequential. Now I am graced with a life of service and meaning." When people praise Hal Taussig for his generosity, he tells them, "Frankly, it's my way of getting kicks out of life."

The 50 Percent League sets the bar high—perhaps too high for most people. James Hong started www.hotornot. com, a website that allows people to rate how "hot" other people are. It made him rich. He has pledged to give away 10 percent of everything he earns over $100,000. Hong's website, www.10over100.org, invites others to do likewise. So far, more than 3,500 people have.

Hong sets the bar low. If you earn less than $100,000, you don't have to give away anything at all, and if you earn, say, $110,000, you would be required to give away only $1,000—less than 1 percent of your income. That is not generous at all. Many of those earning less than $100,000 can also afford to give something. Still, Hong's formula is simple, and it starts to bite when earnings get really big. If you earn a million dollars a year, you have pledged to give $90,000, or 9 percent of what you earn, which is more than most rich people give.

We need to get over our reluctance to speak openly about the good we do. Silent giving will not change a culture that deems it sensible to spend all your money on yourself and your family, rather than to help those in greater need—even though helping others is likely to bring more fulfillment in the long run.

from Project Syndicate, June 13, 2008

Postscript: Bolder Giving is still flourishing, and its 50 percent pledge helped to inspire Bill and Melinda Gates to set up the Giving Pledge (www.givingpledge.org) asking the world's wealthiest people to pledge to give half of their wealth to charity before they die. (My own book, *The Life You Can Save,* was also an influence on the Gates's thinking.) As of January 2016, more than 130 billionaires have pledged to

give away a total of more than $170 billion. 10over100.org is
defunct, but Giving What We Can (www.givingwhatwecan.
org) invites people to make a similar pledge, while The Life
You Can Save, based on my book, uses a progressive scale,
starting at a lower percentage but ending at a higher one,
depending on earnings (www.thelifeyoucansave.org).

GOOD CHARITY, BAD CHARITY

YOU ARE THINKING OF DONATING to a worthy cause. Good. But to which cause should you give?

If you seek help from professional philanthropy advisers, the chances are that they won't have much to say about this vital question. They will guide you, to be sure, through an array of charitable options. But the prevailing assumption in their field is that we shouldn't, or perhaps can't, make objective judgments about which options are better than others.

Take Rockefeller Philanthropy Advisors, one of the world's largest philanthropic service organizations. Its website offers a downloadable pamphlet with a chart showing areas to which a philanthropist might give: health and safety; education; arts, culture, and heritage; human and civil rights; economic security; and environment. The website then asks, "What is the most urgent issue?" and answers by saying, "There's obviously no objective answer to that question."

Is this true? I don't think so. Compare, for instance, two of the Rockefeller Philanthropy Advisors' categories: "health and safety" and "arts, culture and heritage." To me it seems clear that there are objective reasons for thinking we may be able to do more good in one of these areas than in another.

Suppose your local art museum is seeking funds to build a new wing to better display its collection. The museum asks you for a donation for that purpose. Let's say that you could afford to give $100,000. At the same time, you are asked to donate to an organization seeking to reduce the incidence of trachoma, an eye disease caused by an infectious micro-organism that affects children in developing countries. Trachoma causes people to slowly lose their sight, typically culminating in their becoming blind between 30 and 40 years of age. It is preventable. You do some research and learn that each $100 you donate could prevent a person's experiencing 15 years of impaired vision followed by another 15 years of blindness. So for $100,000 you could prevent 1,000 people from losing their sight.

Given this choice, where would $100,000 do the most good? Which expenditure is likely to lead to the bigger improvement in the lives of those affected by it?

On one side we have 1,000 people spared 15 years of impaired vision followed by 15 years of blindness, with all the ensuing problems that that would cause for poor people with no social security. What do we have on the other side?

Suppose the new museum wing will cost $50 million, and over the 50 years of its expected usefulness, one million people will enjoy seeing it each year, for a total of 50 million enhanced museum visits. Since you would contribute 1/500 of the cost, you could claim credit for the enhanced aesthetic experiences of 100,000 visitors. How does that compare with saving 1,000 people from 15 years of blindness?

To answer, try a thought experiment. Suppose you have a choice between visiting the art museum, including its new wing, or going to see the museum without visiting the new wing. Naturally, you would prefer to see it with the new wing. But now imagine that an evil demon declares that out of every 100 people who see the new wing, he will choose one, at random, and inflict 15 years of blindness on that person. Would you still visit the new wing? You'd have to be nuts. Even if the evil demon blinded only one person in every 1,000, in my judgment, and I bet in yours, seeing the new wing still would not be worth the risk.

If you agree, then you are saying, in effect, that the harm of one person's becoming blind outweighs the benefits received by 1,000 people visiting the new wing. Therefore a donation that saves one person from becoming blind would be better value than a donation that enables 1,000 people to visit the new wing. But your donation to the organization preventing trachoma will save not just one but 10 people from becoming blind for every 1,000 people it could provide with an enhanced museum experience. Hence a donation to prevent trachoma offers at least 10 times the value of giving to the museum.

This method of comparing benefits is used by economists to judge how much people value certain states of affairs. It's open to criticism because many people appear to have irrational attitudes toward the small risks of very bad things happening. (That's why we need legislation requiring people to fasten their seat belts.) Still, in many cases, including the one we are now considering, the answer is clear enough.

This is, of course, only one example of how we ought to choose between areas of philanthropy. Some choices are relatively easy and others are much more difficult. In general, where human welfare is concerned, we will achieve more if we help those in extreme poverty in developing countries, as our dollars go much further there. But the choice between, say, helping the global poor directly, and helping them, and all future generations, by trying to reduce greenhouse gas emissions, is more difficult. So, too, is the choice between helping humans and reducing the vast amount of suffering we inflict on nonhuman animals.

But new developments are making these decisions easier. Until recently, it wasn't even possible to find out which charities were the most effective within their own fields. Serious evaluation of charities helping people in extreme poverty began six years ago with the creation of the nonprofit charity evaluator GiveWell.

Now we can be highly confident that a donation to, for example, the Against Malaria Foundation will save lives and reduce the incidence of malaria, and that giving to the Schistosomiasis Control Initiative will, at very low cost, reduce the incidence of neglected tropical diseases, especially those caused by parasites. More experimental is GiveDirectly, which will transfer at least 90 cents of every dollar you give to an extremely low-income African family. Initial studies show that these donations have long-term benefits for the recipients.

"Effective altruism," as this evidence-based approach to charity is known, is an emerging international movement. Not content with merely making the world a better place, its adherents want to use their talents and resources to make the biggest possible positive difference to the world. Thinking about which fields offer the most positive impact for your time and money is still in its infancy, but with more effective altruists researching the issues, we are starting to see real progress.

from The New York Times, *August 10, 2013*

HEARTWARMING CAUSES ARE NICE, BUT LET'S GIVE TO CHARITY WITH OUR HEADS

YOU'D HAVE TO BE A REAL SPOILSPORT not to feel good about Batkid. If the sight of 20,000 people joining in last month to help the Make-A-Wish Foundation and the city of San Francisco fulfill the superhero fantasies of a five-year-old—and not just any five-year-old, but one who has been battling a life-threatening disease—doesn't warm your heart, you must be numb to basic human emotions.

Yet we can still ask if these emotions are the best guide to what we ought to do. According to Make-A-Wish, the average cost of realizing the wish of a child with a life-threatening illness is $7,500. That sum, if donated to the Against Malaria Foundation and used to provide bed nets to families in malaria-prone regions, could save the lives of at least two or three children (and that's a conservative estimate). If donated to the Fistula Foundation, it could pay for surgeries for approximately 17 young mothers who, without that assistance, will be unable to prevent their bodily wastes from leaking through their vaginas and hence are likely to be outcasts for the rest of their lives. If donated to the Seva Foundation to treat trachoma and other common causes of blindness in developing countries, it could protect 100 children from losing their sight as they grow older.

It's obvious, isn't it, that saving a child's life is better than fulfilling a child's wish to be Batkid? If Miles's parents had been offered that choice—Batkid for a day or a cure for their son's leukemia—they surely would have chosen the cure.

Why then do so many people give to Make-A-Wish, when there are more practical ways of using their charitable dollars? The answer lies, at least in part, in those above-mentioned emotions, which, as psychological research shows, make the plight of a single identifiable individual much more salient to us than that of a large number of people we cannot identify.

In one study, people who had earned money for participating in an experiment were given the opportunity to donate some of it to Save the Children, an organization that helps poor children. One group was told things like: "Food shortages in Malawi are affecting more than three million children." A second group was shown a photo of a seven-year-old African girl, told that her name was Rokia, and urged that "her life will be changed for the better as a result of your financial gift." The second group gave significantly more. It seems that seeing a photo of Rokia triggered an emotional desire to help, whereas learning facts about millions of people in need did not.

Similarly, the unknown and unknowable children who will be infected with malaria without bed nets just don't grab our emotions like the kid with leukemia we can watch on TV. That is a flaw in our emotional make-up, one that developed over millions of years when we could help only people we could see in front of us. It is not justification for ignoring the needs of distant strangers.

Some people object that it's harder to track what happens to money sent far away. That was a concern expressed by callers when I was a guest on NPR's *On Point* this month. Edna, clearly a generous person, told us that she volunteers one day a week at a hospital and gives to several local charities. Asked about my argument that donations go furthest when we give to impoverished people in developing countries, she said that she would do that "if I truly believed that the residents who needed that money received it, but no one's ever convinced me of that, so I give where I can see the results." Fortunately, she was followed by Meg, a family-practice doctor who talked about her experiences in Haiti working with kids living on less than $2 a day. Meg pointed out that most of these children had never seen a doctor, except when they got their government vaccinations, and that $1,200 was enough to provide them with regular visits by a Haitian health-care worker for a year.

We don't have to take the word of charitable organizations that the money we give does benefit people in other countries. Technology has made it not only easier to give but easier to give effectively. Websites such as GiveWell or my own The Life You Can Save offer independent evaluations and can direct people to organizations that do not hand over money to corrupt governments but see that it gets to those who need it.

Some Americans may believe that they already do enough, through their taxes, to help poor people abroad. Polls consistently find that Americans think we spend too much on foreign aid—but when asked how much should be spent, they suggest a figure that is many times more than we actually give. In the Kaiser Family Foundation's "2013 Survey of Americans on the U.S. Role in Global Health," the median answer to the question "What percentage of the federal budget is spent on foreign aid?" was 28 percent. That result is broadly in line with a 1997 poll carried out by Kaiser, in conjunction with Harvard University and the *Washington Post*. In that poll, the median answer was 20 percent. The correct answer, both then and now, is approximately 1 percent.

Americans commonly think that the United States is a particularly generous nation, but when it comes to official foreign aid, the United States gives much less, as a percentage of its income, than other wealthy countries. According to 2012 figures from the Organization for Economic Cooperation and Development, Sweden and Luxembourg gave five times as much, while Denmark gave four times as much, and Belgium and Ireland gave more than twice as much. Charitable donations by individuals and foundations do not come anywhere near making up for this shortfall.

Perhaps if Americans knew how stingy we are when it comes to helping the world's poorest people, and were aware of opportunities to do good, we would do more. In an admittedly unscientific test of this belief, my the Life You Can Save organization has been offering cash to surprised strangers on street corners from Wall Street to Santa Monica and then telling them that they have a choice: keep it for themselves or donate it to the Against Malaria Foundation. Almost all of them chose to give it away—and some even added their own money to what they had just been given. Altogether, we have given away $2,500—and the Against Malaria Foundation has received back $2,421.

People who get money as a gift are likely to be more willing to give it away than those who do not receive this unexpected bounty. Nevertheless, the "giving experiment" shows not only that many Americans would like to help the global poor but also that they are genuinely happy to do so. All they need is the knowledge to be able to do so effectively.

from The Washington Post, *December 19, 2013*

THE ETHICAL COST OF HIGH-PRICE ART

IN NEW YORK LAST MONTH, Christie's sold $745 million worth of postwar and contemporary art, the highest total that it has ever reached in a single auction. Among the higher-priced works sold were paintings by Barnett Newman, Francis Bacon, Mark Rothko, and Andy Warhol, each of which sold for more than $60 million. According to the *New York Times*, Asian collectors played a significant part in boosting prices.

No doubt some buyers regard their purchases as an investment, like stocks or real estate or gold bars. In that case, whether the price they paid was excessive or modest will depend on how much the market will be willing to pay for the work at some future date.

But if profit is not the motive, why would anyone want to pay tens of millions of dollars for works like these? They are not beautiful, nor do they display great artistic skill. They are not even unusual within the artists' oeuvres. Do an image search for "Barnett Newman" and you will see many paintings with vertical color bars, usually divided by a thin line. Once Newman had an idea, it seems, he liked to work out all of the variations. Last month, someone bought one of those variations for $84 million. A small image of Marilyn Monroe by Andy Warhol—there are many of those, too—sold for $41 million.

Ten years ago, the Metropolitan Museum of Art in New York paid $45 million for a small *Madonna and Child* by

Duccio. Subsequently, in *The Life You Can Save*, I wrote that there were better things that the donors who financed the purchase could have done with their money. I haven't changed my mind about that, but the Met's Madonna is beautifully executed and 700 years old. Duccio is a major figure who worked during a key transitional moment in the history of Western art, and few of his paintings have survived. None of that applies to Newman or Warhol.

Perhaps, though, the importance of postwar art lies in its ability to challenge our ideas. That view was firmly expressed by Jeff Koons, one of the artists whose work was on sale at Christie's. In a 1987 interview with a group of art critics, Koons referred to the work that was sold last month, calling it "the 'Jim Beam' work." Koons had exhibited this piece—an oversized stainless steel toy train filled with bourbon—in an exhibition called "Luxury and Degradation," that, according to the *New York Times,* examined "shallowness, excess and the dangers of luxury in the high-flying 1980s."

In the interview, Koons said that the Jim Beam work "used the metaphors of luxury to define class structure." The critic Helena Kontova then asked him how his "socio-political intention" related to the politics of then-President Ronald Reagan. Koons answered: "With Reaganism, social mobility is collapsing, and instead of a structure composed of low, middle, and high income levels, we're down to low and high only. . . . My work stands in opposition to this trend."

Art as a critique of luxury and excess! Art as opposition to the widening gap between the rich and the poor! How noble and courageous that sounds. But the art market's greatest strength is its ability to co-opt any radical demands that a work of art makes, and turn it into another consumer good for the super-rich. When Christie's put Koons's work up for auction, the toy train filled with bourbon sold for $33 million.

If artists, art critics, and art buyers really had any interest in reducing the widening gap between the rich and the poor, they would be focusing their efforts on developing countries, where spending a few thousand dollars on the purchase of works by indigenous artists could make a real difference to the well-being of entire villages.

Nothing I have said here counts against the importance of creating art. Drawing, painting, and sculpting, like singing or playing a musical instrument, are significant forms of self-expression, and our lives would be poorer without them. In all cultures, and in all kinds of situations, people produce art, even when they cannot satisfy their basic physical needs.

But we don't need art buyers to pay millions of dollars to encourage people to do that. In fact, it would not be hard to argue that sky-high prices have a corrupting influence on artistic expression.

As for why buyers pay these outlandish sums, my guess is that they think that owning original works by well-known artists will enhance their own status. If so, that may provide a means to bring about change: a redefinition of status along more ethically grounded lines.

In a more ethical world, to spend tens of millions of dollars on works of art would be status-lowering, not status-enhancing. Such behavior would lead people to ask: "In a world in which more than six million children die each year because they lack safe drinking water or mosquito nets, or because they have not been immunized against measles, couldn't you find something better to do with your money?"

from Project Syndicate, June 4, 2014

PREVENTING HUMAN EXTINCTION

(with Nick Beckstead and Matt Wage)

MANY SCIENTISTS BELIEVE that a large asteroid impact caused the extinction of the dinosaurs. Could humans face the same fate?

It's a possibility. NASA has tracked most of the large nearby asteroids and many of the smaller asteroids. If a large asteroid were found to be on a collision course with Earth, that could give us time to deflect the asteroid. NASA has analyzed multiple options for deflecting an asteroid in this kind of scenario, including using a nuclear strike to knock the asteroid off course, and it seems that some of these strategies would be likely to work. The search is, however, not yet complete. The new B612 Foundation has recently begun a project to track the remaining asteroids in order to "protect the future of civilization on this planet." Finding one of these asteroids could be the key to preventing a global catastrophe.

Fortunately, the odds of an extinction-sized asteroid hitting the Earth this century are low, on the order of one in a million. Unfortunately, asteroids aren't the only threats to humanity's survival. Other potential threats stem from bioengineered diseases, nuclear war, extreme climate change, and dangerous future technologies.

Given that there is some risk of humanity going extinct over the next couple of centuries, the next question is whether we can do anything about it. We will first explain what we can do about it, and then ask the deeper ethical question: How bad would human extinction be?

The first point to make here is that if the risks of human extinction turn out to be "small," this shouldn't lull us into complacency. No sane person would say, "Well, the risk of a nuclear meltdown at this reactor is only 1 in 1,000, so we're not going to worry about it." When there is some risk of a truly catastrophic outcome and we can reduce or eliminate that risk at an acceptable cost, we should do so. In general, we can measure how bad a particular risk is by multiplying the probability of the bad outcome by how bad the outcome would be. Since human extinction would, as we shall shortly argue, be extremely bad, reducing the risk of human extinction by even a very small amount would be very good.

Humanity has already done some things that reduce the risk of premature extinction. We've made it through the Cold War and scaled back our reserves of nuclear weapons. We've tracked most of the large asteroids near Earth. We've built underground bunkers for "continuity of government" purposes, which might help humanity survive certain catastrophes. We've instituted disease surveillance programs that track the spread of diseases, so that the world could respond more quickly in the event of a large-scale pandemic. We've identified climate change as a potential risk and developed some plans for responding, even if the actual response so far has been lamentably inadequate. We've also built institutions that reduce the risk of extinction in subtler ways, such as decreasing the risk of war or improving the government's ability to respond to a catastrophe.

One reason to think that it is possible to further reduce the risk of human extinction is that all these things we've done could probably be improved. We could track more asteroids, build better bunkers, improve our disease surveillance programs, reduce our greenhouse gas emissions, encourage non-proliferation of nuclear weapons, and strengthen world institutions in ways that would probably further decrease the risk of human extinction. There is still a substantial challenge in identifying specific worthy projects to support, but it is likely that such projects exist.

So far, surprisingly little work has been put into systematically understanding the risks of human extinction and how best to reduce them. There have been a few books and papers on the topic of low-probability, high-stakes catastrophes, but there has been very little investigation into the most effective methods of reducing these risks. We know of no in-depth, systematic analysis of the different strategies for reducing these risks. A reasonable first step toward reducing the risk of human extinction is to investigate these issues more thoroughly, or support others in doing so.

If what we've said is correct, then there is some risk of human extinction and we probably have the ability to reduce this risk. There are a lot of important related questions, which are hard to answer: How high a priority should we place on reducing the risk of human extinction? How much should we be prepared to spend on doing so? Where does this fit among the many other things that we can and should be doing, like helping the global poor? (On that, see www.the-lifeyoucansave.org.) Does the goal of reducing the risk of extinction conflict with ordinary humanitarian goals, or is the best way of reducing the risk of extinction simply to improve the lives of people alive today and empower them to solve the problem themselves?

We won't try to address those questions here. Instead, we'll focus on this question: How bad would human extinction be?

One very bad thing about human extinction would be that billions of people would likely die painful deaths. But in our view, this is, by far, not the worst thing about human extinction. The worst thing about human extinction is that there would be no future generations.

We believe that future generations matter just as much as our generation does. Since there could be so many generations in our future, the value of all those generations together greatly exceeds the value of the current generation.

Considering a historical example helps to illustrate this point. About 70,000 years ago, there was a supervolcanic eruption known as the Toba eruption. Many scientists believe that this eruption caused a "volcanic winter" which brought our ancestors close to extinction. Suppose that this is true. Now imagine that the Toba eruption had eradicated humans from the Earth. How bad would that have been? Some 3,000 generations and 100 billion lives later, it is plausible to say that the death and suffering caused by the Toba eruption would have been trivial in comparison with the loss of all the human lives that have been lived from then to now, and everything humanity has achieved since that time.

Similarly, if humanity goes extinct now, the worst aspect of this would be the opportunity cost. Civilization began only a few thousand years ago. Yet Earth could remain habitable for another billion years. And if it is possible to colonize space, our species may survive much longer than that.

Some people would reject this way of assessing the value of future generations. They may claim that bringing new people into existence cannot be a benefit, regardless of what kind of life these people have. On this view, the value of avoiding human extinction is restricted to people alive today and people who are already going to exist, and who may want to have children or grandchildren.

Why would someone believe this? One reason might be that if people never exist, then it can't be bad for them that they don't exist. Since they don't exist, there's no "them" for it to be bad for, so causing people to exist cannot benefit them.

We disagree. We think that causing people to exist can benefit them. To see why, first notice that causing people to exist can be bad for those people. For example, suppose some woman knows that if she conceives a child during the next few months, the child will suffer from multiple painful diseases and die very young. It would obviously be bad for her child if she decided to conceive during the next few months. In general, it seems that if a child's life would be brief and miserable, existence is bad for that child.

If you agree that bringing someone into existence can be bad for that person and if you also accept the argument that bringing someone into existence can't be good for that person, then this leads to a strange conclusion: being born could harm you but it couldn't help you. If that is right, then it appears that it would be wrong to have children, because there is always a risk that they will be harmed, and no compensating benefit to outweigh the risk of harm.

Pessimists like the nineteenth-century German philosopher Arthur Schopenhauer or the contemporary South African philosopher David Benatar accept this conclusion. But if parents have a reasonable expectation that their children will have happy and fulfilling lives, and having children would not be harmful to others, then it is not bad to have children. More generally, if our descendants have a reasonable chance of having happy and fulfilling lives, it is good for us to ensure that our descendants exist, rather than not. Therefore we think that bringing future generations into existence can be a good thing.

The extinction of our species—and quite possibly, depending on the cause of the extinction, of all life—would be the end of the extraordinary story of evolution that has already led to (moderately) intelligent life, and which has given us the potential to make much greater progress still. We have made great progress, both moral and intellectual, over the last couple of centuries, and there is every reason to hope that, if we survive, this progress will continue and accelerate. If we fail to prevent our extinction, we will have blown the opportunity to create something truly wonderful: an astronomically large number of generations of human beings living rich and fulfilling lives, and reaching heights of knowledge and civilization that are beyond the limits of our imagination.

from www.effective-altruism.com/ea/50/
preventing_human_extinction, August 19, 2013

··· Happiness ···

HAPPINESS, MONEY, AND GIVING IT AWAY

WOULD YOU BE HAPPIER IF YOU WERE RICHER? Many people believe that they would be. But research conducted over many years suggests that greater wealth implies greater happiness only at quite low levels of income. People in the United States, for example, are, on average, richer than New Zealanders, but they are not happier. More dramatically, people in Austria, France, Japan, and Germany appear to be no happier than people in much poorer countries, like Brazil, Colombia, and the Philippines.

Comparisons between countries with different cultures are difficult, but the same effect appears *within* countries, except at very low income levels, such as below $12,000 annually for the United States. Beyond that point, an increase in income doesn't make a lot of difference to people's happiness. Americans are richer than they were in the 1950s, but they are not happier. Americans in the middle-income range today—that is, a family income of $50,000–$90,000—have a level of happiness that is almost identical to well-off Americans, with a family income of more than $90,000.

Most surveys of happiness simply ask people how satisfied they are with their lives. We cannot place great confidence in such studies, because this kind of overall "life satisfaction" judgment may not reflect how much people really enjoy the way they spend their time.

My Princeton University colleague Daniel Kahneman and several co-researchers tried to measure people's subjective well-being by asking them about their mood at frequent intervals during a day. In an article published in *Science* on June 30, they report that their data confirm that there is little correlation between income and happiness. On the contrary, Kahneman and his colleagues found that people with higher incomes spent more time in activities that are associated with negative feelings, such as tension and stress. Instead of having more time for leisure, they spent more time at and commuting to work. They were more often in moods that they described as hostile, angry, anxious, and tense.

Of course, there is nothing new in the idea that money does not buy happiness. Many religions instruct us that attachment to material possessions makes us unhappy. The Beatles reminded us that money can't buy us love. Even Adam Smith, who told us that it is not from the butcher's benevolence that we get our dinner, but from his regard for his self-interest, described the imagined pleasures of wealth as "a deception" (though one that "rouses and keeps in continual motion the industry of mankind").

Nevertheless, there is something paradoxical about this. Why do governments all focus on increasing per capita national income? Why do so many of us strive to obtain more money, if it won't make us happier?

Perhaps the answer lies in our nature as purposive beings. We evolved from beings who had to work hard to feed themselves, find a mate, and raise children. For nomadic societies, there was no point in owning anything that one could not carry, but once humans settled down and developed a system of money, that limit to acquisition disappeared.

Accumulating money up to a certain amount provides a safeguard against lean times, but today it has become an end in itself, a way of measuring one's status or success, and a goal to fall back on when we can think of no other reason for doing anything, but would be bored doing nothing. Making money gives us something to do that feels worthwhile, as long as we do not reflect too much on why we are doing it.

Consider, in this light, the life of the American investor Warren Buffett. For 50 years, Buffett, now 75, has worked at accumulating a vast fortune. According to *Forbes Magazine*, he is the second wealthiest person in the world, after Bill Gates, with assets of $42 billion. Yet his frugal lifestyle shows that he does not particularly enjoy spending large amounts of money. Even if his tastes were more lavish, he would be hard-pressed to spend more than a tiny fraction of his wealth.

From this perspective, once Buffett earned his first few millions in the 1960s, his efforts to accumulate more money can easily seem completely pointless. Is Buffett a victim of the "deception" that Adam Smith described, and that Kahneman and his colleagues have studied in more depth?

Coincidentally, Kahneman's article appeared the same week that Buffett announced the largest philanthropic donation in US history—$30 billion to the Bill and Melinda Gates Foundation and another $7 billion to other charitable foundations. Even when the donations made by Andrew Carnegie and John D. Rockefeller are adjusted for inflation, Buffett's is greater.

At a single stroke, Buffett has given purpose to his life. Since he is an agnostic, his gift is not motivated by any belief that it will benefit him in an afterlife. What, then, does Buffett's life tell us about the nature of happiness?

Perhaps, as Kahneman's research would lead us to expect, Buffett spent less of his life in a positive mood than he would have if, at some point in the 1960s, he had quit working, lived on his assets, and played a lot more bridge. But, in that case, he surely would not have experienced the satisfaction that he can now rightly feel at the thought that his hard work and remarkable investment skills will, through the Gates Foundation, help to cure diseases that cause death and disability to billions of the world's poorest people. Buffett reminds us that there is more to happiness than being in a good mood.

from Project Syndicate, July 12, 2006

CAN WE INCREASE GROSS NATIONAL HAPPINESS?

THE SMALL HIMALAYAN KINGDOM OF BHUTAN is known internationally for two things: high visa fees, which reduce the influx of tourists, and its policy of promoting "gross national happiness" instead of economic growth. The two are related: more tourists might boost the economy, but they would damage Bhutan's environment and culture, and so reduce happiness in the long run.

When I first heard of Bhutan's goal of maximizing its people's happiness, I wondered if it really meant anything in practice, or was just another political slogan. Last month, when I was in the capital, Thimphu, to speak at a conference on "Economic Development and Happiness," organized by Prime Minister Jigme Y. Thinley and co-hosted by Jeffrey Sachs, Director of The Earth Institute at Columbia University and Special Adviser to United Nations Secretary-General Ban Ki-moon, I learned that it is much more than a slogan.

Never before have I been at a conference that was taken so seriously by a national government. I had expected Thinley to open the conference with a formal welcome, and then return to his office. Instead, his address was a thoughtful review of the key issues involved in promoting happiness as a national policy. He then stayed at the conference for the entire two and a half days, and made pertinent contributions to our discussions. At most sessions, several cabinet ministers were also present.

Since ancient times, happiness has been universally seen as a good. Problems arise when we try to agree on a definition of happiness, and to measure it.

One important question is whether we see happiness as the surplus of pleasure over pain experienced over a lifetime, or as the degree to which we are satisfied with our lives. The former approach tries to add up the number of positive moments that people have, and then to subtract the negative ones. If the result is substantially positive, we regard the person's life as happy; if negative, as unhappy. So, to measure happiness defined in that way, one would have to sample moments of people's existence randomly, and try to find out whether they are experiencing positive or negative mental states.

A second approach asks people: "How satisfied are you with the way your life has gone so far?" If they say they are satisfied, or very satisfied, they are happy, rather than unhappy. But the question of which of these ways of understanding happiness best captures what we should promote raises fundamental questions of value.

On surveys that use the first approach, countries like Nigeria, Mexico, Brazil, and Puerto Rico do well, which suggests that the answer may have more to do with the national culture than with objective indicators like health, education, and standard of living. When the second approach is taken, it tends to be the richer countries, like Denmark and Switzerland, that come out on top. But it is not clear whether people's answers to survey questions in different languages and in different cultures really mean the same thing.

We may agree that our goal ought to be promoting happiness, rather than income or gross domestic product, but, if we have no objective measure of happiness, does this make sense? John Maynard Keynes famously said: "I would rather be vaguely right than precisely wrong." He pointed out that when ideas first come into the world, they are likely to be woolly, and in need of more work to define them sharply. That may be the case with the idea of happiness as the goal of national policy.

Can we learn how to measure happiness? The Center for Bhutan Studies, set up by the Bhutanese government 12 years ago, is currently processing the results of interviews with more than 8,000 Bhutanese. The interviews recorded both subjective factors, such as how satisfied respondents are with their lives, and objective factors, like standard of living, health, and education, as well as participation in culture, community vitality, ecological health, and the balance between work and other activities. It remains to be seen whether such diverse factors correlate well with each other. Trying to reduce them to a single number will require some difficult value judgments.

Bhutan has a Gross National Happiness Commission, chaired by the prime minister, which screens all new policy proposals put forward by government ministries. If a policy is found to be contrary to the goal of promoting gross national happiness, it is sent back to the ministry for reconsideration. Without the Commission's approval, it cannot go ahead.

One controversial law that did go ahead recently—and that indicates how willing the government is to take tough measures that it believes will maximize overall happiness—is a ban on the sale of tobacco. Bhutanese may bring into the country small quantities of cigarettes or tobacco from India for their own consumption, but not for resale—and they must carry the import-tax receipt with them any time they smoke in public.

Last July, the UN General Assembly passed, without dissent, a Bhutanese-initiated resolution recognizing the pursuit of happiness as a fundamental human goal and noting that this goal is not reflected in GDP. The resolution invited member states to develop additional measures that better capture the goal of happiness. The General Assembly also welcomed an offer from Bhutan to convene a panel discussion on the theme of happiness and well-being during its 66th session, which opens this month.

These discussions are part of a growing international movement to re-orient government policies toward well-being and happiness. We should wish the effort well, and hope that ultimately the goal becomes global, rather than merely national, happiness.

from Project Syndicate, September 13, 2011

Postscript: In 2011 the UN General Assembly adopted a resolution recognizing happiness as a "fundamental human goal," inviting member nations to measure the happiness of their people, and to make use of this measure as a guide to policy—in other words, to take some small steps toward what Bhutan was already doing. With more scientists working on measuring happiness and understanding what increases it, the idea of happiness as a goal of public policy is gradually gaining support.

THE HIGH COST OF FEELING LOW

DEPRESSION IS, according to a World Health Organization study, the world's fourth worst health problem, measured by how many years of good health it causes to be lost. By 2020, it is likely to rank second, behind heart disease. Yet not nearly enough is being done to treat or prevent it.

The study, led by Saba Moussavi and published last month in *The Lancet*, also revealed that depression has more impact on the *physical* health of those who suffer from it than major chronic diseases like angina, diabetes, arthritis, and asthma. Yet in the same issue of *The Lancet*, Gavin Andrews and Nickolai Titov, researchers at the University of New South Wales, reported that Australians with depression are far less likely to receive an acceptable level of care than patients with arthritis or asthma. This pattern is consistent with reports from other developed nations.

Treating depression is often, if not always, effective, and without it, those who suffer from depression cannot live happy, fulfilling lives. But, even in narrow cost-benefit terms, it makes sense to spend more on treating depression.

A study of 28 European countries found that depression cost them €118 billion in 2004, or 1 percent of their combined GDP. The cost of treating depression accounted for only 9 percent of this huge sum. A much larger share was lost productivity. Richard Layard, of the Centre for Economic Performance at the London School of Economics, has said that mental illness is Britain's biggest social problem, costing

1.5 percent of GDP. He estimates that while treatment may cost £750 per patient over two years, the result is likely to be an extra month of work, worth £1880. Lord Layard advocates more psychotherapy rather than drug treatment.

In the United States, a research team headed by Philip Wang of the National Institute of Mental Health in Rockville, Maryland, reported similar results last month in the *Journal of the American Medical Association*. Wang's team conducted a randomized controlled trial that showed that depression screening—to find workers who could benefit from treatment—was cost-effective, reducing health insurance costs to employers, decreasing absence due to sickness, and increasing job retention and productivity.

Depression is also costly in developing countries. In China, according to a recent article by Teh-wei Hu and colleagues in *Social Psychiatry and Psychiatric Epidemiology*, depression costs 51 billion renminbi, or more than $6 billion, per year at 2002 prices. A few years ago, a research team led by Vikram Patel reported in the *British Medical Journal* that depression is common in Zimbabwe, where it was often known by a Shona word that means "thinking too much."

Around the world, many primary care physicians underestimate the seriousness of depression. Many of them lack adequate training in recognizing mental illness, and may not be up-to-date with treatments options. Patients, too, may fail to seek treatment, because mental illness still carries a stigma that can make it harder to acknowledge than a physical illness.

The problem has been aggravated, in the United States at least, by the refusal of some health insurance policies to cover treatment for mental illness. Thus, the US Senate's recent approval of the Mental Health Parity Act is a significant step forward. The legislation, which still has to pass through the House of Representatives, would require health insurance plans provided by employers to cover treatment for mental illness at a level similar to coverage for general health care. (Unfortunately, the legislation will do nothing for the 47 million Americans who have no health insurance at all.)

Depression is an individual tragedy that is multiplied more than 100 million times worldwide. So, while we can and should do much better at treating it, perhaps the more significant question is whether we can learn to prevent it.

Some depression appears to be genetic, in which case genetic therapy may ultimately offer a solution. But much mental illness appears to depend on environmental factors. Perhaps we need to focus on aspects of living that have a positive effect on mental health. Many recent studies show that spending time relaxing with family and friends contributes to how happy people are with their lives, while long working hours, and especially long commuting times, contribute to stress and unhappiness. Of course, relaxed and happy people can still become depressed, and stressed and unhappy people may not be depressed, but it is a reasonable hypothesis that happier people are less likely to become depressed.

LaSalle Leffall, who chaired the President's Cancer Panel, wrote to President George W. Bush in August, saying, "We can and must empower individuals to make healthy choices through appropriate policy and legislation." If that is true for encouraging healthy diets and discouraging smoking, it is no less true for lifestyle choices that promote greater mental health. Governments can't legislate happiness or ban depression, but public policy can play a role in ensuring that people have time to relax with friends, and pleasant places to do it.

from Project Syndicate, October 15, 2007

NO SMILE LIMIT

IF YOU WERE TO WALK ALONG the streets of your neighborhood with your face up and an open expression, how many of those who passed you would smile, or greet you in some way?

Smiling is a universal human practice, although readiness to smile at strangers varies according to culture. In Australia, where being open and friendly to strangers is not unusual, the city of Port Phillip, an area covering some of the bayside suburbs of Melbourne, has been using volunteers to find out how often people smile at those who pass them in the street. It then put up signs that look like speed limits, but tell pedestrians that they are in, for example, a "10 Smiles Per Hour Zone."

Frivolous nonsense? A waste of taxpayers' money? Mayor Janet Bolitho says that putting up the signs is an attempt to encourage people to smile or say "G'day"—the standard Australian greeting—to both neighbors and strangers as they stroll down the street. Smiling, she adds, encourages people to feel more connected with each other and safer, so it reduces fear of crime—an important element in the quality of life of many neighborhoods.

In a related effort to get its residents to know each other, the city government also facilitates street parties. It leaves the details to the locals, but offers organizational advice, lends out barbecues and sun umbrellas, and covers the public liability insurance. Many people who have lived in the same street for many years meet each other for the first time at a street party.

All of this is part of a larger program that attempts to measure changes in the city's quality of life, so that the city council can know whether it is taking the community in a desirable direction. The council wants Port Phillip to be a sustainable community, not merely in an environmental sense, but also in terms of social equity, economic viability, and cultural vitality.

Port Phillip is serious about being a good global citizen. Instead of seeing private car ownership as a sign of prosperity, the city hails a *declining* number of cars—and rising use of public transport—as a sign of progress in reducing greenhouse gas emissions while encouraging a healthier lifestyle in which people are more inclined to walk or ride a bike. The city is also seeking designs for new buildings that are more energy efficient.

Some local governments see their role as being to provide basic services like collecting the trash and maintaining the roads—and of course, collecting the taxes to pay for this. Others promote the area's economy, by encouraging industry to move to the area, thus increasing jobs and the local tax base. The Port Phillip city government takes a broader and longer-term view. It wants those who live in the community after the present generation has gone to have the same opportunities for a good quality of life as today's residents have. To protect that quality of life, it has to be able to measure all the varied aspects that contribute to it—and friendliness is one of them.

For many governments, both national and local, preventing crime is a far higher priority than encouraging friendship and cooperation. But, as Professor Richard Layard of the London School of Economics has argued in his recent book *Happiness: Lessons from a New Science*, promoting friendship is often easy and cheap, and can have big payoffs in making people happier. So why shouldn't that be a focus of public policy?

Very small positive experiences can make people not only feel better about themselves, but also be more helpful to others. In the 1970s, American psychologists Alice Isen and Paula Levin conducted an experiment in which some randomly selected people making a phone call found a ten-cent coin left behind by a previous caller, and others did not. All subjects were then given an opportunity to help a woman pick up a folder of papers she dropped in front of them.

Isen and Levin claimed that of the 16 who found a coin, 14 helped the woman, while of the 25 who did not find a coin, only one helped her. A further study found a similar difference in willingness to mail an addressed letter that had been left behind in the phone booth: those who found the coin were more likely to mail the letter.

Although later research has cast doubt on the existence of such dramatic differences, there is little doubt that being in a good mood makes people feel better about themselves and more likely to help others. Psychologists refer to it as the "glow of goodwill." Why shouldn't taking small steps that may produce such a glow be part of the role of government?

Here is one measure of success: over the past year and a half, the proportion of people who smile at you in Port Phillip has risen, from 8 percent to 10 percent.

from Project Syndicate, April 16, 2007

HAPPY, NEVERTHELESS

Harriet McBryde Johnson | 1957–2008

I MET HARRIET MCBRYDE JOHNSON in the spring of 2001, when I was giving a lecture at the College of Charleston. Her brand of Southern etiquette prescribed that if you're not prepared to shoot on sight, you have to be prepared to shake hands, so when I held out mine, she reached up from her powered wheelchair and took it with the three working fingers on her right hand. She added that she was attending my lecture as a supporter of Not Dead Yet, the disability rights organization that a year and a half earlier block-aded Princeton University's Nassau Hall in protest against my appointment as a professor of bioethics. I told her I looked forward to an interesting exchange.

My lecture, "Rethinking Life and Death," was a defense of the position that had aroused such vehement opposition. I pointed out that physicians routinely withdraw life support from severely disabled newborns, and I argued that this is not very different from allowing parents to decide, in consul-tation with their doctors, to end the life of a baby when the child has disabilities so serious that the family believes this will be best for the child or for the family as a whole.

When I finished, Johnson, who was born with a muscle-wasting disease, spoke up. I was saying, she pointed out, that her parents should have been permitted to kill her shortly after her birth. But she was now a lawyer, enjoying her life as much as anyone. It is a mistake, she said, to believe that having a disability makes life less worth living.

Our exchange of views continued for a few minutes in the lecture theater, and by e-mail afterward. Years later, when I read her autobiographical book, *Too Late to Die Young*, I wasn't surprised to see "arguing hard" listed among the pleasures of her life.

The following year, I invited her to Princeton to speak to a large undergraduate class I was teaching. She accepted but on condition that in public we avoid the informality of using first names that I had, in my Australian way, adopted over e-mail. She was also unwilling to accept the inequality implied in "Professor Singer" and "Ms. Johnson." I agreed that she could address me as Mr. Singer.

She described the visit to Princeton in "Unspeakable Conversations," her memorable cover article for the *New York Times Magazine* in 2003. She wrote beautifully, her powers of recollection were remarkable (she wasn't taking notes at the time), and she was more generous to me than I had a right to expect from someone whose very existence I had questioned. She even wrote that she found me good company, as indeed I found her.

After she spoke, I arranged for her to have dinner with a group of undergraduates who met regularly to discuss ethical questions. I sat on her right, and she occasionally asked me to move things to where she could reach them. At one point her right elbow slipped out from under her, and as she was not able to move it back, she asked me to grasp her wrist and pull it forward. I did so, and she could then again reach her food with her fork. I thought nothing of the incident, but when she told some of her friends in the disability movement about it, they were appalled that she had called on me to help her. I'm pleased that she had no difficulty with it. It suggests that she saw me not simply as "the enemy" but as a person with whom it was possible to have some forms of human interaction.

My students talked about Johnson's visit for a long time, and our conversations stayed with me, too. Her life was evidently a good one, and not just for herself, because her legal work and political activism on behalf of the disabled was valuable to others as well. I know that surveys have found that people living with disabilities show a level of satisfaction with their lives that is not very different from that of people who are not disabled. Have people with long-term disabilities adjusted their expectations downward, so that they are satisfied with less? Or do even severe disabilities really make no difference to our happiness, once we get used to them?

Over the next six years we e-mailed sporadically. If I wrote or spoke on disability issues, she would send me her criticisms, and that would lead to a flurry of e-mail messages that at least clarified the points on which we disagreed. I tried to persuade Johnson that her attribution of rights to humans with severe intellectual disabilities had implications for how we should think about animals too, since they could enjoy their lives as much as, or more than, the people whose right to life she was defending. She didn't object to the argument but felt she had enough issues to handle without getting into a new area altogether. We found it easier to agree on religion, for neither of us had any, and on our dislike for the direction the country was taking under the presidency of George W. Bush.

According to her sister, Beth, what most concerned Harriet about dying was "the crap people would say about her." And sure enough, among the tributes to her were several comments about how she can now run and skip through the meadows of heaven—doubly insulting, first because Johnson did not believe in a life after death, and second, why assume that heavenly bliss requires you to be able to run and skip?

from The New York Times Magazine, *December 28, 2008*

... Politics ...

BENTHAM'S FALLACIES, THEN AND NOW

IN 1809, JEREMY BENTHAM, the founder of utilitarianism, set to work on *The Book of Fallacies.* His goal was to expose the fallacious arguments used to block reforms like the abolition of "rotten boroughs"—electorates with so few electors that a powerful lord or landowner could effectively select the member of Parliament, while newer cities like Manchester remained unrepresented.

Bentham collected examples of fallacies, often from parliamentary debates. By 1811, he had sorted them into nearly 50 different types, with titles like "Attack us, you attack Government," the "No precedent argument," and the "Good in theory, bad in practice" fallacy. (One thing on which both Immanuel Kant and Bentham agree is that this last example is a fallacy: if something is bad in practice, there must be a flaw in the theory.)

Bentham was thus a pioneer of an area of science that has made considerable progress in recent years. He would have relished the work of psychologists showing that we have a confirmation bias (we favor and remember information that supports, rather than contradicts, our beliefs); that we systematically overestimate the accuracy of our beliefs (the overconfidence effect); and that we have a propensity to respond to the plight of a single identifiable individual rather than a large number of people about whom we have only statistical information.

Bentham did not rush to publish his work. An abridged version appeared in French in 1816, and in English in 1824, but the complete work remained in manuscript form until its publication this year as part of an ongoing project, under the editorship of Philip Schofield of University College, London, to publish Bentham's collected works.

Some of the fallacies Bentham identified still make frequent appearances, while others are less relevant. The "wisdom of our ancestors" fallacy has often been invoked in debates over same-sex marriage. Anyone familiar with political discussion in the United States will instantly recognize a more specific version that could be called the "wisdom of the Founding Fathers" fallacy.

Another fallacy popular both in Bentham's day and in ours is what he characterized as "What? More jobs?" By "jobs," he meant government spending, and he considered this a fallacy because blanket opposition to more government spending fails to take into account the good that the extra employees will be able to achieve.

The "fallacies" that really challenge the modern reader, however, are those that characterize arguments that today are widely accepted even in the most educated and enlightened circles. One of these, Bentham says, in a jarring juxtaposition, "may be termed Anarchy-preacher's fallacy—or *The Rights of Man* fallacy."

When people argue against a proposed measure on the grounds that it violates "the rights of man"—or, as we would say today, human rights—they are, Bentham claims, using vague generalities that distract us from assessing the measure's utility. Bentham accepts that it may be to the advantage of the community that the law should confer certain rights on people. What threatens to bring us closer to anarchy, he argues, is the idea that I have certain rights already, independent of the law. Whereas the principle of utility calls for inquiry and argument, Bentham believes that those who advocate such pre-existing rights disdain both and are more likely to stir people up to use force.

Bentham's objection to "natural rights" is often cited. Less frequently discussed is what he calls "the Posterity-chainer's device." One example is the Act of Union between England and Scotland, which requires all succeeding sovereigns of the United Kingdom to take an oath to maintain the Church of Scotland and the Church of England. If future generations feel themselves bound by such provisions, they are, Bentham thinks, enslaved by long-dead tyrants.

Bentham's objection to such attempts to bind posterity applies not only to the union that created the United Kingdom, but also to the one that formed the United States: Why should the current generation consider itself bound by what was decided hundreds of years earlier? Unlike the framers of the US Constitution, we have had centuries of experience to judge whether it does or does not "promote the general welfare."

If it does, we have all the reason we need to retain it; but if it does not, don't we have as much power and as much right to change the arrangements under which we are governed as the framers had to prescribe them in the first place? If we do, why should provisions that make the constitution so difficult to amend bind a majority of the electorate?

In the case of the unification of two or more previously sovereign states, Bentham is sensitive to the problem of providing assurances to the smaller states that the larger ones will not dominate them. Given what he takes to be the impossibility of tying future generations' hands, he places his trust in the belief that sooner or later, after having been under one government, "the two communities will have become melted into one."

Public support for independence in Scotland and Catalonia shows that this is not always the case. Bentham, of course, would have accepted that he might be mistaken. After all, the "Authority-worshipper's argument" was another of the fallacies he rejected.

from Project Syndicate, August 12, 2015

THE FOUNDING FATHERS' FISCAL CRISIS

AMERICANS ARE FOND OF SPEAKING in reverential tones about "the wisdom of the Founding Fathers"—that is, the men who wrote the United States Constitution. But the manner in which the House of Representatives has been able to bring the government—or, at least, its non-essential services—to a halt is making the Founding Fathers look rather foolish.

The fundamental cause of the fiscal crisis lies in the Founding Fathers' belief in the doctrine of the separation of powers. That doctrine has always been philosophically controversial.

Thomas Hobbes, writing during the English Civil War, opposed the separation of powers, believing that only a strong and unified central government could ensure peace. John Locke, for his part, was more concerned with curbing monarchical power and regarded the separation of legislative and executive powers as one way to do that.

Having fought against what they regarded as the tyranny of George III, the American revolutionaries wanted to ensure that no such tyranny could arise in the new nation that they were establishing. To do so, they wrote the doctrine of the separation of powers into its constitution.

As a result, neither the US president nor cabinet officials are members of the legislature, and they cannot be removed from office by a legislative majority. At the same time, the legislature controls the budget and the government's ability to borrow. The potential for impasse is obvious.

We might think that the Founding Fathers deserve the credit for the fact that the US government has never devolved into tyranny. But the same can be said of Britain's government, despite the absence of a constitutional separation of powers between the legislature and the executive—indeed, despite the absence of a written constitution altogether.

Nor have former British colonies like Australia, New Zealand, and Canada become tyrannies. In contrast to the United States, however, the prime minister and cabinet officials in all of these countries are members of the legislature, and governments hold office only so long as they retain the confidence of a majority of the parliament's lower house (or, in New Zealand, of its only house). If the legislature denies the executive the money that it needs to run the government, the government falls and is replaced by a new government, perhaps on a caretaker basis pending an early election.

Given the US Constitution's fundamental flaw, what seems improbable is not the current crisis, but the fact that such impasses between the legislature and the executive have not caused chaos more often. That is testimony to most US legislators' common sense and to their willingness to compromise in order to avoid doing serious harm to the country they serve—until now, that is.

Constitutional amendments in the United States must be ratified by three-quarters of the states, which means that at present there is no realistic prospect of changing the constitution sufficiently to overcome the flaw that has made the current crisis possible. But a different factor that contributes to the hyper-partisan nature of US politics today could be changed without amending the constitution. We can best grasp this problem by asking why many members of the

Republican Party who have voted in the House of Representatives to force the government to shut down are not worried that their tactics—which will undoubtedly harm many of their constituents—will fuel an electoral backlash.

The answer is that the districts from which House members are elected are gerrymandered to an extent that citizens of most other democracies would consider preposterous. This happens because responsibility for drawing the districts' boundaries generally falls to state legislatures, where the party in control is free to draw them to its own advantage. Nowadays, the Republicans control most state legislatures, enabling them to win a majority of House seats despite lacking the support of a majority of the American public; in the 2012 congressional election, Democratic Party candidates countrywide received 1.4 percent more votes than Republicans.

The gerrymandering of US electoral districts means more than that the House of Representatives is not representative of the population as a whole; it also means that many incumbents are in no danger of losing their seat in an election. The real danger—especially in the Republican Party—comes largely from those who are further to the right than the incumbent. To be seen as a moderate is to risk defeat, not at the hands of voters as a whole, but in the Republican Party's nomination contests, in which high turnout among the party's most fervently committed members gives them disproportionate influence over outcomes.

One could imagine cool heads in both parties cutting a deal based on an understanding that it is in America's interest to establish an impartial commission to draw fair boundaries for all House electoral districts. There is no constitutional barrier to such an arrangement. In America's current environment of extreme political polarization, however, such an outcome is almost as unlikely as a constitutional amendment preventing the House of Representatives from denying the government the funds that it needs to govern.

from Project Syndicate, October 2, 2013

WHY VOTE?

As an Australian citizen, I voted in the recent federal election there. So did about 95% of registered Australian voters. That figure contrasts markedly with elections in the United States, where the turnout in the 2004 presidential election barely exceeded 60%. In congressional elections that fall in the middle of a president's term, usually fewer than 40% of eligible Americans bother to vote.

There is a reason why so many Australians vote. In the 1920s, when voter turnout fell below 60%, Parliament made voting compulsory. Since then, despite governments of varying political complexions, there has been no serious attempt to repeal the law, which polls show is supported by about 70% of the population.

Australians who don't vote receive a letter asking why. Those without an acceptable excuse, like illness or travel abroad, must pay a small fine, but the number fined is less than 1% of eligible voters.

In practice, what is compulsory is not casting a valid vote, but going to the polling place, having one's name checked off, and putting a ballot paper in the box. The secrecy of the ballot makes it impossible to prevent people writing nonsense on their ballot papers or leaving them blank. While the percentage of invalid votes is a little higher where voting is compulsory, it comes nowhere near offsetting the difference in voter turnout.

Compulsory voting is not unique to Australia. Belgium and Argentina introduced it earlier, and it is practiced in many other countries, especially in Latin America, although both sanctions and enforcement vary.

Because I was in the United States at the time of the Australian election, I was under no compulsion to vote. I had many reasons to hope for the defeat of John Howard's conservative government, but that doesn't explain why I went to some trouble to vote, since the likelihood that my vote would make any difference was miniscule (and, predictably, it did not).

When voting is voluntary, and the chance that the result will be determined by any single person's vote is extremely low, even the smallest cost—for example, the time it takes to stroll down to the polling place, wait in line, and cast a ballot—is sufficient to make voting seem irrational. Yet if many people follow this line of reasoning, and do not vote, a minority of the population can determine a country's future, leaving a discontented majority.

Poland's recent electoral history provides an example. In the 2005 national elections, barely 40% of those eligible voted, the lowest total since the advent of free elections after the communist period. As a result, Jaroslaw Kaczynski was able to become prime minister with the support of a coalition of parties that gained a majority of seats in Parliament, despite receiving only six million votes, out of a total of 30 million eligible voters.

When Kaczynski was forced to go to the polls again only two years later, it became evident that many of those who had not voted in 2005 were unhappy with the outcome. Turnout rose to nearly 54%, with the increase especially marked among younger and better-educated voters. Kaczynski's government suffered a heavy defeat.

If we don't want a small minority to determine our government, we will favor a high turnout. Yet since our own vote makes such a tiny contribution to the outcome, each of us still faces the temptation to get a free ride, not bothering to vote while hoping that enough other people will vote to keep democracy robust and to elect a government that is responsive to the views of a majority of citizens.

But there are many possible reasons for voting. Some people vote because they enjoy it, and would have nothing better to do with the time saved if they did not. Others are motivated by a sense of civic duty that does not assess the rationality of voting in terms of the possible impact of one's own ballot.

Still others might vote not because they imagine that they will determine the outcome of the election, but because, like football fans, they want to cheer their team on. They may vote because if they don't, they will be in no position to complain if they don't like the government that is elected. Or they may calculate that while the chances of their determining the outcome are only one in several million, the result is of such importance that even that tiny chance is enough to outweigh the minor inconveniences of voting.

If these considerations fail to get people to the polls, however, compulsory voting is one way of overcoming the free-rider problem. The small cost imposed on not voting makes it rational for everyone to vote and at the same time establishes a social norm of voting. Australians want to be coerced into voting. They are happy to vote, knowing that everyone else is voting, too. Countries worried about low voter turnout would do well to consider their compulsory model.

from Project Syndicate, December 14, 2007

FREE SPEECH, MUHAMMAD, AND THE HOLOCAUST

THE TIMING OF AUSTRIA'S CONVICTION and imprisonment of David Irving for denying the Holocaust could not have been worse. Coming after the deaths of at least 30 people in Syria, Lebanon, Afghanistan, Libya, Nigeria, and other Islamic countries during protests against cartoons ridiculing Muhammad, the Irving verdict makes a mockery of the claim that in democratic countries, freedom of expression is a basic right.

We cannot consistently hold that cartoonists have a right to mock religious figures but that it should be a criminal offense to deny the existence of the Holocaust. I believe that we should stand behind freedom of speech. And that means that David Irving should be freed.

Before you accuse me of failing to understand the sensitivities of victims of the Holocaust, or the nature of Austrian anti-Semitism, I should say that I am the son of Austrian Jews. My parents escaped Austria in time, but my grandparents did not.

All four of my grandparents were deported to ghettos in Poland and Czechoslovakia. Two of them were sent to Lodz, in Poland, and then probably murdered with carbon monoxide at the extermination site at Chelmno. One fell ill and died in the disease-ridden ghetto at Theresienstadt. My maternal grandmother was the only survivor.

So I have no sympathy for David Irving's absurd denial of the Holocaust—which he now claims was a mistake. I support efforts to prevent any return to Nazism in Austria or anywhere else. But how is the cause of truth served by prohibiting Holocaust denial? If there are still people crazy enough to deny that the Holocaust occurred, will they be persuaded by imprisoning people who express that view? On the contrary, they will be more likely to think that people are being imprisoned for expressing views that cannot be refuted by evidence and argument alone.

In his classic defense of freedom of speech in *On Liberty*, John Stuart Mill wrote that if a view is not "fully, frequently, and fearlessly discussed," it will become "a dead dogma, not a living truth." The existence of the Holocaust should remain a living truth, and those who are skeptical about the enormity of the Nazi atrocities should be confronted with the evidence for it.

In the aftermath of World War II, when the Austrian republic was struggling to establish itself as a democracy, it was reasonable, as a temporary emergency measure, for Austrian democrats to suppress Nazi ideas and propaganda. But that danger is long past. Austria is a democracy and a member of the European Union. Despite the occasional resurgence of anti-immigrant and even racist views—an occurrence that is, lamentably, not limited to countries with a fascist past – there is no longer a serious threat of any return to Nazism in Austria.

By contrast, freedom of speech is essential to democratic regimes, and it must include the freedom to say what everyone else believes to be false, and even what many people find offensive. We must be free to deny the existence of God, and to criticize the teachings of Jesus, Moses, Muhammad, and Buddha, as reported in texts that millions of people regard as sacred. Without that freedom, human progress will always run up against a basic roadblock.

Article 10 of the European Convention on Human Rights and Fundamental Freedoms states: "Everyone has the right to freedom of expression. This right shall include freedom to hold opinions and to receive and impart information and ideas without interference by public authority and regardless of frontiers."

To be consistent with that clear statement, Austria should repeal its law against Holocaust denial. Other European nations with similar laws—for example, Germany, France, Italy, and Poland—should do the same, while maintaining or strengthening their efforts to inform their citizens about the reality of the Holocaust and why the racist ideology that led to it should be rejected.

Laws against incitement to racial, religious, or ethnic hatred, in circumstances where that incitement is intended to—or can reasonably be foreseen to—lead to violence or other criminal acts, are different, and are compatible with maintaining freedom to express any views at all.

Only when David Irving has been freed will it be possible for Europeans to turn to the Islamic protesters and say: "We apply the principle of freedom of expression even-handedly, whether it offends Muslims, Christians, Jews, or anyone else."

from Project Syndicate, March 1, 2006

THE USE AND ABUSE OF RELIGIOUS FREEDOM

WHAT ARE THE PROPER LIMITS of religious freedom? Marianne Thieme, leader of the Party for the Animals in the Netherlands, offers this answer: "Religious freedom stops where human or animal suffering begins."

The Party for the Animals, the only animal-rights party to be represented in a national parliament, has proposed a law requiring that all animals be stunned before slaughter. The proposal has united Islamic and Jewish leaders in defense of what they see as a threat to their religious freedom, because their religious doctrines prohibit eating meat from animals that are not conscious when killed.

The Dutch Parliament has given the leaders a year to prove that their religions' prescribed methods of slaughter cause no more pain than slaughter with prior stunning. If they cannot do so, the requirement to stun before slaughtering will be implemented.

Meanwhile, in the United States, Catholic bishops have claimed that President Barack Obama is violating their religious freedom by requiring all big employers, including Catholic hospitals and universities, to offer their employees health insurance that covers contraception. And, in Israel, the ultra-orthodox, who interpret Jewish law as prohibiting men from touching women to whom they are not related or married, want separate seating for men and women on buses, and to halt the government's plan to end exemption from military service for full-time religious students (63,000 in 2010).

When people are prohibited from practicing their religion—
for example, by laws that bar worshiping in certain ways—
there can be no doubt that their freedom of religion has been
violated. Religious persecution was common in previous
centuries, and still occurs in some countries today.

But prohibiting the ritual slaughter of animals does not
stop Jews or Muslims from practicing their religion. During
the debate on the Party for the Animals' proposal, Rabbi
Binyomin Jacobs, Chief Rabbi of the Netherlands, told members of Parliament: "If we no longer have people who can do
ritual slaughter in the Netherlands, we will stop eating
meat." And that, of course, is what one should do, if one
adheres to a religion that requires animals to be slaughtered
in a manner less humane than can be achieved by modern
techniques.

Neither Islam nor Judaism upholds a requirement to eat
meat. And I am not calling upon Jews and Muslims to do any
more than I have chosen to do myself, for ethical reasons,
for more than 40 years.

Restricting the legitimate defense of religious freedom to
rejecting proposals that stop people from practicing their religion makes it possible to resolve many other disputes in
which it is claimed that freedom of religion is at stake. For
example, allowing men and women to sit in any part of a bus
does not violate orthodox Jews' religious freedom, because
Jewish law does not command that one use public transport.
It's just a convenience that one can do without—and orthodox Jews can hardly believe that the laws to which they
adhere were intended to make life maximally convenient.

Likewise, the Obama administration's requirement to
provide health insurance that covers contraception does
not prevent Catholics from practicing their religion. Ca-
tholicism does not oblige its adherents to run hospitals and

universities. (The government already exempts parishes and dioceses, thereby drawing a distinction between institutions that are central to the freedom to practice one's religion and those that are peripheral to it.)

Of course, the Catholic Church would be understandably reluctant to give up its extensive networks of hospitals and universities. My guess is that, before doing so, they would come to see the provision of health-insurance coverage for contraception as compatible with their religious teachings. But, if the Church made the opposite decision, and handed over its hospitals and universities to bodies that were willing to provide the coverage, Catholics would still be free to worship and follow their religion's teachings.

Religious exemption from military service can be more difficult to resolve, because some religions teach pacifism. That problem is usually resolved by providing alternative service that is no less arduous than military service (so that such religions do not attract adherents for that reason alone), but that does not involve fighting or killing.

Judaism, however, is not pacifist, so, once again, there is no real issue of religious freedom at stake. The ultra-orthodox want exemption for those who spend their time studying the Torah on the grounds that Torah study is as important as military service to Israel's well-being. Providing the option of non-combatant national service thus will not resolve this dispute, unless it consists of Torah study. But there is no reason why Israel's secular majority should share the belief that having tens of thousands of ultra-orthodox scholars studying the Torah provides any benefit at all to the nation, and it is certainly not as arduous as military service.

Not all conflicts between religion and the state are easy to resolve. But the fact that these three issues, all currently causing controversy in their respective countries, are not really about the freedom to practice one's religion, suggests that the appeal to religious freedom is being misused.

from Project Syndicate, June 11, 2012

Postscript: Although the lower house of the Dutch Parliament overwhelmingly passed a ban on ritual slaughter, the upper house rejected it. The issue was resolved by the government brokering a characteristic Dutch compromise: ritual slaughter continues, but a veterinarian must be present, and must stun the animal if it is still conscious 40 seconds after its throat is cut.

The United States Supreme Court ruled, in 2014, that the contraceptive coverage requirement of the Affordable Care Act violated the religious freedom of "closely held" for-profit corporations run on religious principles. This decision does not apply to Catholic hospitals, but in November 2015 the Supreme Court agreed to consider a new challenge to the contraceptive coverage requirement from the Little Sisters of the Poor, an order of nuns. At the time of writing, no decision on that case has been handed down.

In Israel, although the High Court has said forcing women to sit separately on buses is illegal, many buses serving areas where orthodox Jews live continue to have "voluntary" separate seating. It is questionable how voluntary this segregation really is, however, because women who do not sit in the area for women have been harassed, and orthodox men have stood in the doorway of the bus to prevent it moving.

AN HONEST MAN?

IN HIS GUSHING ACCOUNT of President George W. Bush, the former presidential speechwriter David Frum tells us that his boss "scorned the petty untruths of the politician." We learn, for example, that when asked to prepare a radio broadcast for the following day, he would begin reading, "Today I am in California" and quickly break off, saying with exasperation, "But I'm not in California." Frum thought this a bit pedantic, but concluded that it was emblematic of the president's character and that "the country could trust the Bush administration not to cheat and not to lie."

How wrong Frum now seems.

Bush may naively consider it lying, and therefore wrong, to say that he is in California when he is recording a speech in Washington. But he fails to see anything gravely wrong about misleading his country and the world concerning Iraq's weapons of mass destruction. As we have seen, the White House built its case for war on a highly selective dossier of evidence, and Bush made statements about Iraq's attempt to purchase uranium from Africa that he and his staff knew to be highly doubtful, if not false.

When questions were raised about how the statement about uranium was allowed to remain in Bush's State of the Union address, both National Security Advisor Condoleezza Rice and Secretary of Defense Donald Rumsfeld argued that it was not a lie. Their reasoning indicates that they, like the president, have a childishly literal notion of what it is to lie.

Bush's actual words were these: "The British government has learned that Saddam Hussein recently sought significant quantities of uranium from Africa." Bush's statement took this form because the CIA objected to the original version, which flatly stated that Saddam Hussein had sought to buy uranium from Africa. The White House staff member who discussed it with the CIA then suggested changing the sentence so that it stated that the British reported that Saddam Hussein had sought to buy uranium from Africa.

This was literally true, because the British had reported that. It was nevertheless misleading, for the CIA had informed the British that their information was not reliable. The fact that Bush only referred to a British statement is the basis for Rice and Rumsfeld's defense of it. Rice said that "the statement that [Bush] made was indeed accurate. The British government did say that." Rumsfeld said that Bush's statement was "technically accurate."

In fact, even on the most literal interpretation, Bush's statement was not accurate. Bush did not say merely that the British had "reported" that Iraq had sought to buy uranium from Africa, but that the British had "learned" this. To say that someone has learned something is to endorse what they say they have learned as true. Imagine that the British had said that Saddam Hussein was a peace-loving man about to bring democracy to his country. Would Bush have said that the British had *learned* that?

Quite apart from these weak attempts to justify Bush's statement as "technically accurate," the more serious charge is that even if what Bush said really were technically accurate, it still would have been designed to mislead the world into thinking that Iraq had been trying to buy uranium in Africa. Bush and his staff had good reason to believe that this was not true.

Bush's response to the issue after it became public shows him to be focused on the trivial and morally reckless about

the essential. A person who is morally sensitive to the seriousness of starting a war on the basis of misleading information
would take appropriate steps. He would ensure that the
American public knew how the error occurred, and that who-
ever was responsible for it suffered the usual consequences
that befall senior officials who make what was—to put the
best possible interpretation on it—a grave error of judgment.

But Bush did nothing of the sort. When the issue became
public, Bush's response was to condemn his critics as "revi-
sionist historians" and to evade questions about the credibil-
ity of the information he had provided by asserting that the
removal of Saddam was a good outcome. Then he said that
the CIA had cleared his speech, as if that absolved him of all
responsibility. After CIA Director George Tenet took responsibility for the inclusion of the misleading material, Bush
said that he "absolutely" had confidence in Tenet and the
CIA, and that he considered the matter closed.

Belief in Bush's honesty led many voters to prefer him to
Albert Gore in the 2000 presidential election. Among voters
who rated "honesty" as an important factor influencing their
choice of candidate, 80 percent said that they voted for Bush.
These voters were disgusted with Clinton, not only for his
sexual relationship with White House intern Monica Lewin-
sky, but for lying about it.

That Clinton did lie about his sexual activities is clear, and
he was wrong to do so. But his lies did not lead his country
into a war that has cost thousands of lives. Bush's excessively
literal interpretation of the requirements of honesty conceals
a deeper dishonesty the consequences of which have been far
more morally serious.

from Project Syndicate, July 30, 2003

IS CITIZENSHIP A RIGHT?

SHOULD YOUR GOVERNMENT be able to take away your citizenship?

In the United Kingdom, the government has had the legal authority to revoke naturalized Britons' citizenship since 1918. But, until the terrorist bombings on the London transport system in 2005, this power was rarely exercised. Since then, the British government has revoked the citizenship of 42 people, including 20 cases in 2013. British Home Secretary Theresa May has said that citizenship is "a privilege, not a right."

Most of the 42 held dual nationality. Mohamed Sakr, however, did not. His parents came to Britain from Egypt, but he was not an Egyptian citizen. Therefore, by stripping him of citizenship, the UK government made him stateless.

Sakr appealed the decision from Somalia, where he was living. His case was strong, because the UK Supreme Court subsequently ruled in a different case that the government does not have the power to make a person stateless. Nevertheless, Sakr discontinued his appeal, apparently because he was concerned that the use of his cellphone was revealing his location to US intelligence services. Months later, while still in Somalia, he was killed in an American drone attack.

Now, partly in response to fears that Britons who have joined the fighting in Syria may return to carry out terrorism at home, the government has proposed legislation enabling it to revoke the citizenship of naturalized Britons suspected of involvement in terrorist activities—even if this makes them stateless. (Since the start of the year, more than 40 Britons have been arrested on suspicion of engaging in military activities in Syria.) The House of Commons passed the legislation in January, but in April the House of Lords voted to send it to a joint parliamentary committee for additional scrutiny.

In the United States, citizenship can be revoked only on limited grounds, such as fraud committed in the citizenship application or service in another country's military. Arguably, joining a terrorist organization hostile to the US is even worse than joining a foreign army, because terrorist organizations are more likely to target civilians.

But one important difference is that if people who join other countries' military forces lose their US citizenship, they can presumably become citizens of the country for which they are fighting. Terrorist organizations usually have no such ties to a particular government.

The 1961 United Nations Convention on the Reduction of Statelessness, to which Britain is a signatory, does allow countries to declare their citizens stateless if it is proved that they have done something "prejudicial to the vital interests of the country." The legislation currently before the UK Parliament does not require any judicial or public proof even of the weaker claim that someone's presence in the country is not conducive to the public good.

Should the person whose citizenship is revoked mount an appeal, the government is not required to disclose to the appellant the evidence on which it has based its decision. Though governments are bound to make mistakes from time to time in such cases, judges or tribunals will be unable to probe the evidence put before them. Another, more sinister possibility is deliberate abuse of these powers to get rid of citizens whose presence in the country is merely inconvenient.

There is a strong case for an appeal system that allows for full and fair review of decisions to revoke citizenship. But governments will respond that to make the evidence available to a person believed to be involved with a terrorist organization could reveal intelligence sources and methods, thus jeopardizing national security.

The ability to revoke citizenship without presenting any evidence in public is one reason why a government may prefer this course to arresting and trying terrorism suspects. And yet simply revoking citizenship does not solve the problem of leaving at large a suspected terrorist, who may then carry out an attack elsewhere—unless, as with Sakr, he is killed.

The larger question raised by the UK's proposed legislation is the desirable balance between individual rights, including the right to citizenship, and the public good. Suppose that the government gets it right 19 times out of 20 when it relies on suspicion of involvement in terrorist activities to revoke people's citizenship. If that were the case with the decisions made by the UK government in 2013, there would still be a high probability that an innocent naturalized citizen was made stateless. That is a grave injustice.

Suppose, however, that the 19 people correctly suspected of involvement in terrorism were able to return to Britain, and one carried out a terrorist attack similar to the London transport bombings, which killed 52 innocent people (the four bombers also died). In the face of such atrocities, it is difficult to insist that individual rights are absolute. Is it better to have one innocent person unjustly made stateless, or to have 52 innocent people killed and many others injured?

The much greater harm done by the terrorist attack cannot be ignored; but when a democratic government starts to revoke citizenship and make people stateless, it sets a precedent for authoritarian regimes that wish to rid themselves of dissidents by expelling them, as the former Soviet Union did to the poet and later Nobel laureate Joseph Brodsky—among many others. In the absence of global citizenship, it may be best to retain the principle that citizenship is not to be revoked without a judicial hearing.

from Project Syndicate, May 6, 2014

THE SPYING GAME

THANKS TO EDWARD SNOWDEN, I now know that the US National Security Agency is spying on me. It uses Google, Facebook, Verizon, and other Internet and communications companies to collect vast amounts of digital information, no doubt including data about my e-mails, cellphone calls, and credit card usage.

I am not a United States citizen, so it's all perfectly legal. And, even if I were a US citizen, it is possible that a lot of information about me would have been swept up anyway, though it may not have been the direct target of the surveillance operation.

Should I be outraged at this intrusion on my privacy? Has the world of George Orwell's *1984* finally arrived, three decades late? Is Big Brother watching me?

I don't feel outraged. Based on what I know so far, I don't really care. No one is likely to be reading my e-mails or listening in on my Skype calls. The volume of digital information that the NSA gathers would make that an impossible task.

Instead, computer programs mine the data for patterns of suspicious activity that intelligence analysts hope will lead them to terrorists. The process is not all that different from the data collection and analysis that many corporations use to target their ads at us more effectively, or that give us the online search results that we are most likely to want.

The question is not what information a government, or business, gathers, but what they do with it. I would be outraged if there were evidence that—for example—the US government was using the private information that it scoops up to blackmail foreign politicians into serving US interests, or if such information were leaked to newspapers in an effort to smear critics of US policies. That would be a real scandal.

If, however, nothing of that sort has happened, and if there are effective safeguards in place to ensure that it does not happen, then the remaining question is whether this huge data-gathering effort really does protect us against terrorism, and whether we are getting value for money from it. The NSA claims that communications surveillance has prevented more than 50 terrorist attacks since 2001. I don't know how to evaluate that claim, or whether we could have prevented those attacks in other ways.

The value-for-money question is even more difficult to assess. In 2010, the *Washington Post* produced a major report on "Top Secret America." After a two-year investigation involving more than a dozen journalists, the *Post* concluded that no one knows how much US intelligence operations cost—or even how many people American intelligence agencies employ.

At the time, the *Post* reported that 854,000 people held "top secret" security clearances. Now that figure is reported to be 1.4 million. (The sheer number of people does make one wonder whether misuse of personal data for blackmail or other private purposes is inevitable.)

Whatever we think of the NSA surveillance program itself, the US government has clearly overreacted to the release of information about it. It revoked Snowden's passport, and wrote to governments asking them to reject any asylum request that he might make. Most extraordinary of all, it seems that the United States was behind the apparent refusal of France, Spain, Italy, and Portugal to permit Bolivian

President Evo Morales's airplane to enter their airspace en route home from Moscow, on the grounds that Snowden might have been aboard. Morales had to land in Vienna, and Latin American leaders were furious at what they took to be an insult to their dignity.

Supporters of democracy ought to think long and hard before prosecuting people like Julian Assange, Bradley Manning, and Snowden. If we think that democracy is a good thing, then we must believe that the public should know as much as possible about what the government it elects is doing. Snowden has said that he made the disclosures because "the public needs to decide whether these programs and policies are right or wrong."

He's right about that. How can a democracy determine whether there should be government surveillance of the kind that the NSA is conducting if it has no idea that such programs exist? Indeed, Snowden's leaks also revealed that National Intelligence Director James Clapper misled the US Congress about the NSA's surveillance practices in his testimony at a hearing held in March by the Senate Intelligence Committee.

When the *Washington Post* (along with *The Guardian*) published the information that Snowden provided, it asked Americans whether they support or oppose the NSA's intelligence-gathering program. Some 58% of those surveyed supported it. Yet the same poll found that only 43% supported prosecuting Snowden for disclosing the program, while 48% were opposed.

The poll also indicated 65% support for public hearings by the US Congress on the NSA surveillance program. If that happens, we will all be much better informed because of Snowden's disclosures.

from Project Syndicate, July 5, 2013

A STATUE FOR STALIN?

HITLER AND STALIN WERE RUTHLESS DICTATORS who committed murder on a vast scale. But, while it is impossible to imagine a Hitler statue in Berlin, or anywhere else in Germany, statues of Stalin have been restored in towns across Georgia (his birthplace), and another is to be erected in Moscow as part of a commemoration of all Soviet leaders.

The difference in attitude extends beyond the borders of the countries over which these men ruled. In the United States, there is a bust of Stalin at the National D-Day Memorial in Virginia. In New York, I recently dined at a Russian restaurant that featured Soviet paraphernalia, waitresses in Soviet uniforms, and a painting of Soviet leaders in which Stalin was prominent. New York also has its KGB Bar. To the best of my knowledge, there is no Nazi-themed restaurant in New York; nor is there a Gestapo or SS bar.

So, why is Stalin seen as relatively more acceptable than Hitler?

At a press conference last month, Russian President Vladimir Putin attempted a justification. Asked about Moscow's plans for a statue of Stalin, he pointed to Oliver Cromwell, the leader of the Parliamentarian side in the seventeenth-century English Civil War, and asked: "What's the real difference between Cromwell and Stalin?" He then answered his own question: "None whatsoever," and went on to describe Cromwell as a "cunning fellow" who "played a very ambiguous role in Britain's history." (A statue of Cromwell stands outside the House of Commons in London.)

"Ambiguous" is a reasonable description of the morality of Cromwell's actions. While he promoted parliamentary rule in England, ended the civil war, and allowed a degree of religious toleration, he also supported the trial and execution of Charles I and brutally conquered Ireland in response to a perceived threat from an alliance of Irish Catholics and English Royalists.

But, unlike Cromwell, Stalin was responsible for the deaths of very large numbers of civilians, outside any war or military campaign. According to Timothy Snyder, author of *Bloodlands*, 2–3 million people died in the forced labor camps of the Gulag and perhaps a million were shot during the Great Terror of the late 1930s. Another 5 million starved in the famine of 1930–1933, of whom 3.3 million were Ukrainians who died as a result of a deliberate policy related to their nationality or status as relatively prosperous peasants known as kulaks.

Snyder's estimate of the total number of Stalin's victims does not take into account those who managed to survive forced labor or internal exile in harsh conditions. Including them might add as many as 25 million to the number of those who suffered terribly as a result of Stalin's tyranny. The total number of deaths that Snyder attributes to Stalin is lower than the commonly cited figure of 20 million, which was estimated before historians had access to the Soviet archives. It is nonetheless a horrendous total—similar in magnitude to the Nazis' killings (which took place during a shorter period).

Moreover, the Soviet archives show that one cannot say that the Nazis' killings were worse because victims were targeted on the basis of their race or ethnicity. Stalin, too, selected some of his victims on this basis—not only

Ukrainians, but also people belonging to ethnic minorities associated with countries bordering the Soviet Union. Stalin's persecutions also targeted a disproportionately large number of Jews.

There were no gas chambers, and arguably the motivation for Stalin's killings was not genocide, but rather the intimidation and suppression of real or imaginary opposition to his rule. That in no way excuses the extent of the killing and imprisonment that occurred.

If there is any "ambiguity" about Stalin's moral record, it may be because communism strikes a chord with some of our nobler impulses, seeking equality for all and an end to poverty. No such universal aspiration can be found in Nazism, which, even on its face, was not concerned about what was good for all, but about what was good for one supposed racial group, and which was clearly motivated by hatred and contempt for other ethnic groups.

But communism under Stalin was the opposite of egalitarian, for it gave absolute power to a few, and denied all rights to the many. Those who defend Stalin's reputation credit him with lifting millions out of poverty; but millions could have been lifted out of poverty without murdering and incarcerating millions more.

Others defend Stalin's greatness on the basis of his role in repelling the Nazi invasion and ultimately defeating Hitler. Yet Stalin's purge of military leaders during the Great Terror critically weakened the Red Army, his signing of the Nazi-Soviet Non-Aggression Pact in 1939 paved the way for the start of World War II, and his blindness to the Nazi threat in 1941 left the Soviet Union unprepared to resist Hitler's attack.

It remains true that Stalin led his country to victory in war, and to a position of global power that it had not held before and from which it has since fallen. Hitler, by contrast, left his country shattered, occupied, and divided.

People identify with their country and look up to those who led it when it was at its most powerful. That may explain why Muscovites are more willing to accept a statue of Stalin than Berliners would be to have one of Hitler.

But that can be only part of the reason for the different treatment given to these mass murderers. It still leaves me puzzled about New York's Soviet-themed restaurant and KGB Bar.

from Project Syndicate, January 9, 2014

SHOULD WE HONOR RACISTS?

IN THE MIDST OF MY PRACTICAL ETHICS CLASS last month, several students stood up and walked out. They were joining hundreds of others in a protest led by the Black Justice League (BJL), one of many student groups that have emerged across the United States in response to the fatal shooting of Michael Brown in Ferguson, Missouri, in August 2014, and subsequent police killings of unarmed African Americans.

Later that day, members of the BJL occupied the office of Princeton University President Christopher Eisgruber, vowing not to leave until their demands were met.

These demands included "cultural competency training" for both academic and non-academic staff; a requirement that students take classes on the history of marginalized people; and the provision of a "cultural affinity space" on campus dedicated specifically to African American culture.

The demand that received national attention was for the university's Woodrow Wilson School of Public and International Affairs, and Wilson College, one of its residential colleges, to be renamed. The college dining hall features a large photo of Wilson, which the BJL also wants removed. Honoring Wilson, the League says, is offensive to African American students, because Wilson was a racist.

Wilson was a progressive in domestic affairs and an idealist in foreign policy. His administration passed laws against child labor and granted new rights to workers, as well as reforming banking laws and challenging monopolies. In the aftermath of World War I, he insisted that foreign policy be guided by moral values, and advocated democracy and national self-determination in Europe.

Yet his policies for African Americans were reactionary. In 1913, when he became US president, he inherited a federal government that employed many African Americans, some working alongside whites in mid-level management positions. Under his administration, racially segregated workplaces and washrooms, which had been abolished at the end of the Civil War, were re-introduced. African American managers were demoted to more menial positions. When a delegation of African Americans protested, he told them that they should regard segregation as a benefit.

Wilson's name features prominently at Princeton not only because he is one of the university's most famous alumni (and the only one to receive the Nobel Peace Prize). It is also because, before he was US president, he was Princeton's president, and in the words of Anne-Marie Slaughter, a former dean of the Woodrow Wilson School, the person who "perhaps did more than anyone else to transform [Princeton] from a preppie gentlemen's preserve into a great research university."

Wilson is famous worldwide for the "Fourteen Points" that he proposed as the basis of a peace treaty to end World War I. He called for autonomy for the peoples of the Austro-Hungarian and Ottoman Empires, as well as an independent Polish state. No wonder, then, that there is a Wilson Square in Warsaw, that Prague's main train station is named after him, and that there are Wilson streets in both Prague and Bratislava.

Among the other Fourteen Points are calls for open covenants—no secret treaties plotting the postwar division of another country's territory—and for a reduction in trade barriers. Perhaps most momentous is the proposal for the formation of "a general association of nations . . . for the purpose of affording mutual guarantees of political independence and territorial integrity to great and small states alike."

That call led to the founding of the League of Nations, the predecessor of the United Nations, which from 1920 until 1936 had its headquarters in the Palais Wilson, in Geneva. The building retains that name, and is today the headquarters of the UN High Commissioner for Human Rights.

History is full of deeply flawed people who did great things. In the United States, we have only to look at slave-owning Founding Fathers and early presidents like George Washington, Thomas Jefferson, and James Madison. One might plead on their behalf that, in contrast to Wilson, they were at least no worse than the standards that prevailed in their time. But is that sufficient grounds to continue commemorating them?

A New Orleans school board thought not. After adopting a resolution declaring that no school should be named after a slaveholder, it renamed George Washington Elementary School after an African American surgeon who fought for desegregation of blood transfusions. Should the name of the country's capital city be reconsidered, too?

In his book *Veil Politics in Liberal Democratic States,* Ajume Wingo describes how "political veils" gloss over a political system's historical details, creating an idealized visage. The same happens to great—or not-so-great—political leaders, who become symbolic vehicles for inculcating civic virtues.

As our moral standards shift, however, different characteristics of the historical person become more relevant, and the symbol can develop a different meaning. When Wilson's name was added to Princeton's School of Public and International Affairs in 1948, Rosa Parks's famous bus ride was still seven years away, and segregation in the American South was not under serious challenge. Now it is unthinkable. Wilson's racism therefore becomes more salient, and he ceases to embody the values that are important to Princeton University today.

Wilson's contributions to the university, the US, and the world cannot and should not be erased from history. They should, instead, be recognized in a manner that creates a nuanced conversation about changing values, and includes both his positive achievements and his contributions to America's racist policies and practices.

At Princeton, one outcome of that conversation should be the education of students and faculty who would otherwise be unaware of the complexity of an important figure in the university's history. (I certainly have benefited: I have taught at Princeton for 16 years, and I have admired some of Wilson's foreign-policy positions for much longer; but I owe my knowledge of Wilson's racism to the BJL.) The end result of the conversation we should be having may well be the recognition that to attach Wilson's name to a college or school sends a message that misrepresents the values for which the institution stands.

from Project Syndicate, December 11, 2015

Postscript: After holding an inquiry into campus views, Princeton University's Board of Trustees acknowledged Wilson's racism but voted to retain his name on Wilson College and the Woodrow Wilson School of Public and International Affairs. The head of Wilson College has decided to remove the photo of Wilson that occupies one wall of the college dining hall.

··· Global Governance ···

ESCAPING THE REFUGEE CRISIS

IN JULY, THE NUMBER OF MIGRANTS reaching the borders of the European Union passed 100,000—the third consecutive month in which a new record was set. In one week in August, 21,000 migrants arrived in Greece. Tourists complained that the summer holiday they had planned on a Greek island was now in the midst of a refugee camp.

Of course, the refugee crisis has far more serious implications. Last week, Austrian authorities found the decomposing bodies of 71 migrants in a Hungarian truck abandoned near Vienna. And more than 2,500 would-be migrants have drowned in the Mediterranean this year, most of them attempting to cross from North Africa to Italy.

Migrants who have made it as far as France are living in tents near Calais, waiting for a chance to get to England by scrambling aboard a freight train passing through the Channel Tunnel. Some of them die, too, falling off trains or getting run over.

Nevertheless, the number of refugees in Europe is still small compared to some other countries. Germany has received more applications for asylum than any other European country, but its six refugees per thousand inhabitants is less than a third of Turkey's 21 per thousand, which in turn is dwarfed by Lebanon's 232 per thousand.

At the end of 2014, UNHCR, the United Nations agency for refugees, estimated that there were 59.5 million forcibly displaced people worldwide, the highest level ever recorded.

Of these, 1.8 million are awaiting a decision on their asylum applications, 19.5 million are refugees, and the rest are displaced inside their own countries.

Syria, Afghanistan, and Somalia are the largest sources of refugees, but many more come from Libya, Eritrea, the Central African Republic, South Sudan, Nigeria, and the Democratic Republic of Congo. In Asia, the persecution of the Muslim Rohingya minority in Myanmar has contributed to a recent increase in the number of refugees.

We cannot blame people for wishing to leave conflict-ridden, impoverished countries and find a better life elsewhere. In their situation, we would do the same. But there must be a better way of responding to their needs.

A few bold thinkers advocate a world with open borders, arguing that this would greatly boost both global GDP and average global happiness. (See, for example, http://openborders.info.) Such arguments ignore our species' lamentable xenophobic tendencies, evidenced all too clearly by the surge in popularity of far-right extremist political parties in Europe.

For the foreseeable future, no government will open its borders to all who want to enter. Indeed, there is only movement in the opposite direction: Serbia and Hungary are building fences to keep migrants out, and there has been talk of reinstating border controls within the Schengen Area, which currently guarantees freedom of movement among 26 European countries.

Instead of simply sealing themselves off, affluent countries should be giving much more support to less affluent countries that are supporting large numbers of refugees: Lebanon, Jordan, Ethiopia, and Pakistan are obvious examples. Refugees living securely in countries that border their own are less likely to attempt hazardous journeys to remote regions and more likely to return home once a conflict is resolved. International support for countries bearing the greatest refugee burden also makes economic sense: it costs Jordan about €3,000 ($3,350) to support one refugee for a year; in Germany, the cost is at least €12,000.

Ultimately, however, we need to reconsider what for many is a sacred and immutable text: the UN Convention and Protocol Relating to the Status of Refugees. The Convention, concluded in 1951, was originally limited to persons within Europe fleeing events before that date. It required the signatory countries to allow refugees who reached their territory to stay there, without discrimination or penalty for breaching immigration laws. Refugees were defined as those unable or unwilling to return to their country because of a well-founded fear of persecution on the grounds of "race, religion, nationality, membership of a particular social group, or political opinion."

In 1967, the restrictions of time and geography were removed, making the Convention universal. That was a noble thing to do, but a key question was never asked: Why should someone who is able to travel to another country have priority over others who are in refugee camps and unable to travel?

Affluent countries have a responsibility to take refugees, and many of them can and should accept more than they do. But as the number of people seeking asylum has grown, it has become difficult for tribunals and courts to determine who is a refugee, as defined by the Convention, and who is a well-coached migrant seeking a better life in a more affluent country.

The Convention has also given rise to the new, often unscrupulous, and sometimes lethal industry of people smuggling. If those who claim asylum in a nearby country were sent to a refugee camp, safe from persecution, and supported financially by aid from affluent countries, people smuggling—and deaths in transit—would be eliminated. Moreover, the incentive for economic migrants to seek asylum would be reduced, and affluent countries could fulfill their responsibility to accept more refugees from the camps, while maintaining control of their borders.

That may not be the best solution, but it may be the most workable. And it looks a lot better than the chaos and tragedy that many refugees are facing now.

Turning away people who manage to reach one's country is emotionally difficult, even if they are being sent to a safe haven. But we should also have compassion for the millions of people who are waiting in refugee camps. We need to give them hope, too.

from Project Syndicate, September 1, 2015

IS OPEN DIPLOMACY POSSIBLE?

AT PRINCETON UNIVERSITY, Woodrow Wilson, who was president of the university before he became president of the United States, is never far away. His larger-than-life image looks out across the dining hall at Wilson College, where I am a fellow, and Prospect House, the dining facility for academic staff, was his family home when he led the university.

So when the furor erupted over WikiLeaks' recent release of a quarter-million diplomatic cables, I was reminded of Wilson's 1918 speech in which he put forward "Fourteen Points" for a just peace to end World War I. The first of those fourteen points reads: "Open covenants of peace must be arrived at, after which there will surely be no private international action or rulings of any kind, but diplomacy shall proceed always frankly and in the public view."

Is this an ideal that we should take seriously? Is Wikileaks founder Julian Assange a true follower of Woodrow Wilson?

Wilson was unable to get the Treaty of Versailles to reflect his fourteen points fully, although it did include several of them, including the establishment of an association of states that proved to be the forerunner of today's United Nations. But Wilson then failed to get the US Senate to ratify the treaty, which included the covenant of the League of Nations.

Writing in the *New York Times* earlier this month, Paul Schroeter, an emeritus professor of history, argued that open diplomacy is often "fatally flawed," and gave as an example the need for secret negotiations to reach agreement on the Treaty of Versailles. Since the treaty bears substantial responsibility for the resurrection of German nationalism that led to the rise of Hitler and World War II, it has a fair claim to being the most disastrous peace treaty in human history.

Moreover, it is hard to imagine that if Wilson's proposals had formed the basis of the peace, and set the tone for all future negotiations, the history of Europe in the twentieth century would have been worse than it actually was. That makes the Treaty of Versailles a poor example to use to demonstrate the desirability of secrecy in international negotiations.

Open government is, within limits, an ideal that we all share. US President Barack Obama endorsed it when he took office in January 2009. "Starting today," he told his cabinet secretaries and staff, "every agency and department should know that this administration stands on the side not of those who seek to withhold information but those who seek to make it known." He then noted that there would have to be exceptions to this policy to protect privacy and national security.

Even Secretary of Defense Robert Gates has admitted, however, that while the recent leaks are embarrassing and awkward for the United States, their consequences for its foreign policy are modest.

Some of the leaked cables are just opinion, and not much more than gossip about national leaders. But, because of the leak, we know, for example, that when the British government set up its supposedly open inquiry into the causes of the Iraq War, it also promised the US government that it would "put measures in place to protect your interests." The

British government appears to have been deceiving the public and its own parliament.

Similarly, the cables reveal that President Ali Abdullah Saleh of Yemen lied to his people and parliament about the source of US airstrikes against al-Qaeda in Yemen, telling them that Yemen's military was the source of the bombs.

We have also learned more about the level of corruption in some of the regimes that the United States supports, like those in Afghanistan and Pakistan, and in other countries with which the US has friendly relations, notably Russia. We now know that the Saudi royal family has been urging the US to undertake a military attack on Iran to prevent it from becoming capable of producing nuclear weapons. Here, perhaps, we learned something for which the US government deserves credit: it has resisted that suggestion.

Knowledge is generally considered a good thing; so, presumably, knowing more about how the United States thinks and operates around the world is also good. In a democracy, citizens pass judgment on their government, and if they are kept in the dark about what their government is doing, they cannot be in a position to make well-grounded decisions. Even in non-democratic countries, people have a legitimate interest in knowing about actions taken by the government.

Nevertheless, it isn't always the case that openness is better than secrecy. Suppose that US diplomats had discovered that democrats living under a brutal military dictatorship were negotiating with junior officers to stage a coup to restore democracy and the rule of law. I would hope that WikiLeaks would not publish a cable in which diplomats informed their superiors of the plot.

Openness is in this respect like pacifism: just as we cannot embrace complete disarmament while others stand ready to use their weapons, so Woodrow Wilson's world of open diplomacy is a noble ideal that cannot be fully realized in the world in which we live.

We could, however, try to get closer to that ideal. If governments did not mislead their citizens so often, there would be less need for secrecy, and if leaders knew that they could not rely on keeping the public in the dark about what they are doing, they would have a powerful incentive to behave better.

It is therefore regrettable that the most likely outcome of the recent revelations will be greater restrictions to prevent further leaks. Let's hope that in the new WikiLeaks age, that goal remains out of reach.

from Project Syndicate, December 13, 2010

THE ETHICS OF BIG FOOD

LAST MONTH, OXFAM, the international aid organization, launched a campaign called "Behind the Brands." The goal is to assess the transparency of the world's ten biggest food and beverage companies concerning how their goods are produced, and to rate their performance on sensitive issues like the treatment of small-scale farmers, sustainable water and land use, climate change, and exploitation of women.

Consumers have an ethical responsibility to be aware of how their food is produced, and the big brands have a corresponding obligation to be more transparent about their suppliers, so that their customers can make informed choices about what they are eating. In many cases, the biggest food companies themselves do not know how they perform on these issues, betraying a profound lack of ethical responsibility on their part.

Nestlé scored highest on transparency, as they provide information on at least some of their commodity sources and audit systems. But even its rating is only "fair." General Mills was at the bottom of the ranking.

In addition to this lack of transparency, Oxfam's report identifies several deficiencies common to all of the Big 10 food companies. They are not providing small-scale farmers with an equal opportunity to sell into their supply chains, and when small-scale farmers do have the opportunity to sell to the big brands' suppliers, they may not receive a fair price for their product.

The Big 10 are also not taking sufficient responsibility to ensure that their larger-scale farm suppliers pay a decent living wage to their workers. There are 450 million wage workers in agriculture worldwide, and in many countries they are often inadequately paid, with 60 percent living in poverty.

Some of the Big 10 are doing more than others to develop ethical policies in these areas. Unilever has committed itself to sourcing more raw materials from small-scale farmers, and has pledged 100 percent sustainable sourcing for all of its main commodities by 2020. This policy gave Unilever the highest score on openness to small farmers, with a rating of "fair." Danone, General Mills, and Kellogg's were at the bottom, with a rating of "very poor."

For many years, Nestlé was criticized for marketing infant formula in developing countries, where breast-feeding was available and much healthier than bottle-feeding. It revised its policies in response to that criticism, but more recently has been targeted again for using child and forced labor to produce its cocoa.

In 2011, the company used the Fair Labor Association to assess its supply chain. The assessment confirmed that many of Nestlé's suppliers were using child and forced labor, and the company has now begun to address the problem. As a result, Nestlé, along with Unilever and Coca-Cola, scored "fair" on workers' rights. None of the Big 10 did better. Kellogg's received the lowest score in this category.

Agriculture is a major source of greenhouse gas emissions, accounting for more than the entire transport sector, and it is also one of the sectors most at risk from climate change, as recent changes in rainfall patterns have made evident. Clearing tropical forests for grazing or palm-oil production releases large quantities of stored carbon into the atmosphere. Grazing ruminant animals, like cattle and sheep, also contribute significantly to climate change.

Here, too, the big brands receive low grades from Oxfam, mostly for failing even to track the emissions for which they are directly or indirectly responsible. Nestlé was the only company to achieve a "fair" rating, with Associated British Foods at the bottom, with a "very poor" rating.

Anyone with Internet access can visit Oxfam's website and see how the big brands rank on each of seven ethically significant indicators. The highest scores currently are in the "fair" range, with not a single Big 10 company receiving a "good" rating in any category.

Individual consumers are encouraged to contact the companies directly and urge them to demonstrate greater responsibility for the way in which they obtain the ingredients for their products. In this way, Oxfam hopes, its "Behind the Brands" campaign will trigger a "race to the top" in which big corporations compete to achieve the highest possible score, and to become known as truly transparent actors that produce food and beverages with a high degree of ethical responsibility.

The changes that have already occurred show that if big corporations know that their consumers want them to act more ethically, they will do so. To be effective, such a campaign requires individual consumers to take it upon themselves to become better informed about the food and beverages that they consume, to make their voices heard, and to make purchasing choices that are influenced by ethics as well as by taste and price.

from Project Syndicate, March 12, 2013

FAIRNESS AND CLIMATE CHANGE

(with Teng Fei)

A SENSE OF FAIRNESS IS universal among human beings, but people often differ about exactly what fairness requires in a specific situation. Nowhere is this more apparent than in the debate over the need to reduce greenhouse gas emissions to avoid dangerous climate change.

China and the United States are the two largest emitters of GHGs, and it seems unlikely that any global agreement to reduce emissions will be effective unless both participate. Yet in international climate negotiations, they seem to be far apart in their views of what each nation should do. We are professors interested in the issue of climate change, one from a leading university in China, and one from a leading university in the United States. We thought it would be interesting to see if we can reach agreement on what would be a fair principle for regulating GHG emissions.

We decided to use the Gini coefficient, a common measure of inequality in income distribution, to measure inequality in carbon emissions. The Gini coefficient is a number between 0 and 1, where 0 indicates that everyone has exactly the same income, and 1 indicates that a single person has all the income and no one else has any. Naturally, all existing societies fall somewhere between these two extremes, with relatively egalitarian countries like Denmark at around 0.25

and less egalitarian countries like the United States and Turkey closer to 0.4.

Different equity principles will generate different emission distributions over the population and different "carbon Gini coefficients." We use the 1850–2050 time span to calculate the carbon Gini coefficient. This allows us analyze the principle of historical accountability, advocated by countries like China and Brazil, which takes into account past emissions that have had an impact on the atmosphere.

We have selected three widely discussed methods of allocating GHG emission quotas to different countries:

The equal per capita emission rights approach allocates emission rights to countries in proportion to their population, but only for the remaining portion of the global carbon budget, that is, for the amount that can still be emitted, between now and 2050, consistently with avoiding dangerous change to our climate. (This limit is usually stated as avoiding more than 2°C of warming.)

The equal per capita cumulative emission approach seeks equality over time, rather than just from now on. Thus it combines the dimensions of responsibility for past emissions, and equal per capita rights. It allocates an equal share of the overall global budgets taking into account the portion that has already been consumed.

The grandfathering approach bases emission rights on existing patterns. This allocation scheme has become the *de facto* approach applied to developed countries in the Kyoto Protocol which requires these countries to achieve an emissions target based on a percentage reduction from what they emitted in 1990. Thus those countries that emitted more in 1990 have an entitlement to emit more in future than other countries that emitted less in 1990.

The equal per capita cumulative emissions approach is, by definition, a way of producing perfect equality among all countries in the contribution they will have made, over time, to climate change. It thus leads to a carbon Gini coefficient of 0.0. The equal per capita principle applied to annual emission flows, from now on, results in a carbon Gini coefficient of about 0.4. The difference shows that the dispute between developed and developing countries over the principle of historical responsibility accounts for about 40% of the global GHG emissions that can occur from 1850 to 2050, compatibly with avoiding more than 2°C of warming. The grandfathering principle leads to the largest carbon Gini coefficient, of about 0.7.

These widely different carbon Gini coefficients indicate that the world lacks a common understanding on what would be a fair solution to climate change. Success in international climate negotiations will hinge on how parties— and the citizens they represent—consider a few vital equity principles, especially historical responsibility and equal per capita rights. In the negotiations so far, it is already clear that long-term equity concerns are not being adequately addressed. When the *de facto* grandfathering principle is included, our carbon Gini coefficient indicates that as much as 70% of the global carbon budget is still in dispute between rich and poor countries.

If it proves too difficult to reach agreement on a substantive principle of equity, then an agreement that some carbon Gini coefficients are too extreme to be fair could form the basis of a minimum consensus. For example, the grandfathering principle has a very high Gini coefficient of 0.7. We can compare this with the Gini coefficient of the income distribution of the United States, which most people think of as highly inegalitarian, and yet which is, at about 0.38, much lower.

On the other hand, equal per capita annual emissions is based on a principle that at least has a claim to be considered fair, and has a Gini coefficient of less than 0.4. We therefore propose that any fair solution should fall within a Gini coefficient "fair range" of 0.0–0.4. Although any choice of a precise number is somewhat arbitrary, this may serve as a boundary of those proposals that would be discussed by parties committed to a fair solution to the problem of climate change.

from Project Syndicate, April 11, 2013

WILL THE POLLUTERS PAY FOR CLIMATE CHANGE?

I AM WRITING THIS IN NEW YORK in early August, when the mayor declared a "heat emergency" to prevent widespread electricity outages from the expected high use of air conditioners. City employees could face criminal charges if they set their thermostats below 78 degrees Fahrenheit (25.5 Celsius). Nevertheless, electricity usage has reached near-record levels.

Meanwhile California has emerged from its own record-breaking heat wave. For the United States as a whole, the first six months of 2006 were the hottest in more than a century. Europe is experiencing an unusually hot summer, too. July set new records in England and the Netherlands, where weather data go back more than 300 years.

The hot northern summer fits well with the release of *An Inconvenient Truth*, a documentary film featuring former US Vice President Al Gore. Using some remarkable graphs, images, and other information, the film makes a compelling case that our carbon dioxide emissions are causing global warming, or, at the very least, contributing to it, and that we must urgently address the issue.

Americans tend to talk a lot about morality and justice. But most Americans still fail to realize that their country's refusal to sign the Kyoto Protocol, and their subsequent business-as-usual approach to greenhouse gas emissions, is a moral failing of the most serious kind. It is already having harmful consequences for others, and the greatest inequity is that it is the rich who are using most of the energy that leads to the emissions that cause climate change, while it is the poor who will bear most of the costs. (To see what you can do to reduce your own contribution, go to www.climate-crisis.net.)

To see the inequity, I merely have to glance up at the air conditioner that is keeping my office bearable. While I've done more than the mayor requested, setting it at 82°F (27°C), I'm still part of a feedback loop. I deal with the heat by using more energy, which leads to burning more fossil fuel, putting more greenhouse gases into the atmosphere and heating up the planet more. It even happened when I watched *An Inconvenient Truth*: on a warm evening, the cinema was so chilly that I wished I had brought a jacket.

Heat kills. A heat wave in Europe in 2003 caused an estimated 35,000 deaths in France and more than 2,000 deaths in Britain, according to official estimates. Although no particular heat wave can be directly attributed to global warming, it will make such events more frequent. Moreover, if global warming continues unchecked, the number of deaths that occur when rainfall becomes more erratic, causing both prolonged droughts and severe floods, will dwarf the death toll from hot weather in Europe. More frequent intense hurricanes will kill many more. Melting polar ice will cause rising seas to inundate low-lying fertile delta regions on which hundreds of millions of people grow their food. Tropical diseases will spread, killing still more people.

Overwhelmingly, the dead will be those who lack the resources to adapt, to find alternative sources of food, and who do not have access to health care. Even in rich countries, it usually isn't the rich who die in natural disasters. When

Hurricane Katrina hit New Orleans, those who died were the poor in low-lying areas who lacked cars to escape. If this is true in a country like the United States, with a reasonably efficient infrastructure and the resources to help its citizens in times of crisis, it is even more evident when disasters strike developing countries, because their governments lack the resources needed, and because, when it comes to foreign assistance, rich nations still do not count all human lives equally.

According to United Nations figures, in 2002 per capita emissions of greenhouse gases in the United States were 16 times higher than in India, 60 times higher than in Bangladesh, and more than 200 times higher than in Ethiopia, Mali, or Chad. Other developed nations with emissions close to those of the United States include Australia, Canada, and Luxembourg. Russia, Germany, Britain, Italy, France, and Spain all have levels between a half and a quarter that of the United States. This is still significantly above the world average, and more than 50 times that of the poorest nations in which people will die from global warming.

If a polluter harms others, those who are harmed normally have a legal remedy. For example, if a factory leaks toxic chemicals into a river that I use to irrigate my farm, killing my crops, I can sue the factory owner. If the rich nations pollute the atmosphere with carbon dioxide, causing my crops to fail because of changing rainfall patterns, or my fields are inundated by a rise in the sea level, shouldn't I also be able to sue?

Camilla Toulmin, who directs the International Institute for Environment and Development, a London-based NGO, was present at a lecture on climate change that Al Gore gave in June. She asked him what he thought about compensation for those who are hit hardest by climate change, but who have done the least to cause it. The question, she reports on www.opendemocracy.net, seemed to take him by surprise, and he did not support the idea. Like Toulmin, I wonder if this is a truth that is just too inconvenient, even for him.

from Project Syndicate, August 5, 2006

WHY ARE THEY SERVING MEAT AT A CLIMATE CHANGE CONFERENCE?

(with Frances Kissling)

MORE THAN 50,000 UN OFFICIALS, scientists, environmental advocates, and a few heads of state will gather this coming week in Rio de Janeiro for a conference on sustainable development. They're assembling 20 years after the first Earth Summit was held in the same city, and the goal now, as it was then, is to figure out how to cut dangerous greenhouse gases and help the 1.3 billion people living in extreme poverty. Or, to put it more starkly, how we can live ethically without threatening the ability of future generations to live at all.

That's what's on the agenda.

But what we want to know is: What's on the menu? Specifically, will this large gathering on climate change be serving meat—whose production and consumption are major contributors to climate change?

We tried to find out.

The first answer to our e-mail inquiries ignored the question and pointed with pride to the event's effort to be green. A UN spokesperson responded: "There have been quite a few actions taken by both the Brazilian Government and the UN secretariat to 'green' the Rio conference. For one thing, the conference will be 'papersmart,' with no hard documentation issued unless a special request is made for print on demand. I also know that the Brazilian Government has been addressing plastics issues."

Pressing further, we found out from another UN spokesperson that priority will be given to "organic foods in catering services." Which sounds nice enough, except that "organic" cattle typically produce even more methane per pound of beef than their less-well-treated brothers and sisters.

The United Nations has been holding environmental conferences since 1972. Initially these events focused on industrialization, economic growth, and their impact on the environment. By the 1990s, the focus shifted to the effects of global warming. At the first Rio meeting in 1992, 189 nations, including the United States, promised to stabilize the level of greenhouse gases and prevent dangerous changes to the climate system.

They have failed miserably. Since then, the concentration of greenhouse gases in the atmosphere has risen to a level that many scientists think is already dangerous. Many climate experts suggest that we have less than two decades before we reach a point of no return—after that, nothing we can do will prevent climate changes from spiraling into disaster.

No one really believes that the Rio+20 meeting will result in a new agreement to limit greenhouse gas emissions. In that case, the best thing the conference could do for the climate is to remove meat from the menu—and to make a big deal about it. Everyone at that meeting should know that meat is a major contributor to climate change. It is also one problem that can be solved more quickly than others. Cutting out meat would do more to help combat climate change than any other action we could feasibly take in the next 20 years.

A 2006 UN Food and Agriculture Organization (FAO) report, "Livestock's Long Shadow," called raising animals for food "one of the top two or three most significant contributors to the most serious environmental problems, at every scale from local to global." Since then, climate researchers Robert Goodland and Jeff Anhang have estimated that livestock and their methane-rich byproducts account for even more greenhouse gas emissions than the earlier report estimated—a whopping 51 percent. More conservative estimates say that meat accounts for about a third of greenhouse gas emissions.

If the United Nations and all the national delegations and activist groups at Rio+20 were to insist on eliminating meat at all the buffets, private dinners, embassy receptions, luncheons, and breakfast briefings, people might start to think that the United Nations takes seriously the damage that human activity is causing to the planet. Yet, at a meeting that prides itself on being "green," and where environmental advocates will be pushing their agenda, talking about meat seems to be an afterthought, or possibly even taboo.

While environmental groups campaign around the dangers of global warming, it's rare to hear prominent leaders suggest that people stop eating meat—or even seriously cut back. At a recent UN meeting that one of us attended, one speaker, who was from a top environmental organization, spoke fervently about the need to reduce population growth. Then, at the meal that followed his speech, he enjoyed several helpings of osso bucco. Asked about the unsustainable aspects of a high-meat diet, he unabashedly said that he "could never give up" his meat.

And that is part of the problem. In the developed world, eating meat is a sign of the good life. It's a diet that developing countries aspire to, although it undercuts efforts to reduce poverty. As the number of affluent people in countries such as China and India increases, so does the demand for meat.

To meet that demand, the FAO predicts that the number of farm animals raised each year will double from 60 billion today to 120 billion by 2050. Apart from the implications for global warming, this increase will put more pressure on grain, as vast quantities of it have to be produced to be fed to animals. Scholar Vaclav Smil, author of *Feeding the World*, has calculated that it is impossible for everyone on the planet to eat as people in the affluent world do now. It would require 67 percent more agricultural land than the Earth possesses.

A 2007 report from the Intergovernmental Panel on Climate Change spelled out some likely consequences of continuing high levels of greenhouse gas emissions over the next few decades: In Latin America, 70 million people could lack enough water, and many farmers will have to abandon traditional crops as the soil becomes more saline; in Africa, 250 million people would be at risk of water shortages, and the wheat crop could be wiped out; in Asia, 100 million people would face floods from rising sea levels, and less rain could mean reduced rice crops in China and Bangladesh. By the end of the century, the seas are expected to rise between seven and 23 inches. Islands and low-lying countries may simply disappear. Maldives is already saving money in the hope of buying a new country when theirs goes under.

There is clear evidence that reducing meat production and consumption would limit greenhouse gas emissions and possibly stave off these tragedies. However, after multiple revisions and weeks of negotiating, the word "meat" does not appear in the draft conference document for the Rio meeting. Instead, the paper discusses the need to reduce production and consumption of other products that cause global warming, without singling out that key culprit.

Global climate leaders will have a lot of pressing challenges on the table at the Rio+20 conference. It's time to take the meat off their plates.

from The Washington Post, *June 15, 2012*

DETHRONING KING COAL

EARLIER THIS YEAR, THE CONCENTRATION of carbon dioxide in the atmosphere reached 400 parts per million (ppm). The last time there was that much CO_2 in our atmosphere was three million years ago, when sea levels were 24 meters higher than they are today. Now sea levels are rising again. Last September, Arctic sea ice covered the smallest area ever recorded. All but one of the ten warmest years since 1880, when global records began to be kept, have occurred in the twenty-first century.

Some climate scientists believe that 400 ppm of CO_2 in the atmosphere is already enough to take us past the tipping point at which we risk a climate catastrophe that will turn billions of people into refugees. They say that we need to get the amount of atmospheric CO_2 back down to 350 ppm. That figure lies behind the name taken by 350.org, a grassroots movement with volunteers in 188 countries trying to solve the problem of climate change.

Other climate scientists are more optimistic: they argue that if we allow atmospheric CO_2 to rise to 450 ppm, a level associated with a two-degree Celsius temperature rise, we have a 66.6% chance of avoiding catastrophe. That still leaves a one-in-three chance of catastrophe—worse odds than playing Russian roulette. And we are forecast to surpass 450 ppm by 2038.

One thing is clear: if we are not to be totally reckless with our planet's climate, we cannot burn all the coal, oil, and

274 • GLOBAL GOVERNANCE

natural gas that we have already located. About 80% of it—especially the coal, which emits the most CO_2 when burned—will have to stay in the ground.

In June, US President Barack Obama told students at Georgetown University that he refused to condemn them and their children and grandchildren to "a planet that's beyond fixing." Saying that climate change cannot wait for Congress to overcome its "partisan gridlock," he announced measures using his executive power to limit CO_2 emissions, first from new fossil-fuel power plants, and then from existing ones.

Obama also called for an end to public financing of new coal plants overseas, unless they deploy carbon-capture technologies (which are not yet economically viable), or else there is, he said, "no other viable way for the poorest countries to generate electricity."

According to Daniel Schrag, Director of Harvard University's Center for the Environment and a member of a presidential science panel that has helped to advise Obama on climate change, "Politically, the White House is hesitant to say they're having a war on coal. On the other hand, a war on coal is exactly what's needed."

Schrag is right. His university, like mine and many others, has a plan to reduce its greenhouse gas emissions. Yet most of them, including Schrag's and mine, continue to invest part of their multi-billion-dollar endowments in companies that extract and sell coal.

But pressure on educational institutions to stop investing in fossil fuels is beginning to build. Student groups have formed on many campuses, and a handful of colleges and universities have already pledged to end their investment in fossil fuels. Several US cities, including San Francisco and Seattle, have agreed to do the same.

Now financial institutions, too, are coming under fire for their involvement with fossil fuels. In June, I was part of a group of prominent Australians who signed an open letter to the heads of the country's biggest banks asking them to stop lending to new fossil-fuel extraction projects, and to sell their stakes in companies engaged in such activities.

Speaking at Harvard earlier this year, former US Vice President Al Gore praised a student group that was pushing the university to sell its investments in fossil-fuel companies, and compared their activities to the divestment campaign in the 1980s that helped to end South Africa's racist apartheid policy.

How fair is that comparison? The dividing lines may be less sharp than they were with apartheid, but our continued high level of greenhouse gas emissions protects the interests of one group of humans—mainly affluent people who are alive today—at the cost of others. (Compared to most of the world's population, even the American and Australian coal miners who would lose their jobs if the industry shut down are affluent.) Our behavior disregards most of the world's poor, and everyone who will live on this planet in centuries to come.

Worldwide, the poor leave a very small carbon footprint, but they will suffer the most from climate change. Many live in hot places that are getting even hotter, and hundreds of millions of them are subsistence farmers who depend on rainfall to grow their crops. Rainfall patterns will vary, and the Asian monsoon will become less reliable. Those who live on this planet in future centuries will live in a hotter world, with higher sea levels, less arable land, and more extreme hurricanes, droughts, and floods.

In these circumstances, to develop new coal projects is unethical, and to invest in them is to be complicit in this unethical activity. While this applies, to some extent, to all fossil fuels, the best way to begin to change our behavior is by reducing coal consumption. Replacing coal with natural gas does reduce greenhouse gas emissions, even if natural gas itself is not sustainable in the long term. Right now, ending investment in the coal industry is the right thing to do.

from Project Syndicate, August 6, 2013

PARIS AND THE FATE OF THE EARTH

THE LIVES OF BILLIONS OF PEOPLE, for centuries to come, will be at stake when world leaders and government negotiators meet at the United Nations Climate Change Conference in Paris at the end of the month. The fate of an unknown number of endangered species of plants and animals also hangs in the balance.

At the "Earth Summit" in Rio de Janeiro in 1992, 189 countries, including the United States, China, India, and all European countries, signed on to the UN Framework Convention on Climate Change (UNFCCC), and agreed to stabilize greenhouse gas emissions "at a low enough level to prevent dangerous anthropogenic interference with the climate system."

So far, however, no such stabilization has taken place, and without it, climate feedback loops could boost rising temperatures further still. With less Arctic ice to reflect sunlight, the oceans will absorb more warmth. Thawing Siberian permafrost will release vast quantities of methane. As a result, large areas of our planet, currently home to billions of people, could become uninhabitable.

Earlier conferences of the UNFCCC signatories sought to reach legally binding agreements on emission reductions, at least for the industrialized countries that have produced most of the greenhouse gases now in the atmosphere. That strategy faltered—partly owing to US intransigence under President George W. Bush—and was abandoned when the

2009 Copenhagen conference failed to produce a treaty to replace the expiring Kyoto Protocol (which the US never signed). Instead, the Copenhagen Accord merely asked countries for voluntary pledges to cut their emissions by specific amounts.

Those pledges have now come in, from 154 countries, including the major emitters, and they fall far short of what is required. To fathom the gap between what the pledges would achieve and what is required, we need to go back to the language that everyone accepted in Rio.

The wording was vague in two key respects. First, what would constitute "dangerous anthropogenic interference with the climate system"? And, second, what level of safety is assumed by the term "prevent"?

The first ambiguity has been resolved by the decision to aim for a level of emissions that would cap the increase in average surface temperature at 2° Celsius above the pre-industrial level. Many scientists consider even a lower increase dangerous. Consider that even with a rise of only 0.8°C so far, the planet has experienced record-high temperatures, more extreme weather events, and substantial melting of the Greenland ice sheet, which contains enough water to cause a seven-meter rise in sea levels. In Copenhagen, the pleas of representatives of small island states (some of which will cease to exist if sea levels continue to rise) for a target of 1.5°C went unheeded, essentially because world leaders thought the measures required to meet such a target were politically unrealistic.

The second ambiguity remains. The London School of Economics' Grantham Research Institute has analyzed the submissions made by all 154 countries and concluded that even if they are all implemented, global carbon emissions will rise from their current level of 50 billion tons per year to

55–60 billion tons by 2030. But, to have even a 50% chance of keeping to the 2°C limit, annual carbon emissions need to come down to 36 billion tons.

A report from Australia's National Centre for Climate Restoration is no less alarming. The level of emissions in the atmosphere today already means that we have a 10% chance of exceeding 2°C, even if we stopped adding further emissions right now (which is not going to happen).

Imagine if an airline slashed its maintenance procedures to a level at which there was a 10% chance that its planes would not safely complete their flights. The company could not claim that it had prevented dangerous planes from flying, and it would find few customers, even if its flights were much cheaper than anyone else's. Similarly, given the scale of the catastrophe that could result from "dangerous anthropogenic interference with the climate system," we ought not to accept a 10% chance—if not many times higher—of exceeding 2°C.

What is the alternative? Developing countries will argue that their need for cheap energy to lift their people out of poverty is greater than rich countries' need to maintain their often wasteful levels of energy consumption—and they will be right. That is why rich countries should aim at decarbonizing their economies as soon as possible, and by 2050 at the latest. They could start by closing down the dirtiest form of energy production, coal-fired power stations, and refuse licenses to develop new coal mines.

Another quick gain could come from encouraging people to eat more plant-based foods, perhaps by taxing meat and using the revenue to subsidize more sustainable alternatives. According to the UN Food and Agriculture Organization, the livestock industry is the second largest source of greenhouse gas emissions, ahead of the entire transport sector. This implies great scope for emission reductions, and in ways that would have a smaller impact on our lives than ceasing all fossil-fuel use. Indeed, according to a recent World Health Organization report, a reduction in the consumption of processed and red meat would have the additional benefit of reducing cancer deaths.

These proposals may sound unrealistic. Anything less, however, would be a crime against billions of people, living and yet to be born, and against the entire natural environment of our planet.

from Project Syndicate, November 11, 2015

Postscript: The Paris conference produced a more encouraging outcome than I had dared to hope for when writing the essay above. At the insistence of some of the countries most at risk from climate change, the text of the agreement commits the signatories to holding the increase in global temperatures to "well below" 2°C and even "to pursue efforts to limit the temperature increase to 1.5°C." More importantly, there was a consensus that all countries, developed and developing, should play their part in reducing greenhouse gas emissions. As noted above, the pledges made by all the parties to the agreement are insufficient to meet that target. The Paris agreement does, however, require all signatories to renew their emission reduction targets every five years, and to be given a "global stocktake" that will show whether the world is on track to meet the conference's agreed goals. Inevitably, the first stocktake will indicate that global warming is likely to exceed 2°C. At that point the key question will be whether the signatories then commit themselves to reducing their emissions beyond their own 2015 targets.

... Science and Technology ...

A CLEAR CASE FOR GOLDEN RICE

GREENPEACE, THE GLOBAL ENVIRONMENTAL NGO, typically leads protests. Last month, it became the target.

Patrick Moore, a spokesperson for the protesters—and himself an early Greenpeace member—accused the organization of complicity in the deaths of two million children per year. He was referring to deaths resulting from vitamin A deficiency, which is common among children for whom rice is the staple food.

These deaths could be prevented, Moore claims, by the use of "golden rice," a form of the grain that has been genetically modified to have a higher beta-carotene content than ordinary rice. Greenpeace, along with other organizations opposed to the use of genetically modified organisms (GMOs), has campaigned against the introduction of beta-carotene, which is converted in the human body into vitamin A.

Moore's mortality figures seem to be on the high side, but there is no doubting the seriousness of vitamin A deficiency among children, especially in parts of Africa and Southeast Asia. According to the World Health Organization, it causes blindness in about 250,000–500,000 pre-school children every year, about half of whom die within 12 months.

The deficiency also increases susceptibility to diseases like measles, still a significant cause of death in young children, although one that is declining as a result of vaccination. In some countries, lack of vitamin A is also a major factor in high rates of maternal mortality during pregnancy and childbirth.

First developed 15 years ago by Swiss scientists, golden rice specifically addresses vitamin A deficiency, and the first field trials were conducted a decade ago. But it is still not available to farmers. Initially, there was a need to develop improved varieties that would thrive where they are most needed. Further field trials had to be carried out to meet the strict regulations governing the release of GMOs. That hurdle was raised higher when activists destroyed fields in the Philippines where trials were being conducted.

Critics have suggested that golden rice is part of the biotech industry's plans to dominate agriculture worldwide. But, although the agribusiness giant Syngenta did assist in developing the genetically modified rice, the company has stated that it is not planning to commercialize it. Low-income farmers will own their seeds and be able to retain seed from their harvests.

Indeed, Syngenta has given the right to sublicense the rice to a nonprofit organization called the Golden Rice Humanitarian Board. The board, which includes the two co-inventors, has the right to provide the rice to public research institutions and low-income farmers in developing countries for humanitarian use, as long as it does not charge more for it than the price for ordinary rice seeds.

When genetically modified crops were first developed in the 1980s, there were grounds for caution. Would these crops be safe to eat? Might they not cross-pollinate with wild plants, passing on the special qualities they were given, such as resistance to pests, and so create new "superweeds"? In the 1990s, as a Senate candidate for the Australian Greens, I was among those who argued for strong regulations to prevent biotech companies putting our health, or that of the environment, at risk in order to increase their profits.

Genetically modified crops are now grown on about one-tenth of the world's cropland, and none of the disastrous consequences that we Greens feared have come to pass. There is no reliable scientific evidence that GM foods cause illness, despite the fact that they receive much more intense scrutiny than more "natural" foods. (Natural foods can also pose health risks, as was shown recently by studies establishing that a popular type of cinnamon can cause liver damage.)

Although cross-pollination between GM crops and wild plants can occur, so far no new superweeds have emerged. We should be pleased about that—and perhaps the regulations that were introduced in response to the concerns expressed by environmental organizations played a role in that outcome.

Regulations to protect the environment and the health of consumers should be maintained. Caution is reasonable. What needs to be rethought, however, is blanket opposition to the very idea of GMOs.

With any innovation, risks need to be weighed against possible benefits. Where the benefits are minor, even a small risk may not be justified; where those benefits are great, a more significant risk may well be worth taking.

Regulations should, for instance, be sensitive to the difference between releasing a GM crop that is resistant to the herbicide glyphosate (making it easier for farmers to control weeds) and releasing GM crops that can resist drought and are suitable for drought-prone regions of low-income countries. Similarly, a GM crop that has the potential to prevent blindness in a half-million children would be worth growing even if it does involve some risks. The irony is that glyphosate-resistant crops are grown commercially on millions of hectares of land, whereas golden rice (which has not been shown to pose any risk at all to human health or the environment) still cannot be released.

In some environmental circles, blanket opposition to GMOs is like taking a loyalty oath—dissidents are regarded as traitors in league with the evil biotech industry. It is time to move beyond such a narrowly ideological stance. Some GMOs may have a useful role to play in public health, and others in fighting the challenge of growing food in an era of climate change. We should consider the merits of each genetically modified plant on a case-by-case basis.

from Project Syndicate, February 17, 2014

LIFE MADE TO ORDER

IN THE SIXTEENTH CENTURY, the alchemist Paracelsus offered a recipe for creating a living being that began with putting sperm into putrefying *venter equinus*. This is usually translated as "horse manure," but the Latin *venter* means abdomen or uterus.

So occultists now will no doubt have a fine time with the fact that Craig Venter was the driving force behind the team of scientists that last month announced that they had created a synthetic form of life: a bacterium with a genome designed and created from chemicals in a laboratory.

The new bacterium, nicknamed "Synthia," replicates and produces proteins. By any reasonable definition, it is alive. Although it is very similar to a natural bacterium from which it was largely copied, the creators put distinctive strings of DNA into its genome to prove that it is not a natural object. These strings spell out, in code, a website address, the names of the researchers, and apt quotations, such as Richard Feynman's "What I cannot build, I cannot understand."

For some years now, synthetic biology has been looming as the next big issue in bioethics. The scientists at the J. Craig Venter Institute expected to be told that they were "playing God," and they were not disappointed. Yes, if one believes that life was created by God, then this comes as close to "playing God" as humans have come, so far.

Well-known University of Pennsylvania bioethicist Art Caplan says that the achievement ranks as a discovery of historic significance, because it "would seem to extinguish the argument that life requires a special force or power to exist." Asked about the significance of what the team had done, Venter described it as bringing about "a giant philosophical change in how we view life."

Others have pointed out that, although the team produced a synthetic genome, they put it into a cell from another bacterium, replacing that cell's DNA. We have yet to build a living organism entirely from bottles of chemicals, so anyone who believes in a "life force" that only a divine being could imbue into inert matter will no doubt continue to believe in it.

At a more practical level, Venter said, the team's work has produced "a very powerful set of tools" for redesigning life. He has been criticized for the fact that the research was funded by Synthetic Genomics, a company that he cofounded, which will hold the intellectual property rights resulting from the research—and has already filed for 13 patents related to it. But the work has taken 20 scientists a decade to complete, at an estimated cost of $40 million, and commercial investors are an obvious source for such funds.

Others object that living things should not be patented. That battle was lost in 1980, when the United States Supreme Court decided that a genetically modified micro-organism designed to clean up oil spills could be patented. (Obviously, given the damage caused by the BP spill in the Gulf of Mexico, there is still some work to be done on that particular organism.)

Patenting life was taken a step further in 1984, when Harvard University successfully applied for a patent on its "oncomouse," a laboratory mouse specifically designed to get cancer easily, so that it would be more useful as a research tool. There are good grounds for objecting to turning a sentient being into a patented laboratory tool, but it is not so easy to see why patent law should not cover newly designed bacteria or algae, which can feel nothing and may be as useful as any other invention.

Indeed, Synthia's very existence challenges the distinction between living and artificial that underlies much of the opposition to "patenting life"—though pointing this out is not to approve the granting of sweeping patents that prevent other scientists from making their own discoveries in this important new field.

As for the likely usefulness of synthetic bacteria, the fact that Synthia's birth had to compete for headlines with news of the world's worst-ever oil spill made the point more effectively than any public-relations effort could have done. One day, we may be able to design bacteria that can quickly, safely, and effectively clean up oil spills. And, according to Venter, if his team's new technology had been available last year, it would have been possible to produce a vaccine to protect ourselves against H1N1 influenza in 24 hours, rather than several weeks.

The most exciting prospect held out by Venter, however, is a form of algae that can absorb carbon dioxide from the atmosphere and use it to create diesel fuel or gasoline. Synthetic Genomics has a $600 million agreement with ExxonMobil to obtain fuel from algae.

Obviously, the release of any synthetic organism must be carefully regulated, just like the release of any genetically modified organism. But any risk must be weighed against other grave threats that we face. For example, international climate-change negotiations appear to have reached an impasse, and public skepticism about global warming is rising, even as the scientific evidence continues to show that it is real and will endanger the lives of billions of people.

In such circumstances, the admittedly very real risks of synthetic biology seem decisively outweighed by the hope that it may enable us to avert a looming environmental catastrophe.

from Project Syndicate, June 11, 2010

RIGHTS FOR ROBOTS?

(with Agata Sagan)

LAST MONTH, GECKO SYSTEMS ANNOUNCED that it had been running trials of its "fully autonomous personal companion home care robot," also known as a "carebot," designed to help elderly or disabled people to live independently. A woman with short-term memory loss broke into a big smile, the company reported, when the robot asked her, "Would you like a bowl of ice cream?" The woman answered "yes," and presumably the robot did the rest.

Robots already perform many functions, from making cars to defusing bombs—or, more menacingly, firing missiles. Children and adults play with toy robots, while vacuum-cleaning robots are sucking up dirt in a growing number of homes and—as evidenced by YouTube videos— entertaining cats. There is even a Robot World Cup, though, judging by the standard of the event held in Graz, Austria, last summer, footballers have no need to feel threatened just yet. (Chess, of course, is a different matter.)

Most of the robots being developed for home use are functional in design—Gecko System's home-care robot looks rather like the *Star Wars* robot R2-D2. Honda and Sony are designing robots that look more like the same movie's "android" C-3PO. There are already some robots, though, with soft, flexible bodies, human-like faces and expressions, and a large repertoire of movement. Hanson Robotics has a demonstration model called Albert, whose face bears a striking resemblance to that of Albert Einstein.

Will we soon get used to having humanoid robots around the home? Noel Sharkey, professor of artificial intelligence and robotics at the University of Sheffield, has predicted that busy parents will start employing robots as babysitters. What will it do to a child, he asks, to spend a lot of time with a machine that cannot express genuine empathy, understanding, or compassion? One might also ask why we should develop energy-intensive robots to work in one of the few areas—care for children or elderly people—in which people with little education can find employment.

In his book *Love and Sex with Robots*, David Levy goes further, suggesting that we will fall in love with warm, cuddly robots, and even have sex with them. (If the robot has multiple sexual partners, just remove the relevant parts, drop them in disinfectant, and, voilà, no risk of sexually transmitted diseases!) But what will the presence of a "sexbot" do to the marital home? How will we feel if our spouse starts spending too much time with an inexhaustible robotic lover?

A more ominous question is familiar from novels and movies: Will we have to defend our civilization against intelligent machines of our own creation? Some consider the development of superhuman artificial intelligence inevitable, and expect it to happen no later than 2070. They refer to this moment as "the singularity," and see it as a world-changing event.

Eliezer Yudkowsky, one of the founders of The Singularity Institute for Artificial Intelligence, believes that singularity will lead to an "intelligence explosion" as super-intelligent machines design even more intelligent machines, with each generation repeating this process. The more cautious

Association for the Advancement of Artificial Intelligence has set up a special panel to study what it calls "the potential for loss of human control of computer-based intelligences."

If that happens, the crucial question for the future of civilization is: Will the super-intelligent computers be friendly? Is it time to start thinking about what steps to take to prevent our own creations from becoming hostile to us?

For the moment, a more realistic concern is not that robots will harm us, but that we will harm them. At present, robots are mere items of property. But what if they become sufficiently complex to have feelings? After all, isn't the human brain just a very complex machine?

If machines can and do become conscious, will we take their feelings into account? The history of our relations with the only nonhuman sentient beings we have encountered so far—animals—gives no ground for confidence that we would recognize sentient robots not just as items of property, but as beings with moral standing and interests that deserve consideration.

The cognitive scientist Steve Torrance has pointed out that powerful new technologies, like cars, computers, and phones, tend to spread rapidly, in an uncontrolled way. The development of a conscious robot that (who?) was not widely perceived as a member of our moral community could therefore lead to mistreatment on a large scale.

The hard question, of course, is how we could tell that a robot really was conscious, and not just designed to mimic consciousness. Understanding how the robot had been programmed would provide a clue—did the designers write the code to provide only the appearance of consciousness? If so, we would have no reason to believe that the robot was conscious.

But if the robot was designed to have human-like capacities that might incidentally give rise to consciousness, we would have a good reason to think that it really was conscious. At that point, the movement for robot rights would begin.

from Project Syndicate, December 14, 2009

A DREAM FOR THE DIGITAL AGE

FIFTY YEARS AGO, MARTIN LUTHER KING dreamed of an America that would one day deliver on its promise of equality for all of its citizens, black as well as white. Today, Facebook founder Mark Zuckerberg has a dream, too: he wants to provide Internet access to the world's five billion people who do not now have it.

Zuckerberg's vision may sound like a self-interested push to gain more Facebook users. But the world currently faces a growing technological divide, with implications for equality, liberty, and the right to pursue happiness that are no less momentous than the racial divide against which King preached.

Around the world, more than two billion people live in the Digital Age. They can access a vast universe of information, communicate at little or no cost with their friends and family, and connect with others with whom they can cooperate in new ways. The other five billion are still stuck in the Paper Age in which my generation grew up.

In those days, if you wanted to know something but did not own an expensive encyclopedia (or your encyclopedia was no longer sufficiently up-to-date to tell you what you wanted to know), you had to go to a library and spend hours searching for what you needed. To contact friends or colleagues overseas, you had to write them a letter and wait at least two weeks for a reply. International phone calls were prohibitively expensive, and the idea of actually seeing someone while you talked to them was the stuff of science fiction.

Internet.org, a global partnership launched by Zuckerberg last month, plans to bring the two-thirds of the world's population without Internet access into the Digital Age. The partnership consists of seven major information-technology companies, as well as nonprofit organizations and local communities. Knowing that you cannot ask people to choose between buying food and buying data, the partnership will seek new, less expensive means of connecting computers, more data-efficient software, and new business models.

Microsoft founder Bill Gates has suggested that Internet access is not a high priority for the poorest countries. It is more important, he says, to tackle problems like diarrhea and malaria. I have nothing but praise for Gates's efforts to reduce the death toll from these diseases, which primarily affect the world's poorest people. Yet his position seems curiously lacking in big-picture awareness of how the Internet could transform the lives of the very poor. For example, if farmers could use it to get more accurate predictions of favorable conditions for planting, or to obtain higher prices for their harvest, they would be better able to afford sanitation, so that their children do not get diarrhea, and bed nets to protect themselves and their families against malaria.

A friend working to provide family-planning advice to poor Kenyans recently told me that so many women were coming to the clinic that she could not spend more than five minutes with each. These women have only one source of advice, and one opportunity to get it, but if they had access to the Internet, the information could be there for them whenever they wanted it.

Moreover, online consultations would be possible, sparing women the need to travel to clinics. Internet access would also bypass the problem of illiteracy, building on the oral traditions that are strong in many rural cultures and enabling communities to create self-help groups and share their problems with peers in other villages.

What is true for family planning is true for a very wide range of topics, especially those that are difficult to speak about, like homosexuality and domestic violence. The Internet is helping people to understand that they are not alone, and that they can learn from others' experience.

Enlarging our vision still more, it is not absurd to hope that putting the world's poor online would result in connections between them and more affluent people, leading to more assistance. Research shows that people are more likely to donate to a charity helping the hungry if they are given a photo and told the name and age of a girl like those the charity is aiding. If a mere photo and a few identifying details can do that, what might Skyping with the person do?

Providing universal Internet access is a project on a scale similar to sequencing the human genome, and, like the Human Genome Project, it will raise new risks and sensitive ethical issues. Online scammers will have access to a new and perhaps more gullible audience. Breaches of copyright will become even more widespread than they are today (although they will cost the copyright owners very little, because the poor would be very unlikely to be able to buy books or other copyrighted material).

Moreover, the distinctiveness of local cultures may be eroded, which has both a good and a bad side, for such cultures can restrict freedom and deny equality of opportunity. On the whole, though, it is reasonable to expect that giving poor people access to knowledge and the possibility of connecting with people anywhere in the world will be socially transforming in a very positive way.

from Project Syndicate, September 9, 2013

A UNIVERSAL LIBRARY

SCHOLARS HAVE LONG DREAMED of a universal library containing everything that has ever been written. Then, in 2004, Google announced that it would begin digitally scanning all the books held by five major research libraries. Suddenly, the library of utopia seemed within reach.

Indeed, a digital universal library would be even better than any earlier thinker could have imagined, because every work would be available to everyone, everywhere, at all times. And the library could include not only books and articles, but also paintings, music, films, and every other form of creative expression that can be captured in digital form.

But Google's plan had a catch. Most of the works held by those research libraries are still in copyright. Google said that it would scan the entire book, irrespective of its copyright status, but that users searching for something in copyrighted books would be shown only a snippet. This, it argued, was "fair use"—and thus permitted under copyright laws in the same way that one may quote a sentence or two from a book for the purpose of a review or discussion.

Publishers and authors disagreed, and some sued Google for breach of copyright, eventually agreeing to settle their claim in exchange for a share of Google's revenue. Last month, in a Manhattan court, Judge Denny Chin rejected that proposed settlement, in part because it would have given Google a *de facto* monopoly over the digital versions of so-called "orphan" books—that is, books that are still in copyright, but no longer in print, and whose copyright ownership is difficult to determine.

Chin held that the US Congress, not a court, was the appropriate body to decide who should be entrusted with guardianship over orphan books, and on what terms. He was surely right, at least in so far as we are considering matters within US jurisdiction. These are large and important issues that affect not only authors, publishers, and Google, but anyone with an interest in the diffusion and availability of knowledge and culture. So, while Chin's decision is a temporary setback on the way to a universal library, it provides an opportunity to reconsider how the dream can best be realized.

The central issue is this: how can we make books and articles—not just snippets, but entire works—available to everyone, while preserving the rights of the works' creators? To answer that, of course, we need to decide what those rights are. Just as inventors are given patents so that they can profit from their inventions for a limited time, so, too, authors were originally given copyright for a relatively short period—in the United States, it was initially only 14 years from the first publication of the work.

For most authors, that would be enough time to earn the bulk of the income that they would ever receive from their writings; after that, the works would be in the public domain. But corporations built fortunes on copyright, and repeatedly pushed Congress to extend it, to the point that in the United States it now lasts for 70 years after the creator's death. (The 1998 legislation responsible for the last extension was nicknamed the "Mickey Mouse Protection Act" because it allowed the Walt Disney Company to retain copyright of its famous cartoon character.)

It is because copyright lasts so long that as many as three-quarters of all library books are "orphaned." This vast collection of knowledge, culture, and literary achievement is inaccessible to most people. Digitizing it would make it available to anyone with Internet access. As Peter Brantley, Director of Technology for the California Digital Library, has put it: "We have a moral imperative to reach out to our library shelves, grab the material that is orphaned, and set it on top of scanners."

Robert Darnton, Director of the Harvard University Library, has proposed an alternative to Google's plans: a digital public library, funded by a coalition of foundations, working in tandem with a coalition of research libraries. Darnton's plan falls short of a universal library, because works in print and in copyright would be excluded; but he believes that Congress might grant a non-commercial public library the right to digitize orphan books.

That would be a huge step in the right direction, but we should not give up the dream of a universal digital public library. After all, books still in print are likely to be the ones that contain the most up-to-date information, and the ones that people most want to read.

Many European countries, as well as Australia, Canada, Israel, and New Zealand, have adopted legislation that creates a "public lending right"—that is, the government recognizes that enabling hundreds of people to read a single copy of a book provides a public good, but that doing so is likely to reduce sales of the book. The universal public library could be allowed to digitize even works that are in print and in copyright, in exchange for fees paid to the publisher and author based on the number of times the digital version is read.

If we can put a man on the Moon and sequence the human genome, we should be able to devise something close to a universal digital public library. At that point, we will face another moral imperative, one that will be even more difficult to fulfill: expanding Internet access beyond the less than 30% of the world's population that currently has it.

from Project Syndicate, April 13, 2011

THE TRAGIC COST OF BEING UNSCIENTIFIC

THROUGHOUT HIS TENURE as South Africa's president, Thabo Mbeki rejected the scientific consensus that AIDS is caused by a virus, HIV, and that antiretroviral drugs can save the lives of people who test positive for it. Instead, he embraced the views of a small group of dissident scientists who suggested other causes for AIDS.

Mbeki stubbornly continued to embrace this position even as the evidence against it became overwhelming. When anyone—even Nelson Mandela, the heroic resistance fighter against apartheid who became South Africa's first black president—publicly questioned Mbeki's views, Mbeki's supporters viciously denounced them.

While Botswana and Namibia, South Africa's neighbors, provided anti-retrovirals to the majority of its citizens infected by HIV, South Africa under Mbeki failed to do so. A team of Harvard University researchers has now investigated the consequences of this policy. Using conservative assumptions, it estimates that, had South Africa's government provided the appropriate drugs, both to AIDS patients and to pregnant women who were at risk of infecting their babies, it would have prevented 365,000 premature deaths.

That number is a revealing indication of the staggering costs that can arise when science is rejected or ignored. It is roughly comparable to the loss of life from the genocide in Darfur, and close to half of the toll from the massacre of Tutsis in Rwanda in 1994.

One of the key incidents in turning world opinion against South Africa's apartheid regime was the 1961 Sharpeville massacre, in which police fired on a crowd of black protesters, killing 69 and wounding many more. Mbeki, like Mandela, was active in the struggle against apartheid. Yet the Harvard study shows that he is responsible for the deaths of 5,000 times as many black South Africans as the white South African police who fired on the crowd at Sharpeville.

How are we to assess a man like that?

In Mbeki's defense, it can be said that he did not intend to kill anyone. He appears to have genuinely believed—and perhaps still believes—that anti-retrovirals are toxic.

We can also grant that Mbeki was not motivated by malice against those suffering from AIDS. He had no desire to harm them, and for that reason, we should judge his character differently from those who do set out to harm others, whether from hatred or to further their own interests.

But good intentions are not enough, especially when the stakes are so high. Mbeki is culpable, not for having initially entertained a view held by a tiny minority of scientists, but for having clung to this view without allowing it to be tested in fair and open debate among experts. When Professor Malegapuru Makgoba, South Africa's leading black immunologist, warned that the president's policies would make South Africa a laughingstock in the world of science, Mbeki's office accused him of defending racist Western ideas.

Since Mbeki's ouster in September, the new South African government of Kgalema Motlanthe has moved quickly to implement effective measures against AIDS. Mbeki's health minister, who notoriously suggested that AIDS could be cured by the use of garlic, lemon juice, and beetroot, was promptly fired. The tragedy is that the African National Congress, South Africa's dominant political party, was so much in thrall to Mbeki that he was not deposed many years ago.

The lessons of this story are applicable wherever science is ignored in the formulation of public policy. This does not mean that a majority of scientists is always right. The history of science clearly shows the contrary. Scientists are human and can be mistaken. They, like other humans, can be influenced by a herd mentality, and a fear of being marginalized. The culpable failure, especially when lives are at stake, is not to disagree with scientists, but to reject science as a method of inquiry.

Mbeki must have known that, if his unorthodox views about the cause of AIDS and the efficacy of anti-retrovirals were wrong, his policy would lead to a large number of unnecessary deaths. That knowledge put him under the strongest obligation to allow all the evidence to be fairly presented and examined without fear or favor. Because he did not do this, Mbeki cannot escape responsibility for hundreds of thousands of deaths.

Whether we are individuals, corporate heads, or government leaders, there are many areas in which we cannot know what we ought to do without assessing a body of scientific evidence. The more responsibility we hold, the more tragic the consequences of making the wrong decision are likely to be. Indeed, when we contemplate the possible consequences of climate change caused by human activities, the number of human lives that could be lost by the wrong decision dwarfs the number lost in South Africa.

from Project Syndicate, December 15, 2008

... Living, Playing, Working ...

HOW TO KEEP A NEW YEAR'S RESOLUTION

DID YOU MAKE ANY NEW YEAR'S RESOLUTIONS? Perhaps you resolved to get fit, to lose weight, to save more money, or to drink less alcohol. Or your resolution may have been more altruistic: to help those in need, or to reduce your carbon footprint. But are you keeping your resolution?

We are not yet far into 2010, but studies show that fewer than half of those who make New Year's resolutions manage to keep them for as long as one month. What does this tell us about human nature, and our ability to live either prudently or ethically?

Part of the problem, of course, is that we make resolutions to do only things that we are not otherwise likely to do. Only an anorexic would resolve to eat ice cream at least once a week, and only a workaholic would resolve to spend more time in front of the television. So we use the occasion of the New Year to try to change behavior that may be the most difficult to change. That makes failure a distinct possibility.

Nevertheless, presumably we make resolutions because we have decided that it would be best to do whatever it is that we are resolving to do. But if we have already made that decision, why don't we just do it? From Socrates onwards, that question has puzzled philosophers. In the *Protagoras,* one of Plato's dialogues, Socrates says that no one chooses what they know to be bad. Hence choosing what is bad is a kind of error: people will do it only if they think that it is good. If we can teach people what is best, Socrates and Plato seem to have thought, they will do it. But that is a hard doctrine to swallow—much harder than eating the extra slice of cake that you know is not good for you.

Aristotle took a different view, one that fits better with our everyday experience of failing to do what we know to be best. Our reason may tell us what is best to do, he thought, but in a particular moment our reason may be overwhelmed by emotion or desire. Thus, the problem is not lack of knowledge, but the failure of our reason to master other, non-rational aspects of our nature.

That view is supported by recent scientific work showing that much of our behavior is based on very rapid, instinctive, emotionally based responses. Although we are capable of deciding what to do on the basis of rational thought processes, such decisions often prove less powerful than our instinctive feelings in moving us to action.

What does this have to do with keeping resolutions? Richard Holton, a professor of philosophy at MIT and the author of *Willing, Wanting, Waiting,* points out that a resolution is an attempt to overcome the problem of maintaining an intention when we expect that, at some future time, we will face inclinations contrary to our intention. Right now, we want to lose weight and we are rationally convinced that this is more important than the pleasure we will get from that extra slice of cake. But we anticipate that, faced with cake tomorrow, our desire for that rich chocolate texture will distort our reasoning so that we might convince ourselves that putting on just a little more weight doesn't really matter all that much.

To prevent that, we seek to shore up our current intention to lose weight. By making a solemn resolution and telling our family and close friends about it, we tilt the scales against succumbing to temptation. If we fail to keep our resolution,

we will have to admit that we are less in control of our behavior than we had hoped, thus losing face in our own eyes
and in the eyes of others about whom we care.

This fits well with what psychologists have discovered
about how we can improve the odds that we will keep our
resolutions. Richard Wiseman, a professor of psychology at
the University of Hertfordshire, has tracked 5,000 people
who made New Year's resolutions. Only about one in ten
managed to stick to what they had resolved. In his recently
released book *59 Seconds,* Wiseman sets out the things that
you can do to make success more likely:

> Break your resolution into a series of small steps;
>
> Tell your family and friends about your resolution, thus both gaining
> support and increasing the personal cost of failure;
>
> Regularly remind yourself of the benefits of achieving your goal;
>
> Give yourself a small reward each time you achieve one of the steps
> toward your goal;
>
> Keep track of your progress toward your goal, for example by keeping
> a journal or putting a chart on the fridge door.

Individually, each of these factors seems trivial. Collectively,
they are ways of exerting our self-control not only now, but
in the future as well. If we succeed, the behavior we judge to
be better will become habitual—and thus no longer require
a conscious act of will to keep acting in that way.

These tools for keeping a New Year's resolution can help
us to make progress, not only in losing weight or staying out
of debt, but also in living more ethically. We may even find
that that is the best resolution to make, for our own benefit
and that of others.

from Project Syndicate, January 4, 2010

WHY PAY MORE?

WHEN THE POLISH MINISTER of Foreign Affairs, Radoslaw Sikorski, went to the Ukraine for talks last month, his Ukrainian counterparts reportedly laughed at him because he was wearing a Japanese quartz watch that cost only $165. A Ukrainian newspaper reported on the preferences of Ukrainian ministers. Several of them have watches that cost more than $30,000. Even a Communist Member of Parliament was shown wearing a watch retailing at more than $6,000.

The laughter should have gone in the other direction. Wouldn't you laugh (maybe in private, to avoid being impolite) at someone who pays more than 200 times as much as you do, and ends up with an inferior product? That's what the Ukrainians have done. They could have bought an accurate lightweight, maintenance-free quartz watch that can run for five years, telling the time virtually perfectly, without ever being moved or wound. Instead they paid far more for clunkier watches that can lose minutes every month, that will stop if you forget to wind them for a day or two (if they have an automatic mechanism, they will stop if you don't move them). In addition the quartz watches also have integrated alarm, stopwatch, and timer functions that the other watches either lack, or have only as a design-spoiling, hard-to-read attempt to keep up with the competition.

Why would any wise shopper accept such an extremely bad bargain? Out of nostalgia, perhaps? A full-page ad for Patek Philippe has Thierry Stern, the president of the company, saying that he listens to the chime of every watch with a minute repeater that his company makes, as his father and grandfather did before him. That's all very nice, but since the days of Mr. Stern's grandfather, we have made progress in time-keeping. Why reject the improvements that human ingenuity has provided us? I have an old fountain pen that belonged to my grandmother, and it's a nice memento of her, but I wouldn't dream of using it to write this column.

Thorstein Veblen knew the answer. In his classic *Theory of the Leisure Class*, published in 1899, he argued that once the basis of social status became wealth itself—rather than, say, wisdom, knowledge, moral integrity, or skill in battle—the rich needed to find ways of spending money that had no other objective than the display of wealth itself. He termed this "conspicuous consumption." Veblen wrote as a social scientist, refraining from making moral judgments, although he left the reader in little doubt of his attitude to such expenditure, in a time when many lived in poverty.

Wearing a ridiculously expensive watch to proclaim that one has achieved an elevated level of social standing seems especially bad in someone who is in public office, paid by the taxpayers, in a country that still has a significant portion of its population living in real poverty. These officials are wearing the equivalent of four or five years' average Ukrainian salary on their wrists. That suggests either "You poor benighted taxpayers are paying me too much" or "Although my official salary would not permit me to afford this watch, I have other ways of getting such an expensive watch."

The Chinese government knows what those "other ways" might be. As the *International Herald Tribune* reports, one aspect of Beijing's campaign against corruption is a clampdown on expensive gifts. As a result, according to Jon Cox, an analyst at Kepler Capital Markets, "it's no longer acceptable to have a big chunky watch on your wrist." The Chinese market for expensive watches is in steep decline. Ukrainians, take note.

Wearing a watch that costs 200 times more than one that does a better job of keeping the time says something else, even when the watch is worn by people who are not governing a relatively poor country. Andrew Carnegie, the richest man of Veblen's era, was blunt in his moral judgments. "The man who dies rich," he is often quoted as saying, "dies disgraced." We can adapt that judgment to the man or woman who wears a $30,000 watch, or buys similar luxury goods, like a $12,000 handbag. Essentially such a person is saying: "I am either extraordinarily ignorant, or just plain selfish. If I were not ignorant, I would know that children are dying from diarrhea or malaria because they don't have safe drinking water, or a mosquito net, and obviously what I have spent on this watch or handbag would have been enough to help several of them survive; but I care so little about them that I would rather spend my money on something that I wear for ostentation alone."

Of course, we all have our little indulgences. I am not arguing that every luxury is wrong. But to laugh at someone for having a sensible watch at a modest price puts pressure on others to join the race to greater and greater extravagance. That pressure should be turned in the opposite direction, and we should celebrate those with modest tastes and higher priorities than conspicuous consumption.

from Project Syndicate, May 9, 2013

Postscript: The corruption symbolized by the expensive watches on the wrists of Ukrainian ministers was a key issue in the protests that led to the ousting of President Viktor Yanukovych and his cronies in February 2014. Sikorski had the last laugh.

TIGER MOTHERS OR ELEPHANT MOTHERS?

MANY YEARS AGO, MY WIFE AND I were driving somewhere with our three young daughters in the back, when one of them suddenly asked: "Would you rather that we were clever or that we were happy?"

I was reminded of that moment last month when I read Amy Chua's *Wall Street Journal* article, "Why Chinese Mothers Are Superior," which sparked more than 4,000 comments on wsj.com and over 100,000 comments on Facebook. The article was a promotional piece for Chua's book, *Battle Hymn of the Tiger Mother*, which has become an instant bestseller.

Chua's thesis is that, when compared to Americans, Chinese children tend to be successful because they have "tiger mothers," whereas Western mothers are pussycats, or worse. Chua's daughters, Sophia and Louise, were *never* allowed to watch television, play computer games, sleep over at a friend's home, or be in a school play. They had to spend hours every day practicing the piano or violin. They were expected to be the top student in every subject except gym and drama.

Chinese mothers, according to Chua, believe that children, once they get past the toddler stage, need to be told, in no uncertain terms, when they have not met the high standards their parents expect of them. (Chua says that she knows Korean, Indian, Jamaican, Irish, and Ghanaian mothers who are "Chinese" in their approach, as well as some ethnic-Chinese mothers who are not.) Their egos should be strong enough to take it.

But Chua, a professor at Yale Law School (as is her husband), lives in a culture in which a child's self-esteem is considered so fragile that children's sports teams give "Most Valuable Player" awards to every member. So it is not surprising that many Americans react with horror to her style of parenting.

One problem in assessing the tiger-mothering approach is that we can't separate its impact from that of the genes that the parents pass on to their children. If you want your children to be at the top of their class, it helps if you and your partner have the brains to become professors at elite universities. No matter how hard a tiger mom pushes, not every student can finish first (unless, of course, we make everyone "top of the class").

Tiger parenting aims at getting children to make the most of what abilities they have, and so seems to lean toward the "clever" side of the "clever or happy" choice. That's also the view of Betty Ming Liu, who blogged in response to Chua's article: "Parents like Amy Chua are the reason why Asian-Americans like me are in therapy."

Stanley Sue, a professor of psychology at the University of California, Davis, has studied suicide, which is particularly common among Asian-American women (in other ethnic groups, more males commit suicide than females). He believes that family pressure is a significant factor.

Chua would reply that reaching a high level of achievement brings great satisfaction, and that the only way to do it is through hard work. Perhaps, but can't children be encouraged to do things because they are intrinsically worthwhile, rather than because of fear of parental disapproval?

I agree with Chua to this extent: a reluctance to tell a child what to do can go too far. One of my daughters, who now has children of her own, tells me amazing stories about her friends' parenting styles. One of them let her daughter drop out of three different kindergartens, because she didn't want to go to them. Another couple believes in "self-directed learning" to such an extent that one evening they went to bed at 11 p.m., leaving their five-year-old watching her ninth straight hour of Barbie videos.

Tiger mothering might seem to be a useful counterbalance to such permissiveness, but both extremes leave something out. Chua's focus is unrelentingly on solitary activities in the home, with no encouragement of group activities, or of concern for others, either in school or in the wider community. Thus, she appears to view school plays as a waste of time that could be better spent studying or practicing music.

But to take part in a school play is to contribute to a community good. If talented children stay away, the quality of the production will suffer, to the detriment of the others who take part (and of the audience that will watch it). And all children whose parents bar them from such activities miss the opportunity to develop social skills that are just as important and rewarding—and just as demanding to master— as those that monopolize Chua's attention.

We should aim for our children to be good people, and to live ethical lives that manifest concern for others as well as for themselves. This approach to child-rearing is not unrelated to happiness: there is abundant evidence that those who are generous and kind are more content with their lives than those who are not. But it is also an important goal in its own right.

Tigers lead solitary lives, except for mothers with their cubs. We, by contrast, are social animals. So are elephants, and elephant mothers do not focus only on the well-being of their own offspring. Together, they protect and take care of all the young in their herd, running a kind of day-care center.

If we all think only of our own interests, we are headed for collective disaster—just look at what we are doing to our planet's climate. When it comes to raising our children, we need fewer tigers and more elephants.

from Project Syndicate, February 11, 2011

VOLKSWAGEN AND THE FUTURE OF HONESTY

IF YOU USED THE TERM "BUSINESS ETHICS" in the 1970s, when the field was just starting to develop, a common response was: "Isn't that an oxymoron?" That quip would often be followed by a recitation of Milton Friedman's famous dictum that corporate executives' only social responsibility is to make as much money for shareholders as is legally possible.

Over the next 40 years, however, businesspeople stopped quoting Friedman and began to talk of their responsibilities to their companies' *stakeholders*, a group that includes not only shareholders, but also customers, employees, and members of the communities in which they operate.

In 2009, an oath circulated among the first class of Harvard Business School to graduate after the global financial crisis. Those who took it—admittedly, a minority—swore to pursue their work "in an ethical manner" and to run their enterprises "in good faith, guarding against decisions and behavior that advance my own narrow ambitions but harm the enterprise and the societies it serves."

Since then, the idea has spread, with students from 250 business schools taking a similar oath. This year, all Dutch bankers, 90,000 of them, are swearing that they will act with integrity, put the interests of customers ahead of others (including shareholders), and behave openly, transparently, and in accordance with their responsibilities to society. Australia has a voluntary Banking and Finance Oath, which obliges those taking it (more than 300 people have so far) to, among other things, speak out against wrongdoing and encourage others to do the same.

In August, one executive, Véronique Laury, said that her professional ambition is to have "a positive impact in the wider world." You might think she heads a charity, rather than Kingfisher, a home-improvement retailer with some 1,200 stores across Europe and Asia. In September, McDonald's, the largest purchaser of eggs in the United States, showed that it, too, can contribute to ethical progress, by announcing that its US and Canadian operations would phase out the use of eggs from caged hens. According to Paul Shapiro, the US Humane Society's vice president for farm animal protection, the move signals the beginning of the end for the cruel battery cages that have, until now, dominated America's egg industry.

Then came the revelations that Volkswagen installed software on 11 million diesel cars that reduced emissions of nitrogen oxides only when the cars were undergoing emissions tests, enabling them to pass, even though in normal use their emissions levels greatly exceeded permitted levels. In the wake of the ensuing scandal, the *New York Times* invited experts to comment on whether "the pervasiveness of cheating" has made moral behavior passé. The newspaper published their responses under the heading "Is Honesty for Suckers?"

Cynics would say that nothing has changed in the last 40 years, and nothing will change, because in business, all talk of ethics is intended only to camouflage the ultimate aim: profit maximization. Yet Volkswagen's cheating is odd, because, even—or especially—by the standard of profit maximization, it was an extraordinarily reckless gamble. Anyone at Volkswagen who knew what the software was doing should have been able to predict the company was likely to lose.

Indeed, all that was required to lose the bet was an attempt to confirm that the emissions results obtained when the vehicles were undergoing federal emissions tests were similar to those resulting from normal driving. In 2014, the International Council on Clean Transportation commissioned West Virginia University's Center for Alternative Fuels, Engines, and Emissions to do just that. The software ruse quickly unraveled.

Volkswagen's stock has lost more than one-third of its value since the scandal broke. The company will have to recall 11 million cars, and the fines it will have to pay in the United States alone could go as high as $18 billion. Most costly of all, perhaps, will be the damage to the company's reputation.

The market is giving its own answer to the question "Is honesty for suckers?" Its response is: "No, honesty is for those who want to maximize value over the long term." Of course, some corporations will get away with cheating. But the risk is always there that they will be caught. And often—especially for corporations whose brands' reputation is a major asset— the risk just isn't worth taking.

Honesty maximizes value over the long term, even if by "value" we mean only the monetary return to shareholders. It is even more obviously true if value includes the sense of satisfaction that all those involved take from their work. Several studies have shown that members of the generation that has come of age in the new millennium are more interested in having an impact on the world than in earning money for its own sake. This is the generation that has spawned "effective altruism," which encourages giving money away, as long as it is done efficiently.

So we have grounds to hope that as the millennials begin to outnumber those still running Volkswagen and other major corporations, ethics will become more firmly established as an essential component of maximizing the kinds of value that really matter. At least among major corporations, scandals like the one at Volkswagen would then become increasingly rare.

from Project Syndicate, October 7, 2015

IS DOPING WRONG?

THERE IS NOW A REGULAR SEASON for discussing drugs in sports, one that arrives every year with the Tour de France. This year, the overall leader, two other riders, and two teams were expelled or withdrew from the race as a result of failing, or missing, drug tests. The eventual winner, Alberto Contador, is himself alleged to have had a positive test result last year. So many leading cyclists have tested positive for drugs, or have admitted, from the safety of retirement, that they used them, that one can plausibly doubt that it is possible to be competitive in this event otherwise.

In the United States, the debate has been fueled by the baseball player Barry Bonds's march toward the all-time record for home runs in a career. Bonds is widely believed to have been helped by drugs and synthetic hormones. He is frequently booed and mocked by fans, and many thought that baseball's commissioner, Bud Selig, should not attend games at which Bonds might tie or break the record.

At the elite level, the difference between being a champion and an also-ran is so miniscule, and yet matters so much, that athletes are pressured to do whatever they can to gain the slightest edge over their competitors. It is reasonable to suspect that gold medals now go not to those who are drug-free, but to those who most successfully refine their drug use for maximum enhancement without detection.

As events like the Tour de France turn farcical, bioethics professor Julian Savulescu has offered a radical solution.

Savulescu, who directs the Uehiro Centre for Practical Ethics at Oxford University and holds degrees in both medicine and bioethics, says that we should drop the ban on performance-enhancing drugs, and allow athletes to take whatever they want, as long as it is safe for them to do so.

Savulescu proposes that instead of trying to detect whether an athlete has taken drugs, we should focus on measurable indications of whether an athlete is risking his or her health. So, if an athlete has a dangerously high level of red blood cells as a result of taking erythropoietin (EPO), he or she should not be allowed to compete. The issue is the red blood cell count, not the means used to elevate it.

To those who say that this will give drug users an unfair advantage, Savulescu replies that now, without drugs, those with the best genes have an unfair advantage. They must still train, of course, but if their genes produce more EPO than ours, they are going to beat us in the Tour de France, no matter how hard we train. Unless, that is, we take EPO to make up for our genetic deficiency. Setting a maximum level of red blood cells actually levels the playing field by reducing the impact of the genetic lottery. Effort then becomes more important than having the right genes.

Some argue that taking drugs is "against the spirit of sport." But it is difficult to defend the current line between what athletes can and cannot do in order to enhance their performance.

In the Tour de France, cyclists can even use overnight intravenous nutrition and hydration to restore their bodies. Training at high altitude is permitted, though it gives those athletes who can do it an edge over competitors who must train at sea level. The World Anti-Doping Code no longer prohibits caffeine. In any case, performance enhancement is,

Savulescu says, the very spirit of sport. We should allow athletes to pursue it by any safe means.

Moreover, I would argue that sport has no single "spirit." People play sports to socialize, for exercise, to keep fit, to earn money, to become famous, to prevent boredom, to find love, and for the sheer fun of it. They may strive to improve their performance, but often they do so for its own sake, for the sense of achievement.

Popular participation in sport should be encouraged. Physical exercise makes people not only healthier, but also happier. To take drugs will usually be self-defeating. I swim for exercise, and I time myself over a set distance to give myself a goal and encourage myself to work harder. I am pleased when I swim fast, but I would get no sense of achievement from improving my time if the improvement came out of a bottle.

But elite sport, watched by millions but participated in by few, is different. For the sake of fame and glory now, athletes will be tempted to risk their long-term health. So, while Savulescu's bold suggestion may reduce illegal drug use, it will not end it.

The problem is not with the athletes, but with us. We cheer them on. We acclaim them when they win. And no matter how blatant the drug use may be, we don't stop watching the Tour de France. Maybe we should just turn off the television and get on our own bikes.

from Project Syndicate, August 14, 2007

IS IT OK TO CHEAT AT FOOTBALL?

Shortly before half-time in the World Cup elimination match between England and Germany on June 27, the English midfielder Frank Lampard had a shot at goal that struck the crossbar and bounced down onto the ground, clearly over the goal line. The goalkeeper, Manuel Neuer, grabbed the ball and put it back into play. Neither the referee nor the linesman, both of whom were still coming down the field—and thus were poorly positioned to judge—signaled a goal, and play continued.

After the match, Neuer gave this account of his actions: "I tried not to react to the referee and just concentrate on what was happening. I realized it was over the line and I think the way I carried on so quickly fooled the referee into thinking it was not over."

To put it bluntly: Neuer cheated, and then boasted about it.

By any normal ethical standards, what Neuer did was wrong. But does the fact that Neuer was playing football mean that the only ethical rule is "Win at all costs"?

In soccer, that does seem to be the prevailing ethic. The most famous of these incidents was Diego Maradona's goal in Argentina's 1986 World Cup match against England, which he later described as having been scored "a little with the head of Maradona and a little with the hand of God." Replays left no doubt that it was the hand of Maradona that scored the goal. Twenty years later, he admitted in a BBC interview that he had intentionally acted as if it were a goal, in order to deceive the referee.

Something similar happened last November, in a game between France and Ireland that decided which of the two nations went to the World Cup. The French striker Thierry Henry used his hand to control the ball and pass to a teammate, who scored the decisive goal. Asked about the incident after the match, Henry said: "I will be honest, it was a handball. But I'm not the ref. I played it, the ref allowed it. That's a question you should ask him."

But is it? Why should the fact that you can get away with cheating mean that you are not culpable? Players should not be exempt from ethical criticism for what they do on the field, any more than they are exempt from ethical criticism for cheating off the field—for example, by taking performance-enhancing drugs.

Sports today are highly competitive, with huge amounts of money at stake, but that does not mean it is impossible to be honest. In cricket, if a batsman hits the ball and one of the fielders catches it, the batsman is out. Sometimes when the ball is caught the umpire cannot be sure if the ball has touched the edge of the bat. The batsman usually knows and traditionally should "walk"—leave the ground—if he knows that he is out.

Some still do. The Australian batsman Adam Gilchrist "walked" in the 2003 World Cup semi-final against Sri Lanka, although the umpire had already declared him not out. His decision surprised some of his teammates but won applause from many cricket fans.

An Internet search brought me just one clear-cut case of a footballer doing something equivalent to a batsman walking. In 1996, Liverpool striker Robbie Fowler was awarded a

326 • LIVING, PLAYING, WORKING

penalty for being fouled by the Arsenal goalkeeper. He told the referee that he had not been fouled, but the referee insisted that he take the penalty kick. Fowler did so, but in a manner that enabled the goalkeeper to save it.

Why are there so few examples of such behavior from professional footballers? Perhaps a culture of excessive partisanship has trumped ethical values. Fans don't seem to mind if members of their own team cheat successfully; they only object when the other side cheats. That is not an ethical attitude. (Though, to their credit, many French football followers, from President Nicolas Sarkozy down, expressed their sympathy for Ireland after Henry's handball.)

Yes, we can deal with the problem to some extent by using modern technology or video replays to review controversial refereeing decisions. But, while that will reduce the opportunity for cheating, it won't eliminate it, and it isn't really the point. We should not make excuses for intentional cheating in sports. In one important way, it is much worse than cheating in one's private life. When what you do will be seen by millions, revisited on endless video replays, and dissected on television sports programs, it is especially important to do what is right.

How would football fans have reacted if Neuer had stopped play and told the referee that the ball was a goal? Given the rarity of such behavior in football, the initial reaction would no doubt have been surprise. Some German fans might have been disappointed. But the world as a whole— and every fair-minded German fan too—would have had to admit that he had done the right thing.

Neuer missed a rare opportunity to do something noble in front of millions of people. He could have set a positive ethical example to people watching all over the world, including the many millions who are young and impressionable.

Who knows what difference that example might have made to the lives of many of those watching? Neuer could have been a hero, standing up for what is right. Instead, he is just another footballer who is very skillful at cheating.

from Project Syndicate, June 28, 2010

A SURFING REFLECTION

FOR ME, AS FOR MOST AUSTRALIANS, summer holidays have always meant going to the beach. I grew up swimming and playing in the waves, eventually moving on to a body board, but somehow missing out on learning to stand on a surfboard.

I finally made up for that omission when I was in my fifties—too old ever to become good at it, but young enough for surfing to give me a decade of fun and a sense of accomplishment. This southern summer, I'm back in Australia and in the waves again.

At the beach where I surfed today, I heard about a ceremony that had taken place there earlier in the season—a farewell to a local surfer who had died at a ripe old age. His fellow surfers paddled out into the ocean and formed a circle, sitting on their boards, while his ashes were scattered over the surface. Other friends and family stood and watched from the beach and cliff top. I was told that he was one of the best surfers around, but at a time when there was no money in it.

Was it his bad luck, I wondered, to be born too early to take part in today's lucrative professional surfing circuit? Or was it his good luck to be part of a surfing scene that was less about stardom and more about enjoying the waves?

This is not a general rant against the corrupting influence of money. Having money opens up opportunities that, if used well, can be very positive. Surfers have created environmental organizations like the Surfrider Foundation, which has a special concern for the oceans; and SurfAid, which tries to spread some of the benefits of surfing tourism in developing countries to the poorest of the local people. Still, the spirit of surfing's early days (think of the harmony of wave and human action portrayed in the 1971 movie *Morning of the Earth*) contrasts sharply with the razzamatazz of today's professional circuit.

Some sports are inherently competitive. Tennis fans may admire a well-executed backhand; but watching players warm up on court would soon become dull if no match followed. The same is true of football (soccer): who would go to watch a group of people kicking a ball around a field if it wasn't all about winning or losing? Players of these sports cannot exhibit the full range of their skills without being pushed by a competitive opponent.

Surfing is different. It offers opportunities to meet challenges that call on a variety of skills, both physical and mental; but the challenges are intrinsic to the activity and do not involve beating an opponent. In that respect, surfing is closer to hiking, mountaineering, or skiing than to tennis or football: the aesthetic experience of being in a beautiful natural environment is an important part of the activity's attractiveness; there is satisfaction to be found in the sense of accomplishment; and there is vigorous physical exercise without the monotony of running on a treadmill or swimming laps.

To make surfing competitive requires contriving ways to measure performance. The solution is to judge certain skills displayed in riding a wave. There is nothing wrong with surfers competing to see who can do the most difficult maneuvers on a wave—just as there is nothing wrong with seeing who can pull off the most difficult dive from the ten-meter platform.

But when we make surfing competitive, a recreational activity in which millions of people can happily participate is transformed into a spectator sport to be watched, for most, on a screen. It would be highly regrettable if the competitive sport's narrow focus on point-scoring were to limit our appreciation of the beauty and harmony we can experience riding a wave without fitting as many turns as possible into our time on it.

Many of the highlights of my surfing have more to do with experiencing the splendor and power of the waves than with my ability to ride them. In fact, at the time of my single most magical surfing moment, I wasn't on a wave at all. At Byron Bay, Australia's easternmost point, I was paddling out to where the waves were breaking. The sun was shining, the sea was blue, and I was aware of the Pacific Ocean stretching ahead thousands of miles, uninterrupted by land until it reached the coast of Chile.

A pulse of energy generated in that vast expanse of water neared a submerged line of rocks and reared up in front of me in a green wall. As the wave began to break, a dolphin leapt out ahead of the foam, its entire body clear of the water.

It was a sublime moment, but not such an unusual one. As many of my fellow wave riders know, we are the only animal that plays tennis or football, but not the only animal that enjoys surfing.

from Project Syndicate, January 15, 2015

... INDEX ...

France: adult sibling incest in, 135;
heat waves in, 265; personal lives of
politicians in, 146; refugee crisis in,
249; UN Climate Change
Conference in, 277–80
Francis (pope), 129–30
Franz Joseph (Austrian emperor),
154
Fraser, Malcolm, 48
Freddie (steer), 66–67
freedom: individual, vs. public health,
118–21; of religion, misuse of,
225–28; of speech, 118–19, 222–24
free-range chickens, 42
free-rider problem, 221
free will: and morality pill, 21–22;
and suffering, 12
Freud, Sigmund, 27
Friedman, Milton, 317
friendliness, government promotion
of, 202–4
friendship, government promotion
of, 203–4
Frost, Sydney, 47, 48
Frum, David, 229
fuel: algae as, 289; coal as, 273–76,
279

Galileo, 3
Gates, Bill, 169, 193, 296
Gates, Melinda, 74, 169
Gates, Robert, 254
Gates Foundation, 74, 193–94
Gaucher's disease, 115–16
GDI. See Gottlieb Duttweiler
Institute
GDP. See gross domestic product
Gecko Systems, 291
gender: in language, 68; privacy for
information about, 152–53; and
smoking rates, 120; and suicide,
314
gender equality: in Iran, 155;
progress toward, 9–11; religious
views on, 155

gender identities, 150–53
gender segregation, on buses in
Israel, 225–26, 228
General Mills, 257, 258
genetically modified organisms
(GMOs): opposition to, 283, 284–86;
patents for, 288–89; prevention of
vitamin A deficiency with, 283–86
genetics: in athletic performance,
322; of depression, 201; of disease,
103; and human cloning, 106–9
genetic screening, 104–5
genocide, in Darfur and Rwanda,
302. See also Holocaust
genome: human, 103–5; synthetic,
287–88
Gentile, Douglas, *Violent Video
Game Effects on Children and
Adults,* 144
George Washington Elementary
School (New Orleans), 245
German Ethics Council, 135–38
Germany: adult sibling incest in,
135–38; animal welfare in, 68;
refugee crisis in, 249, 251; virtual
sex in, 142
Germany, Nazi: Austria under, 27,
222; vs. Soviet Union, victims of,
240–41; Treaty of Versailles in rise
of, 254. See also Holocaust
gerrymandering, 217–18
gestational age, 77
GHG. See greenhouse gas
Gilchrist, Adam, 325
gill nets, 45
Gini coefficient, 260–63
GiveDirectly, 174
GiveWell, 116, 164–66, 174, 177
Giving Pledge, 169–70
Giving What We Can, 170
Global Thought Leaders, 35–37
global warming. See climate change
glow of goodwill, 204
glyphosate, 285–86
GMOs. See genetically modified
organisms

Irving, David, 222–24
Isen, Alice, 204
Islam: animal slaughter in, 225, 226;
    dominion over animals in, 50;
    homosexuality in, 139; male
    superiority in, 155; religious
    freedom of Muslims, 225, 226
Islamic countries: homosexuality in,
    139; protests again Muhammad
    cartoons in, 222, 224; views on
    equal rights in, 10–11
Israel: military service in, 225, 227;
    religious freedom in, 225–28

Jacobs, Binyomin, 226
Jain, Manoj, 116
Japan, whaling in, 47–49
Jefferson, Thomas, 245
Jews. *See* Judaism
Job, Book of, 14
Johnson, Harriet McBryde, 205–8;
    Too Late to Die Young, 206;
    "Unspeakable Conversations," 206
Jordan, refugee crisis in, 250–51
*Journal of the American Medical
    Association,* 200
journals, peer-reviewed, xi
Judaism: animal slaughter in, 225,
    226; dominion over animals in, 50;
    gender segregation in, 225–26,
    228; in Iran, 155; life support in,
    87–88; male superiority in, 155;
    orthodox, 87, 225–28; religious
    freedom of Jews, 225–28; Stalin's
    killing of Jews, 241. *See also*
    Holocaust

Kaczynski, Jaroslaw, 220
Kahneman, Daniel, 191–92, 193
Kaiser Family Foundation, 177
kangaroos, 49
Kant, Immanuel, 3, 5, 8, 211
Karnofsky, Holden, 163–66
Katrina, Hurricane, 89–92, 266

Kellogg's, 258
Kevorkian, Jack, 95
Keynes, John Maynard, 196–97
KGB Bar (New York), 239, 242
Khamenei, Ali, 156
kidneys: donation of, xi, 37, 111–12;
    sale of, 110–13
King, Martin Luther, Jr., 295
Kingfisher, 318
Kissling, Frances, 268–72
Klebold, Dylan, 143
Kontova, Helena, 180
Koons, Jeff, 180–81
Kravinsky, Zell, 111–12
Krawall.de, 144
Kubrick, Stanley, 21
kulaks, 240
Kyoto Protocol, 261, 264, 278

laboratory animals: chimpanzees as,
    64–65; patents on, 288–89; rise of
    concern for welfare of, 42
Lampard, Frank, 324
Lancet, The (journal), 120, 199
language: gender in, 68; used to refer
    to animals, 66–69
Lappé, Frances Moore, *Diet for a Small
    Planet,* 52–53
last generation of humans, 31–34
Latham, Mark, 148
Latin America: abortion in, 73–74;
    compulsory voting in, 220; future
    effects of climate change in, 271.
    See also specific countries
Laury, Véronique, 318
Layard, Richard, 199–200, 203–4;
    *Happiness: Lessons from a New
    Science,* 204
Lazari-Radek, Katarzyna de, *The
    Point of View of the Universe,* xiii
League of Nations, 245, 253
Lebanon, refugee crisis in, 249, 250
Leffall, LaSalle, 201
left ventricular assist device (LVAD),
    116, 117